we have your ro

Whether you travel for business or pleasure, we have your room ready when you need to be in Rochester, New York.

1 **THE DEL MONTE LODGE, A RENAISSANCE HOTEL AND SPA**
PITTSFORD: (585) 381-9900

LUXURY ACCOMMODATIONS, DYNAMIC CATERING PROGRAM, INDOOR POOL, FITNESS CENTER, THE SPA AT THE DEL MONTE, THE ERIE GRILL SERVING INNOVATIVE CUISINE

2 **MARRIOTT — ROCHESTER AIRPORT**
GREECE: (585) 225-6880

DELUXE ACCOMMODATIONS, SPACIOUS MEETING AND BANQUET ROOMS, POOL, WHIRLPOOL SPA, SAUNA AND FITNESS CENTER, EXCEPTIONAL RESTAURANT DINING

3 **COURTYARD BY MARRIOTT**
BRIGHTON: (585) 292-1000

4 **COURTYARD BY MARRIOTT**
GREECE: (585) 621-6050

5 **COURTYARD BY MARRIOTT**
PENFIELD: (585) 385-1000

SPACIOUS GUEST ROOMS AND SUITES, MEETING FACILITIES FOR GROUPS UP TO 50, POOL, WHIRLPOOL, FITNESS CENTER, THE MARKET WITH SNACKS AND BEVERAGES AVAILABLE 24 HOURS (BRIGHTON AND GREECE LOCATIONS ONLY)

6 **FAIRFIELD INN BY MARRIOTT**
AIRPORT: (585) 529-5000

7 **FAIRFIELD INN BY MARRIOTT**
HENRIETTA: (585) 334-3350

8 **FAIRFIELD INN BY MARRIOTT**
WEBSTER: (585) 671-1500

COMFORTABLE GUEST ROOMS, INDOOR POOL, COMPLIMENTARY CONTINENTAL BREAKFAST

9 **RESIDENCE INN BY MARRIOTT**
GREECE: (585) 865-2090

SPACIOUS STUDIO, ONE & TWO BEDROOM SUITES WITH A FULLY EQUIPPED KITCHEN & LIVING ROOM, POOL, WHIRLPOOL, FITNESS CENTER, SPORT COURT, COMPLIMENTARY HOT BREAKFAST BUFFET

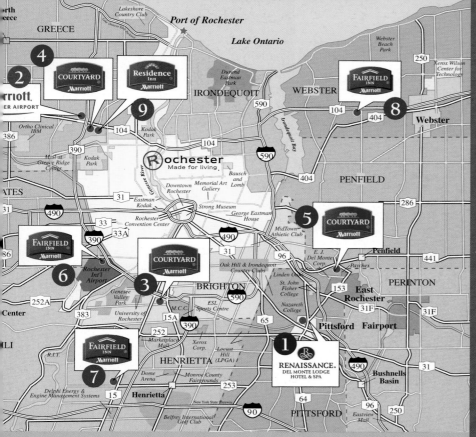

Visit us online at marriott.com

All of our hotels in Rochester have complimentary in-room high speed internet access.

contents

How to use this guide

*All telephone area codes
are 585 unless otherwise
noted. Listings contain
letter-number codes. These
correspond to the grids on
maps found in the Maps
section and can help you
locate the attraction.*

Publisher: Susan R. Holliday

Editor: Paul Ericson

Copy Editors: Karen Beadling, Lynne P. Cody

Writer/Researcher: Sally L. Parker

Editorial Contributors: Ruth German, Sheila Livadas, Debbie Waltzer

Director of Advertising: Suzanne Y. Seldes

Advertising Sales: Michelle Sanfilippo

Advertising Support: April Skolny

Distribution Assistant: Lori Wilkinson

Art/Production Director: Edward C. Fowler

Graphic Designers: Rachel S. Levitan, Melanie A. Watson

Explore Greater Rochester
© 2006 by Rochester Business Journal Inc. All rights reserved. No part of this publication may be reproduced or transmitted in any form or by any means, electronic or mechanical, including photocopy, recording or any information storage or retrieval system, without permission in writing from the publisher.

ISBN 0-9740732-3-7

Printed in the United States of America

boutique

skincare/makeup

yoga

spa

juice bar

nutrition services

natural apothecary

The stories of a city

Like any city, Rochester means something unique to each person who lives here. This place is a collection of the personalities and life stories, all the interests and talents, that have been born or brought here in the last 500 years.

Here's a taste of some of the people and events that have shaped the Rochester region into the community it is today:

Seneca Nation

For hundreds of years before the mill town of Rochesterville was born in 1811, Greater Rochester was home to the Seneca nation. Thousands of Seneca lived in Ganondagan, "town of peace," near modern-day Victor, and many more lived in communities throughout the region. Almost all of the major roads in the area once were Seneca trails created for trade and other activities.

Today's Ganondagan State Historic Site, located where the town once stood, tells the story of the Seneca. It is the only U.S. National Landmark dedicated to Native American culture east of the Mississippi.

The Seneca are one of six nations in the Haudenosaunee (pronounced hoe-dee-noe-sho-nee) Confederacy—called the Iroquois by the French. Some maintain that the Haudenosaunee's democratic ideals served as a model for the U.S. Constitution. While there is some question about how direct this influence was, the confederacy's Great Law of Peace was founded on the principle that disputes can be settled with thinking and negotiations rather than violence and warfare.

The confederacy also figures into the women's rights movement. The Haudenosaunee system of equality helped inspire the 1848 Declaration of Sentiments, written by women's rights activists in nearby Seneca Falls at a time when white women had few legal rights. Traditional Haudenosaunee culture holds that everyone is on equal footing. The Declaration of Sentiments sought similar equality for women everywhere.

The five original nations are recognized in county and city names across central New York: Seneca, Cayuga, Onondaga, Oneida and Mohawk. The Tuscarora from North Carolina joined the confederacy in 1714. Haudenosaunee today live in 16 communities in New York, Ontario, Quebec, Oklahoma and Wisconsin.

The Erie Canal

Before the Erie Canal was built, Rochester was a frontier village. Rochester's early millers and merchants were the first to harness the power of the Genesee River's High Falls and exploit the waterway as a commercial transportation route. Producing flour in mills that hugged the river's gorge, Rochester earned its first nickname, the Flour City.

Though it's hard to imagine today, two centuries ago Rochester sat on the Western frontier. Malaria-carrying mosquitoes infested the swampland and dense forests surrounding the river. This was uncharted territory ripe for opportunity seekers.

When the Erie Canal came to town, it brought a new population of ditch diggers and masons. With the canal's completion in the 1820s, Rochester grew up almost overnight. Products found new markets as the frontier moved west. Businesses multiplied and job seekers flocked from around the world.

A replica Haudenosaunee bark longhouse can be visited at Ganondagan State Historic Site. The structure would have housed several families in the same clan.

THE WORLD'S FINEST BRANDS
CHOOSE MANN'S JEWELERS.

 SCOTT KAY
PLATINUM

 PATEK PHILIPPE
GENEVE

 BREITLING
1884

VERA WANG

JAY STRONGWATER

 BELLA DOLCE

 PRECISION SET
FINE JEWELRY WORKS

ROBERTO COIN®

 JB STAR

 MICHAEL B.
PLATINUM

GUCCI

 ALEX ŠEPKUS®
NEW YORK

 JAEGER-LeCOULTRE

 KWIAT
SINCE 1907

MIKIMOTO.

Cartier

 TAGHeuer
SWISS MADE SINCE 1860

 LESLIE GREENE

 STEPHEN WEBSTER

Di MODOLO
MILANO

BAUME & MERCIER
GENEVE · 1830

DAVID YURMAN

BURBERRY

PENNY PREVILLE

 JOHN HARDY

MANN'S
JEWELERS
2945 MONROE AVENUE · ROCHESTER, NY 14618
585-271-4000 · 800-828-6234
WWW.MANNSJEWELERS.COM

STORE HOURS: MONDAY, WEDNESDAY, FRIDAY: 10:00AM - 5:30PM   TUESDAY, THURSDAY: 10:00AM - 8:30PM
SATURDAY: 10:00AM - 5:00PM   CLOSED SUNDAYS   PLEASE CALL FOR HOLIDAY HOURS

The Erie Canal crossed the Genesee River downtown via an aqueduct (top). After the canal was rerouted to the south, Broad Street was laid above the aqueduct. The old aqueduct is still open for tours, and city officials have plans to reuse the space.

The nation's first boomtown, becoming a city in 1834, began an affinity with exporting that continues today: Greater Rochester out-exports many entire states.

Hiram Sibley

Hiram Sibley was the first president of Western Union Telegraph Co.—and the first of many Rochesterians who made their mark in telecommunications.

Born in 1807 in Massachusetts, he was unschooled but a quick study, and had a mechanical aptitude. He moved to Western New York as a teenager and by his 30s he had helped build a telegraph service from Washington to Baltimore.

Western Union was born in 1851 in Rochester as the New York and Mississippi Valley Printing Telegraph Co. After a series of acquisitions it became Western Union, and by the late 1850s it had a telegraph system that spanned nearly the whole country. During the 16 years Sibley was president, the number of telegraph offices grew from 132 to more than 4,000. Western Union was based in Reynolds Arcade downtown.

Sibley's efforts to run a trans-Siberian telegraph line through the Bering Strait to connect Europe and the United States was beat to the punch by an Atlantic line—and caused the company big losses. It did, however, lead to the United States' purchase of Alaska.

Sibley was Rochester's wealthiest citizen and greatly influenced the community, says Cynthia Howk, architectural research coordinator for the Landmark Society of Western New York. He was an incorporator of Cornell University, where he endowed an engineering school, and he paid for the University of Rochester's first library.

"He built his house on East Avenue, and suddenly East Avenue wasn't just the country road to Pittsford," Howk says. "It became extremely elegant."

Sibley's efforts were the beginning of a telecommunications focus in Rochester. It is fed by a strong infrastructure, skilled labor and

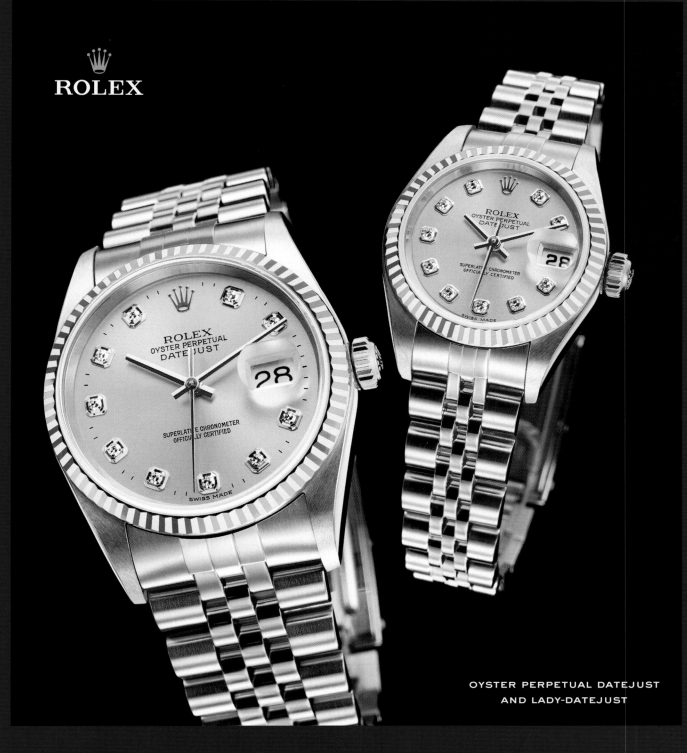

ROLEX

OYSTER PERPETUAL DATEJUST
AND LADY-DATEJUST

MANN'S
JEWELERS

2945 MONROE AVENUE
585-271-4000

Hiram Sibley, president of Western Union Telegraph Co., was the first of many Rochesterians to make their mark in telecommunications.

engineering programs. Monroe County officials count some 75 telecom companies in the Rochester area today with a total payroll approaching $250 million a year. The region outpaces the nation and the rest of New York in telecom payroll growth.

Susan B. Anthony

Of the two world-famous visionaries who lived in Rochester while they led the fight for social justice, only one is remembered here with a museum in her name.

Susan B. Anthony became the leading voice of the women's rights movement shortly after the first Women's Rights Convention in Seneca Falls, held in 1848.

At that meeting, organizers drafted a Declaration of Sentiments. The document, its inspirational spark drawn from Haudenosaunee culture, was modeled after the Declaration of Independence—and its claims were equally controversial, maintaining that "all men and women had been created equal." Some 300 people attended the event, including about 40 men, and 100 signed the declaration.

While hundreds of supporters, both men and women, were eager to see property and marriage laws changed to improve women's standing in society, they focused their battle on one right in particular: the vote.

Three years later, Anthony joined the movement. She traveled the country speaking for the cause, returning home to 17 Madison St. for research and fund raising with her sister Mary. (The house, now a museum, is a National Historic Landmark.) While she did not launch the movement—that credit goes to her friend Elizabeth Cady Stanton—Anthony was its voice and face; Stanton, busy at home with a brood of

children, worked behind the scenes and wrote many of the speeches and articles.

Their efforts brought national attention to Rochester and Central New York. After she and others tried to vote in 1873, Anthony's trial was moved from Rochester to Canandaigua because prosecutors feared she had too much support in her hometown to be convicted.

The judge instructed the jury to find her guilty. Several jurors later indicated they would have found otherwise. If the jury had been allowed to consider her case, the outcome might have been very different, and the right to vote might have come much sooner.

As it is, Anthony died in 1906 at the age of 86, 14 years before the 19th Amendment finally gave women the right to vote. She did live to see the measure pass at the state level in Utah, Wyoming, Colorado and Idaho.

Frederick Douglass

Frederick Douglass escaped his enslaved childhood to become the 19th century's leading voice for the freedom of African-Americans. With his wife, Anna, he moved to Rochester in the late 1840s. He had heard of the area's progressive reputation and wasn't disappointed when he got here. While there were people who opposed his outspoken efforts, Douglass found strong support from the Quaker community and others who fought to abolish slavery.

Douglass spent 25 of his most productive years in Rochester, publishing the North Star newspaper (later Frederick Douglass' Paper) and helping people who had been enslaved find freedom. His editorials directly influenced the public here as well as around the nation.

Douglass was personally involved in two major incidents that were catalysts of the Civil War. In one he sheltered three fugitives who had killed a slave owner. In the other, he had abolitionist John Brown at his house for a week or so, planning the raid on Harpers Ferry. When Douglass later learned of the plan, he declined to participate—but didn't try to stop it.

"Those two incidents would shape the outcome of the 1860 election," says David Anderson, Freedom Trail Commission chairman. "Douglass was right in the middle of that. He was a major player."

He also had the ear of President Abraham

Lincoln. His insistence that black men should be allowed to enlist provided the margin of victory that the Union eventually enjoyed.

"Douglass never shot at a rebel soldier. But to a significant degree he is responsible for changing the nation because he pushed that the Civil War was a war to end slavery," Anderson says.

Douglass was determined, well-known and a success by any measure, but he didn't get there alone. In Rochester he had loyal allies, among them Isaac and Amy Post (who may have ushered more former slaves to safety than anyone else here) and Susan B. Anthony and her family.

"As unique as Douglass is, he is standing on the foundation laid by others," Anderson says.

Those others are Austin Steward, who put slavery behind him and became one of Rochester's first successful business owners; Thomas James, an early member of the AME Zion Church who persuaded Douglass to move to Rochester; and Jacob Morris, a barbershop owner who was busy challenging the status quo, quizzing candidates for elective office on their views about the fugitive slave law, when Douglass met him.

George Eastman

The founder of Eastman Kodak Co. wasn't just any industrialist. George Eastman put the power of photography into the hands of the people. He invented the film that set Hollywood in motion. His company created nothing short of a revolution in storytelling and the documentation of everyday life.

And more than any other businessperson, Eastman shaped Rochester's future. He did this by employing hundreds of thousands of Rochesterians over the years and by sharing his wealth with the community.

Education, medicine and the arts were favorite philanthropies. The University of Rochester benefited substantially from his largesse,

Susan B. Anthony and Frederick Douglass were friends. A statue of the two having tea presides over a park near Anthony's home on Madison Street.

particularly with the creation of the School of Medicine and Dentistry and Eastman School of Music. Eastman also funded the Rochester Philharmonic Orchestra and Eastman Theatre, built dental centers around the world for needy children

George Eastman and Rush Rhees (right) made a good team, a later university president remarked. Thomas Edison adapted Eastman's continuous film for motion picture use (below).

Eastman's first photo, from 1877, shows the Erie Canal aqueduct spanning the Genesee River (above).

and became the Tuskegee Institute's most important benefactor during the 1920s.

Today, the Eastman School is one of the leading conservatories in the world. Its graduates have gone on to performance and teaching careers. Composer David Diamond, soprano Renee Fleming and jazz musician Chuck Mangione are among its alumni.

As a philanthropist, Eastman believed in focusing his contributions. "The progress of the world depends almost entirely upon education," he once said. "I selected a limited number of recipients because I wanted to cover certain kinds of education, and felt I could

get results with those named quicker and more directly than if the money were spread."

As a house museum, Eastman's home on East Avenue is one of the region's leading cultural attractions. Its film industry side contains robust collections of photography, motion pictures and technology— regarded as among the most comprehensive anywhere. It has one of the oldest film archives in the country and one of the top cinematic collections in the world. The personal film collections of Martin Scorsese, Spike Lee and others are housed here.

After Eastman's death in 1932, a New York Times editorial sang his praises, citing his contributions in music, education, science research and teaching, and public health: "Eastman was a stupendous factor in the education of the modern world. Of what he got in return for his great gifts to the human race he gave generously for their good."

Rush Rhees

As generous as he was, Eastman was not always interested in furthering higher education. It wasn't until Rush Rhees was hired as president of the University of Rochester in 1900 that Eastman began moving in that direction.

Rhees, a Baptist minister by training, had a restrained and understated way with people that drew out their talents, says Nancy Martin, the John M. and Barbara Keil university archivist and Rochester collections librarian. "I think his great strength was vision and patience, so that he could work with many different kinds of people."

A few years after his arrival, Rhees had his first opportunity to ask Eastman for money. The school's tiny Prince Street campus needed a science building. Rhees dreaded approaching Eastman, and the business titan initially said no. But Eastman eventually paid for the whole building—and it was the only time Rhees ever had to ask him to contribute, Martin says.

"(Eastman's) turnaround from total disinterest can be traced to his relationship to University of

Rochester president Rush Rhees," she says.

The relationship produced benefits that were not only immediately apparent but remain to this day. The move to the River Campus brought the school to the university level, an expansion that continues. The Eastman School of Music and the Medical Center are world renowned.

In 2005, Eastman's largest beneficiary overtook the company he founded as the leading employer in Rochester, with some 17,000 staffers. Rochester is making the transition from company town to innovative hot spot.

Today, led by the university and Rochester Institute of Technology, the area ranks high for research funding. UR researchers in fiscal 2005 attracted $352.8 million in grants, including $152 million from the National Institutes of Health. Thanks to nationally ranked academic programs and growing lab-to-market efforts, companies in biotechnology, imaging and optics, and fuel-cell research are springing up.

Historic preservation

Rochester has a national reputation as a leader in the preservation field. It was one of the first cities to issue ordinances to preserve existing building stock.

"People from other cities say, 'You're so lucky in Rochester to have this community awareness and support of your built environment and the value that has to the community at large,'" says Howk of the Landmark Society.

During its boom and again in the early part of the 20th century, Rochester's prosperity enabled its residents to build handsome downtown office buildings and grand homes. The region's architecture is of unusually high quality and wide variety, with plenty of intact 19th century streetscapes. The city and surrounding towns have a reputation for seeking new uses for old buildings.

City Hall, for example, is the former federal building. The old armory on Washington Square is the home of Geva Theatre Center. Monroe Community College's downtown campus is in what once was Sibley's department store. Dozens of loft apartments fill former factories, office buildings and a Catholic girls' academy.

But it wasn't always so. After World War II, residents in cities across America moved out to mushrooming suburbs. Rochester was no exception. Urban renewal in the 1960s polished up the public spaces of downtown, and new skyscrapers went up. But superhighways plowed through city neighborhoods, changing them forever. The resulting decline in housing stock sent neighborhoods into a tailspin.

This is when Rochester's signature grassroots activism came into its own. Preservationists battled the wrecking ball in historic districts,

Downtown Rochester is a mix of repurposed industrial buildings and newer office towers. The Genesee River runs through the heart of downtown.

Victorian mansions and cottages in Corn Hill were saved from the wrecking ball by preservationists in the 1960s and '70s (above). Renovation of the Troup Howell Bridge adds a steel arch and other aesthetic elements that have changed the city skyline (right).

including the mansion district on East Avenue and parts of Corn Hill, where the city's earliest business leaders had lived. The most popular areas of the city today are the direct result of preservation efforts and neighborhood involvement that began in earnest 40 years ago.

The Landmark Society was organized in 1937 to protect and preserve the Campbell-Whittlesey mansion in Corn Hill. In the 1960s, as modern office buildings began to replace ornate mansions on East Avenue, the Landmark Society sprang into action. Today's largely intact Mansion Row is one of the rare remaining examples of a "grand American avenue," Howk says, and "is an extremely important stabilizing factor" for the surrounding area.

Corn Hill is another example, she says. "People who are fairly recent to Rochester, they assume Corn Hill has sailed along in history. The death knell was tolling very loudly in the 1960s."

As a collection of mid-

19th century homes, Corn Hill was a unique neighborhood in the region. The society pushed city planners to look at the blighted area's potential for revitalization.

Though many streets and houses were lost, the northern section remains largely intact. Today it is one of the most popular areas to live in the city and draws 200,000 people for a weekend arts festival in July.

Not all corners of the city have fared as well. One of Rochester's architectural treasures, Union Station, designed by architect Claude Bragdon, was torn down in the 1960s. A huge parking lot and tiny Amtrak station replaced it.

Howk says the memory of that building reminds preservationists and city officials to think creatively about reuse. Such an approach reinforces the tax base, draws new construction and stabilizes whole neighborhoods.

"That is not typical in other cities, as our preservation colleagues tell us repeatedly," she says. "That all goes toward quality of life."

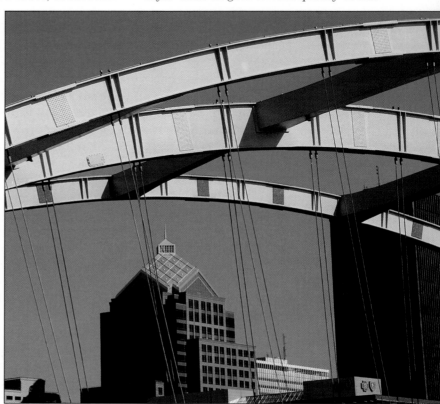

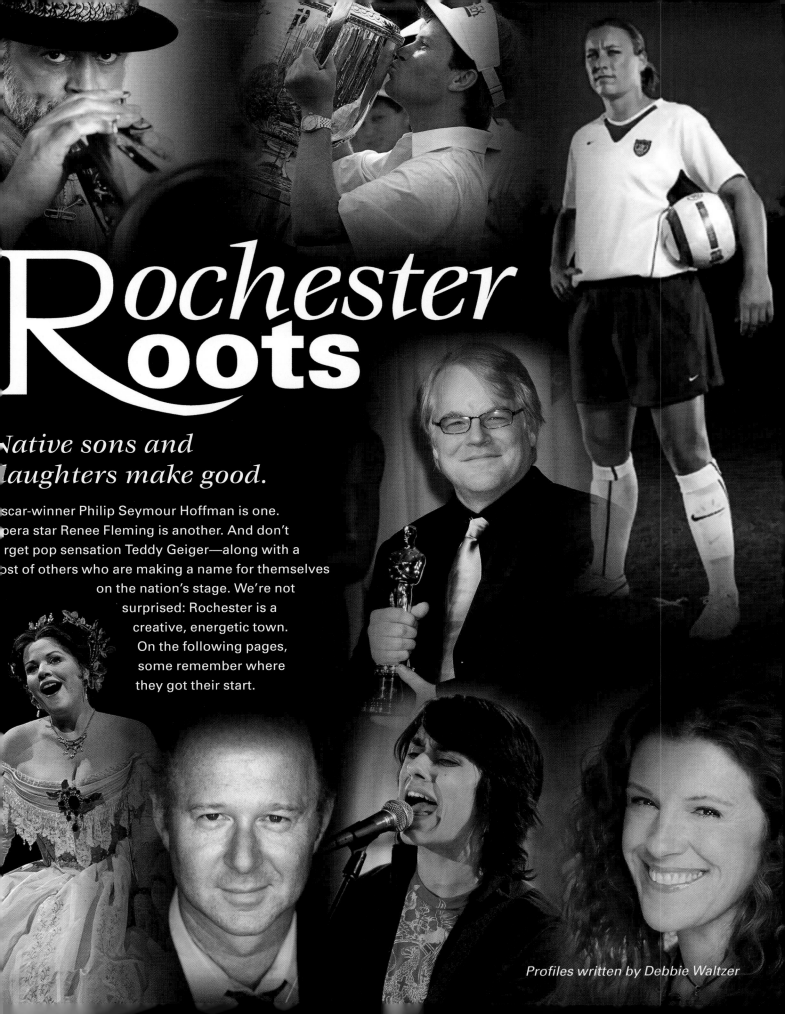

Rochester Roots

Native sons and daughters make good.

Oscar-winner Philip Seymour Hoffman is one. Opera star Renee Fleming is another. And don't forget pop sensation Teddy Geiger—along with a host of others who are making a name for themselves on the nation's stage. We're not surprised: Rochester is a creative, energetic town. On the following pages, some remember where they got their start.

Profiles written by Debbie Waltzer

Chuck Mangione

Mangione—took his children to listen to jazz greats at the Ridgecrest Inn on West Ridge Road.

The children had the chance to watch musical legends in action, such as Dizzy Gillespie, Miles Davis and Billie Holiday.

"My dad wasn't shy," Mangione says. "The first time that we went to the club, he walked up to Dizzy, told him that Gap and I could play, and before long we were invited to sit in with them and jam."

The gregarious Papa Mangione even took it one step further. He invited these musicians over to the house for Sunday night dinners, complete with spaghetti and meatballs, wine and a chance to listen to albums on a stereo. For these traveling musicians in the 1950s, it was an invitation that they couldn't refuse.

"My mom fed them delicious home-cooked meals, and I just assumed that every other kid had folks like Carmen McRae, Sarah Vaughan and Cannonball Adderley in their dining rooms for dinner," recalls Mangione, 66, the father of two daughters and two grandchildren. "It was a glorious childhood."

From there, his musical career took off. After watching baseball games at Silver Stadium on Norton Street, the teen would hop in his mom's car, change into fancier clothes, and head to a playing gig such as a wedding or Bar Mitzvah party.

He enrolled as a music education major at the Eastman School of Music, and began recording. For decades now, Mangione and his fellow musicians have charmed audiences worldwide with their performances of compositions such as "Feels So Good," "Hill Where the Lord Hides," "Chase the Clouds Away," and "Bellavia," which garnered Mangione his first Grammy award.

Throughout it all, Mangione's heroes have been his siblings, the late Dizzy Gillespie and his parents (his father died in 2001, and his mother, 91, is a resident at St. John's Home in Rochester).

With his mom, siblings, daughters, grandchildren, aunts, uncles and numerous good friends still in town, the Manhattan resident and his wife, Rosemarie, visit Rochester a half-dozen times each year. Favorite haunts include Restaurant 2 Vine, Java Joe's Coffee Experience at the Rochester Public Market and Mr. Dominic's on the Lake.

"Growing up in Rochester was idyllic. I didn't have to do anything except honk my horn," Mangione says. "This city brings back lots of great memories because it's home to the people I love most in this world."

If not for the movie, "Young Man with a Horn," two-time Grammy award winner and Rochester native Chuck Mangione might have become a violinist instead.

It all began at Public School No. 20. After testing well on a general music exam, the lad—who grew up with his family on the northeast side of town—was offered his choice of instrument to study.

Having just seen the classic film starring Kirk Douglas and Lauren Bacall—supposedly based on the life of jazz great Bix Beiderbecke—Mangione's choice was easy. He wanted to play the trumpet, just like his hero Beiderbecke.

His passion for music, however, started in the modest Mangione family living room.

Frank and Nancy Mangione—he a grocery store owner and she a homemaker—encouraged their three children's musical passions. The kids—Gap, Chuck and Josephine, in descending order by age—all vied for use of the household piano. Family jam sessions were abundant, and on Sunday afternoons, Frank—fondly known as Papa

Rochester Roots

With a cell phone in one hand and carry-on luggage in the other, Rochester native and international soccer great Abby Wambach is boarding a plane in Los Angeles, heading to the 13th annual Algarve Cup in southern Portugal.

There, she and her teammates on the U.S. Women's National Soccer Team will face opponents from China, France and Denmark in an attempt to win their fourth Cup championship.

"This is my life: I'm either in airports or on the soccer field—and I'm loving every minute of it," says Wambach, 25, considered by many to be one of the most dangerous strikers in the world. Fans will never forget her performance in Athens in 2004, when she became the first U.S. player to score four goals in an Olympic tournament, including a dramatic overtime game-winning goal in the final match against Brazil.

And to think it all started in her hometown back yard, on a quiet cul-de-sac off Clover Street in Pittsford. Wambach was the youngest of seven.

"Sports was the family activity, and I was into everything—baseball, lacrosse and soccer," she recalls. "Growing up in such a big family surrounded by so many jocks, I learned to play by watching my siblings' triumphs and mistakes. Sometimes when we were tired, my parents would lock us out of the house and make us play! But honestly, we didn't mind one bit."

Wambach played her heart out at Our Lady of Mercy High School.

"Catholic school really grounded me," she says. "It helped instill a strong sense of ethics, morals and self-confidence."

These days Wambach owns a home in Hermosa Beach, Calif. But, true to her Rochester roots, she returns to her hometown several times a year. In the summer she runs a soccer camp here.

"The first year, we had way too many kids, something like 600," she says. "So the second year, we cut it by half to make it much more of an intimate experience. I want to get to know every single camper, so that when I run into them at the mall at holiday time, I'll be able to greet them by name."

Wambach donates all proceeds from the camp to Rochester charities. "This is an opportunity for me to give back to my community, which has been so supportive of my career."

Wambach knows she won't be playing professional soccer forever. She's making plans for what comes after, working long distance on a bachelor's degree in family, youth and community sciences from the University of Florida.

Last December, Wambach visited Uganda and Rwanda as part of Right To Play, an athlete-driven humanitarian organization that uses sports and play as a way of reaching children in some of the world's most impoverished nations.

"This is my ultimate goal—to someday do extensive charity work as a foreign aid worker," she says. "There is so much poverty in the world, and I hope that I can make a difference. I think this is what life is about for me—helping others who need a hand."

Aaron Lustig

Anyone who lives 3,000 miles away from his birthplace and uses twelvecorners@aol.com as his e-mail address clearly has a passion for his hometown.

Such is the case with Hollywood actor Aaron Lustig, 49, who grew up in Brighton near the Twelve Corners, and to this day has insatiable cravings for cheeseburgers and French fries with gravy from the now-defunct Don & Bob's Restaurant on Monroe Avenue.

"I have such fond memories of Rochester," says Lustig, who has made guest appearances on dozens of television shows, including "Criminal Minds," "Monk," "Boston Legal" and "The West Wing."

"If I could do this work from Rochester, I'd be back home in a minute," says the South Pasadena resident and single father of Sam, 16, and Abby, 13.

Lustig, who in 1997 was nominated for an Emmy as best supporting actor in the daytime drama "The Young and the Restless" (he played the character Tim Reid), first got bitten by the acting bug while in 8th grade at Twelve Corners Middle School. There, he got to swivel his hips and cause young girls to swoon while playing the character of Conrad Birdie in "Bye Bye Birdie."

As he moved on to Brighton High School, Lustig—the son of a frozen-food company executive and a homemaker, and the youngest of three sons—landed roles in numerous shows including "South Pacific," "The Odd Couple" and "HMS Pinafore."

"I wasn't a jock, so acting was the only way I knew how to get attention from girls," he says.

Acting also satisfied his craving for creative expression. After high school, he enrolled at Ithaca College, earned a bachelor of fine arts degree in theatre, and then headed to New York City, where, he says, "I didn't get work."

For the first few years, he landed only a handful of minor acting gigs that paid minimal wages. But eventually he learned about the more lucrative world of commercials. Suddenly, Lustig was working, recording hundreds of spots during his 10 years in the Big Apple, for clients as diverse as IBM and Perdue Chicken.

In 1988, he decided to take the plunge and head to Hollywood. Despite the competitive acting climate, Lustig has been steadily employed ever since.

He has appeared in movies such as "Ghostbusters II," "Edward Scissorhands" and "Tuesdays with Morrie," and on television shows ranging from "Dallas" to "Without a Trace."

Soon he'll be seen in the feature film "Thank You for Smoking," starring Aaron Eckhart, William H. Macy and Robert Duvall.

Despite his career success, Lustig admits to occasional pangs of homesickness for Rochester.

"I love going back, visiting my family and enjoying the change of seasons," says Lustig, who has toyed with the idea of opening up a hot dog stand in Los Angeles that sells white hots, just like the ones from back home. He is looking forward to Abby's Bat Mitzvah in July, when his entire Rochester clan will come out to South Pasadena for the celebration.

"Rochester was a great place to grow up, even though I was a bit of a troublemaker as a kid," he says. "And believe it or not, I actually miss the snow!"

Rochester Roots

Jeff Sluman

Jeff Sluman took to golf at an early age. Every summer, he and his pals converted their adjoining back yards into a makeshift course, whacking balls between their houses in a Greece suburban tract.

"I can't remember ever *not* golfing," says Sluman, 48, who has played professional golf on the PGA Tour since 1983. He won the coveted PGA Championship in 1988, one of six tournament wins during his 23-year career.

Golf is in his blood. His dad, George Sluman—a retired Eastman Kodak Co. employee—loved nothing more than taking his three sons out for an afternoon at a nearby course.

"By the time I was 10 years old, I broke 80, so I guess I had a certain amount of talent," recalls Sluman, who also remembers long hours bowling with his chums at AMC Dewey Garden Lanes.

A nasty childhood bout with nephritis—inflammation of the kidneys—prevented Sluman from playing contact sports, much to the eventual delight of golf fans worldwide.

Making it to the pros was anything but easy; competition was fierce. After high school, he played for Monroe Community College, then accepted his only golfing scholarship offer—from Tennessee Tech University.

One year in, Tennessee Tech cancelled its golfing program, so Sluman headed south to Florida State University, as a finance major.

A few years after earning his bachelor's degree, he and 2,000 other golfing hopefuls showed up for the PGA's training school. Sluman was accepted on the tour.

"It was a very rigorous, tough road to make it to the tour because the number of acceptances is so minuscule," he says. "I feel so blessed. I always dreamed that I might make it as a pro, but I honestly didn't think I had a chance because of the health hurdles I had to overcome. But that's what dreams and hard work are all about."

These days, Sluman plays in roughly 30 tournaments a year. He and his wife, Linda, a retired oncologist, and their 8-year-old daughter, Katie, make their home in Hinsdale, Ill., near Chicago.

But they get back to Rochester at least a couple of times a year, mostly to visit Sluman's brother, Brad, and his family.

Although Sluman has not lived in Rochester for many years, fond memories linger.

"I used to love those huge snowfalls," he recalls. "My friends and I would play a little

bit of street hockey and pray that the salt trucks wouldn't come by.

"And to this day, no visit to Rochester is complete without a stop at Schaller's Drive-In on Edgemere Drive. It's mandatory. I have to have their cheeseburgers—the best in the world, as far as I'm concerned."

And while on tour, wearing his signature

Paychex cap (the company has been his sponsor for 20 years), not a week goes by that fans don't stop him to say that they, too, are Rochester natives.

"Rochester will always be home to me," he says. "It's a community filled with great, friendly people. That's all anyone can ever ask for."

Mimi Kennedy

Many people know Mimi Kennedy as the hippie-type mom Abby on re-runs of "Dharma & Greg," as Laura Ambrosino in the Oscar-winning film "Erin Brokovich," and as various characters in recent television episodes of "Cold Case," "House" and "Grey's Anatomy."

What might be less known is that Kennedy—an actress, antiwar activist, ardent feminist and environmentalist—got her theatrical start in Rochester, on the stage of Our Lady of Mercy High School, where she played roles as diverse as Jo in "Little Women" and Captain Hook in "Peter Pan."

"Playing my heart out on the stage of Mercy High gave me the first chance to feel loved by an audience," says the 57-year-old married mother of two. "It was like heroin coursing through my veins."

Kennedy is radiant when she speaks about growing up in the Browncroft neighborhood, the third of four children of Daniel and Nancy Kennedy—an attorney and a model-turned-community volunteer. The family later moved to Brighton, near the corners of Highland Avenue and Clover Street.

Kennedy was full of energy from the word "go." Her kindergarten teacher at Public School No. 46 firmly advised her to "learn to lead, but not be so pushy."

She and her pals took weekly gymnastics classes at the Catholic Youth Organization's facility on Chestnut Street, rode horses at Heberle Riding Stables and routinely entertained residents of the Rochester Psychiatric Center with vocal medleys.

And as a teen, Kennedy and her chums hopped a bus for downtown, to take in the sights of Midtown Plaza, buy candy at Fanny Farmer's and stroll their way through Forman's and Sibley's. She still treasures the memory of a magnificent white plastic wallet—adorned with a horse—that she purchased at Neisner's.

"It was a glorious life, a glorious place to grow up," says Kennedy, who now lives with her husband, Larry Dilg—a private high school English teacher—in Van Nuys, Calif. Their son Cisco, 23, teaches at a Catholic school in San Francisco, while daughter Molly, 20, is studying psychology and Spanish at Colorado College.

Kennedy, a Smith College graduate who got her first professional break in the role of Jan in the original Broadway production of "Grease," wrote about her experiences as a Catholic girl coming of age in "Taken to the Stage: The Education of an Actress," a memoir published in 1996.

These days, in addition to acting, doing voiceover work and writing a novel, Kennedy is immersed in social activism, supporting causes such as election reform, protesting U.S. involvement in the Iraq War and working to preserve the environment. She returns to Rochester at least yearly to visit relatives and some favorite former Mercy faculty members.

She is inspired in large part, she says, by Rochester-area historic figures who similarly fought for social justice, such as Susan B. Anthony, Frederick Douglass and Matilda Joslyn Gage.

"I owe my passions to these heroic individuals, as well as to the socially active nuns who helped shape my values," she says. "Rochester will forever be embedded in my brain and in my heart."

Rochester Roots

Where's *that?*

No, this is not the set for Hitchcock's "The Birds." It's St. Joseph's Park downtown. Read about Rochester's walking tours, starting on page 57. ▶

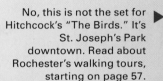

◀ Exhibits highlighting the mighty mastodon are only one reason to visit Rochester Museum and Science Center. See page 41.

▼ Rochester has mounted police officers, but this isn't one of them. Read about the Sterling Renaissance Festival on page 62.

This room could be yours—really! Check out Craft Company No. 6 and other local arts retailers in Shopping on page 131.

Do they really make horses this small? Read about Springdale Farm on page 83. ▶

A Rochesterian ▶ dressed for winter? No, it's a llama who calls Perinton home. See about the town in Neighborhoods, starting on page 27.

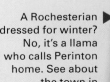

◀ Look at them thar hills ... of ice. The Lake Ontario shore can be surreal in winter. See Sports & Recreation, starting on page 71.

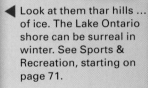

Curious about the front ▶ cover? It's the water fountain by St. Mary's Church and the Excellus Blue Cross Blue Shield building downtown.

maps of Rochester
and the surrounding region

Most listings in the following chapters contain letter-number codes. These correspond to the grids on maps on pages 22 to 26 and can help you locate the attraction.

A bird's-eye view of Rochester

Chilly visitors to downtown Rochester, take note: You can dodge the cold—and gain a different view of the city—by using the Skyway. Follow the round blue signs with the white arrow. The route burrows under streets and through skyscrapers, but its most visible presence is the enclosed bridges that span city streets. These offer some unique views of Rochester.

One of the best is from the bridge over Main Street connecting Rochester Riverside Convention Center and the Four Points Sheraton. From two stories up, you can see Main Street stretching east and west, the Genesee River flowing north under the street, and some of the oldest office buildings in the city.

The Skyway connects dozens of businesses, seven garages, two hotels, the convention center and other major facilities. While the route is considered handicap-accessible, some doors lack automatic openers.

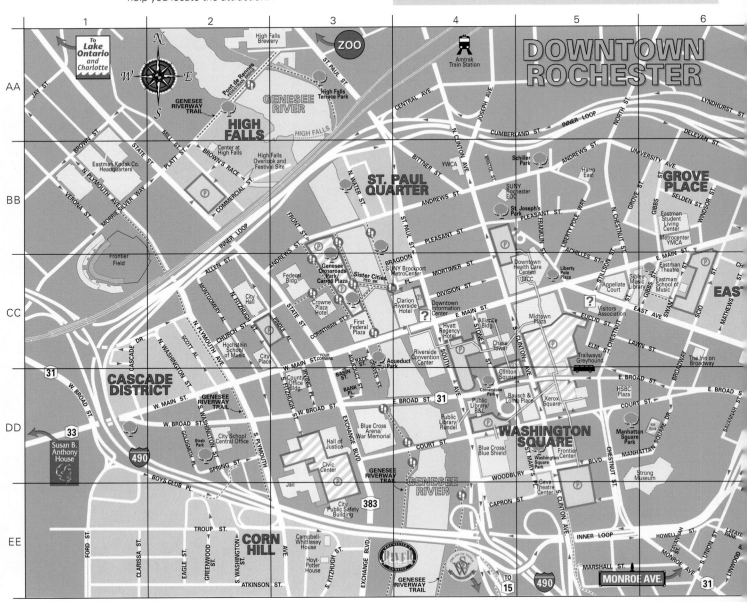

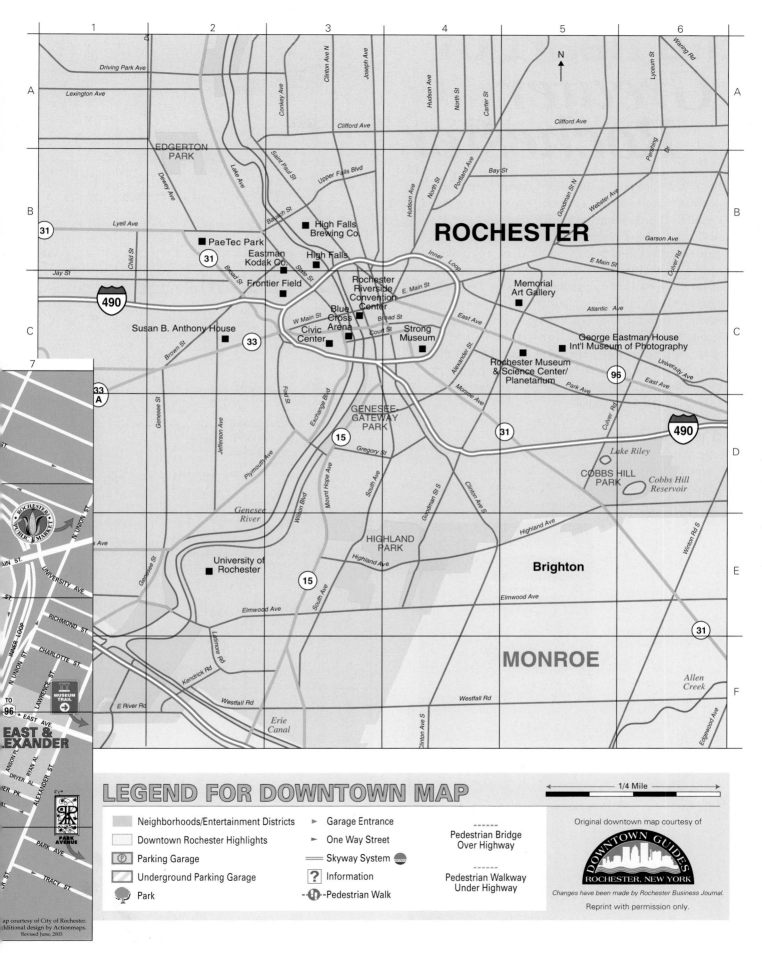

LEGEND FOR DOWNTOWN MAP

Neighborhoods/Entertainment Districts

Downtown Rochester Highlights

Ⓟ Parking Garage

Underground Parking Garage

🌳 Park

▶ Garage Entrance

▶ One Way Street

Skyway System

? Information

-Ⓗ-Pedestrian Walk

Pedestrian Bridge
Over Highway

Pedestrian Walkway
Under Highway

1/4 Mile

Original downtown map courtesy of

DOWNTOWN GUIDES
ROCHESTER, NEW YORK

Changes have been made by Rochester Business Journal.

Reprint with permission only.

ap courtesy of City of Rochester.
dditional design by Actionmaps.
Revised June, 2003

the heart of
Greater Rochester

The city of Rochester and Monroe County are located on the southern shore of Lake Ontario. The county, named for President James Monroe, was created from portions of Ontario and Genesee counties in 1821. In the same year, the Erie Canal reached Bushnell's Basin, near Pittsford. The canal eastward from Rochester to Albany opened in 1823 and the westward link to Buffalo opened in 1825. The original 14 towns in Monroe County were Brighton, Gates, Clarkson, Henrietta, Mendon, Ogden, Parma, Penfield, Perinton, Pittsford, Riga, Rush, Sweden and Wheatland.

Today, Monroe County consists of 19 towns, 10 villages and the city of Rochester. New York's third-largest city, Rochester has some 220,000 residents, and the county's population is roughly 750,000.

Did you know?

- Average summer temperature — 78 degrees
- Average winter temperature — 32 degrees
- Average commuting time — 21 minutes
- Greater Rochester population — 1,099,000
- Median age — 37

No matter where you are in Rochester, you're never far from the Erie Canal (right), Lake Ontario or the rolling countryside of the Finger Lakes region (below).

LAKE ONTARIO

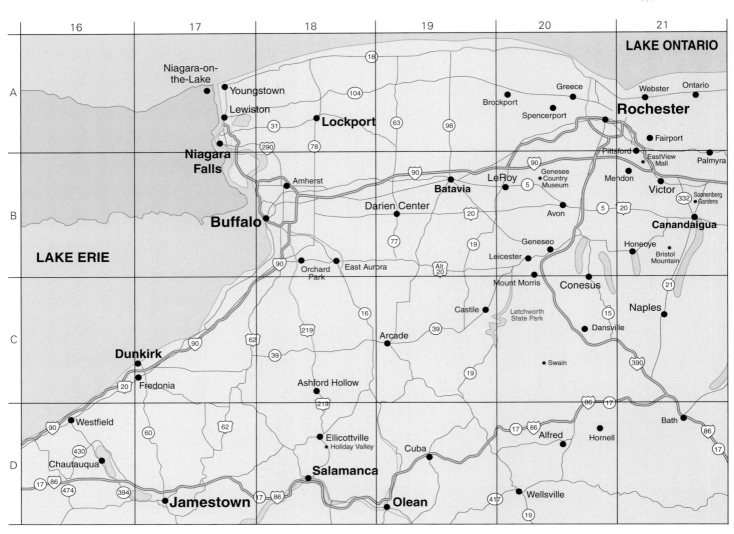

Driving distances from Rochester

Albany: *217 miles*

Batavia: *33 miles*

Binghamton: *152 miles*

Buffalo: *70 miles*

Corning: *86 miles*

Ithaca: *82 miles*

New York City: *354 miles*

Niagara Falls: *82 miles*

Niagara-on-the-Lake: *98 miles*

Syracuse: *82 miles*

Toronto: *167 miles*

Picturesque Niagara-on-the-Lake in Ontario, Canada, is less than two hours by car from Rochester.

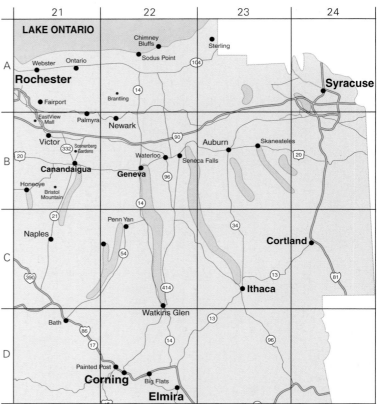

20

Neighborhoods and Towns

You are sitting on a plane and your seatmate introduces himself. He says he's from Rochester. You assume he lives in the city by that name, right?

Not so fast. He's as likely to live in the sprawling town of Greece (one of New York's largest) as he is in the quaint canal village of Fairport or the commercial mecca of Henrietta.

For the most part, people who live in the city of Rochester and the many towns that encircle it in Monroe County identify themselves as Rochesterians. Which isn't to say surrounding communities lack their own flavor—far from it. In fact, many of the towns were incorporated long before Rochester and have rich histories and personalities all their own.

Take a look:

Villages and Towns

Brighton

www.townofbrighton.org
Close to the city's eastern edge, Brighton is known for charming, storybook houses and neighborhood bagel shops, tailors and garages. Depending on what part of town you live in, you'll be near shopping in Pittsford and Henrietta. City nightlife is a five-minute drive away. The Erie Canal towpath is a popular place to ride, run or skate.

Brockport

www.brockportny.org
Like any college town, Brockport is a good place to live if you crave what a campus has to offer—music, lectures, sports and a youthful energy. It's moments from the open road, antique shops and farm markets of the countryside. The canal path is here too, and Lake Ontario is close. The village is a 30-minute drive from the city.

Chili

www.townofchili.org
Chili is a mix of suburban and rural. The western Monroe County town has parks, museums, golf courses and boat launches (one on the Genesee River and the other on Black Creek) on 40 square miles. Some 40,000 people call Chili home. Chili was named for the South American country that won its independence around the same time the town was founded. (The Rochester suburb of Greece was similarly named.) Chili's unusual spelling was common at the time. Historians attribute its odd pronunciation (chie-lie) to the Yankee roots of the town's settlers. Riga, Lima and Castile suffered similar fates.

Churchville

The village of Churchville lies on the west side of Monroe County within the town of Riga. With a population of some 2,000, it is a small village covering only about 1 square mile. Black Creek runs through town and is a

Homes in Irondequoit have the charming architectural details of the early 20th century.

popular fishing destination. Churchville Park on the edge of the village has lodges and shelters for group gatherings. A portion of the park's 742 acres is Churchville Golf Club, a public course operated by the county.

East Rochester

www.eastrochester.org
Despite its name, East Rochester is a village all its own, not an extension of the city. If you like Italian food, you're in luck: East Rochester has several family-run Italian restaurants that have been in business for generations. The village lies in the town of Pittsford and is close to all eastside shopping centers.

Fairport

www.village.fairport.ny.us
This village has pretty Victorians on tree-lined streets. Some have been subdivided into flats, and the surrounding area has plenty of apartment complexes. The Erie Canal cuts right through the center of the village. There are small shops, restaurants and bars, and EastView Mall is about 10 minutes away.

Gates

www.townofgates.org
Gates is the geographic center of Monroe County. It was incorporated in 1813 and is named after the American Revolutionary general Horatio Gates. The town was largely rural until city residents started migrating to outlying areas

in the 1960s. With a population of 30,000, Gates has a solid parks and recreation program, popular big-box retailers and locally owned restaurants favored by generations of Rochesterians.

Greece

www.townofgreece.org
This town has the largest population in the county and one of the biggest in the state. Greece is perhaps best known for its Ridge Road retail strip and as the home of Kodak Park. But its proximity to Lake Ontario and ample rural acres give parts of it a country feel.

Henrietta

www.charityadvantage.com/townofhenrietta/Home.asp
The region's first megamall, the Marketplace, is located here. Surrounding retail has sprung up over the last 20 years, making Henrietta a shopping destination easily accessible from the city and southside towns. Henrietta is about 15 minutes from downtown, and its property taxes are among the lowest in the area.

Greece is the retail hub for towns north and west of Rochester. Greece Ridge Center anchors the commercial strip on West Ridge Road.

Honeoye Falls

www.villageofhoneoyefalls.org
Located in the southeast corner of the county, Honeoye Falls is named for the falls of Honeoye Creek that tumble through town. Gift shops, coffee shops and restaurants contribute to Main Street's small-town feel. Founded in 1791, Honeoye Falls includes plenty of Victorian housing and 19th century buildings. The village is a 30-minute drive from downtown and accessible to nearby Mendon Ponds Park.

Irondequoit

www.irondequoit.org
Newcomers are always a little surprised that Rochester is more of an inland, river-oriented city. Those who love the seafaring ways of the Great Lakes will feel right at home in Irondequoit. Bordered by Lake Ontario and Irondequoit Bay, this town has a flavor all its own. There are rambling mansions, condos and tiny cottages on the waterfront. Houses in Irondequoit have the charming details of the early 20th century.

Mendon

www.townofmendon.org
The heart of Mendon is the intersection of routes 64 and 251. The hamlet bustles with the activity of area businesses, including restaurants, a grocery store, churches and several shops, offices and banks. All this belies the nature of the rest of Mendon, where rolling farmlands stretch for miles. Mendon borders Ontario County and is a 30-minute drive from downtown.

Penfield

www.penfield.org
Penfield is growing all the time. New stores and restaurants are coming to the retail corridors of Route 441 and Panorama Trail. At the busy Four Corners intersection, Penfield is recreating a walkable streetscape that plays off the 19th century buildings. Residential areas of the town continue to expand.

Pittsford

www.villageofpittsford.org
With tony shops and restaurants in restored 19th century buildings, the village of Pittsford has a well-heeled feel about it. Well-kept Victorian houses line neighborhood streets. Wegmans' uber-store and busy shopping plazas are west on Monroe Avenue. Head east and be at EastView Mall in a few minutes. The Erie Canal runs through town.

Spencerport

www.vil.spencerport.ny.us
Like many villages located on the Erie Canal, Spencerport has polished up its waterfront with new paths and a gazebo. The village has early-20th century homes. You can shop for basics right in town; malls and plazas are nearby on Ridge Road in Greece.

Webster

www.ci.webster.ny.us
As their populations grow, the town and village of Webster are expanding as well, with more

Homes front the Erie Canal near the village of Fairport.

stores, restaurants, athletic fields, parks and trails appearing all the time. Lake Ontario borders the town on the northern edge.

City Neighborhoods

Every community in the city of Rochester has the older housing stock typical of Northeastern cities. Rochester's supply is larger than most, despite the loss of some neighborhoods during urban renewal in the 1960s. Many areas of the city have preserved the details and charm these homes were built with. To find out more about city neighborhoods, go to www.rochestercityliving.com.

14621
www.rochestercityliving.com/neighborhoods /14621/index.htm
Named for the district's ZIP code, 14621 is a mosaic of languages and cultures from around the world. Some streets are broad, with gracious homes and large yards. On others are tiny but tidy workers' cottages. Most homes were built in the late 19th and early 20th centuries and have the charming details of that era. Parts of the neighborhood have their challenges. But an exceptionally strong neighborhood association brings concerned citizens together to work on solutions. The 297-acre Seneca Park, designed by Frederick Law Olmsted, lies in 14621.

19th Ward
www.rochestercityliving.com/neighborhoods /19thward/19thward.html
Across the river from the University of Rochester is one of the most ethnically diverse areas of the city. The 19th Ward has more than 22,000 residents, an active neighborhood association and a strong sense of community. It is minutes from the airport, the University of Rochester and I-390 and home to Frederick Law Olmsted's Genesee Valley Park. This is an

affordable neighborhood with homes that retain period charm.

Alexander Street
Alexander Street is one of the city's longest-running nightspots. In the past couple of years, its energy has spread around the corner to East Avenue, making East & Alexander a prime destination for partygoers. A relatively sedate business district by day, the area comes alive at night, drawing professionals from across the age spectrum. Residences include grand homes— both single-family and subdivided—on nearby East Avenue, and Victorian houses on side streets. World War II-era apartment buildings line Alexander Street, including the newly renovated Medical Arts Building in the art deco style.

Browncroft
www.rochestercityliving.com/neighborhoods /browncroft/browncroft.html
A 1920s subdivision of Tudors and other well-appointed homes, Browncroft occupies former nursery land off Winton Road and Browncroft Boulevard. It lies within the North Winton Village neighborhood.

Charlotte
www.rochestercityliving.com/neighborhoods /charlotte
The waterfront community of Charlotte seems more like a village than a city neighborhood. That's because it is 15 miles from downtown, wedged between Greece and Irondequoit on Lake Ontario. Charlotte was established as a port in 1805. One hundred years later, it was a popular summer resort. Grand summer homes and small cottages went up in those years. Charlotte also has plentiful housing built after World War II. In recent years the city has poured millions into a facelift of the harbor district. The popular Ontario Beach Park has a sandy beach, picnic areas, promenade and historic carousel.

Cobbs Hill
www.rochestercityliving.com/neighborhoods /cobbs/cobbs.html
The center of this neighborhood is Cobbs Hill Park, between Culver Road and Highland

Many of Rochester's original architectural jewels dodged the ravages of urban renewal in the 1960s.

Grassroots preservation

During its boom and again in the early part of the 20th century, Rochester's prosperity enabled it to build handsome downtown office buildings and grand homes. Our architecture is of unusually high quality and wide variety, and the city and surrounding towns have a reputation for seeking new uses for old buildings. City Hall, for example, is the former federal building. The old armory on Washington Square is the home of Geva Theatre Center. Monroe Community College's downtown campus is in the former Sibley's department store.

Dozens of loft apartments fill former factory buildings.

But it wasn't always so. After World War II, residents in cities across the country moved out to mushrooming suburbs. Rochester was no exception. Urban renewal in the 1960s polished up the public spaces of downtown, and new skyscrapers went up. But superhighways plowed through city neighborhoods, changing them forever. The resulting decline of housing stock sent neighborhoods into a tailspin.

This is when Rochester's signature grassroots activism came into its own.

Preservationists battled the wrecking ball in historic districts, including the mansion districts on East Avenue and in Corn Hill, where the city's earliest business leaders lived. The most popular areas of the city today, including Park Avenue, are the direct result of preservation efforts and neighborhood involvement that began 40 years ago.

Avenue. Runners use the path encircling the park's reservoir; there are tennis courts and ball fields too. Residents of Cobbs Hill are close to the commercial districts of both Monroe and Park avenues, as well as the suburb of Brighton. Homes in the area are typical of larger early 20th century dwellings.

Corn Hill

www.cornhill.org

Rochester's oldest residential neighborhood is one of its most popular. Corn Hill is right next to downtown and not far from the University of Rochester. The Corn Hill Arts Festival draws 200,000 people every July to see creations by some 500 artists. Homes from mansions to workers' cottages share mid-19th century character, and the 1980s saw the addition of nice town houses. The new Corn Hill Landing apartments, shops and cafes bring the neighborhood right up to the river—and the 21st century.

Culver-Winton-Main

www.rochestercityliving.com/neighborhoods/cwmain/cwmain.html

Farms and nurseries covered this area before a building boom from 1910 to the 1930s, when trolley lines were extended out from the city center. You can still see some old farmhouses (as well as the only cobblestone house in the city), but most of the homes are colonials, American Foursquares and bungalows. The neighborhood's prize possession, and a well-kept secret, is the 80-acre wilderness preserve of Tryon Park. It has trails on steep, wooded terrain loved by birders, hikers and mountain bikers.

East End

www.rochesterseastend.com

The East End is driving a renaissance in 24/7 city living with its own stamp of jazzy/bluesy sophistication. The cultural heart of Rochester, it is centered on East Avenue and stretches through side streets north to Main Street. Recent condos, townhouses and restaurants, some carved out of car dealerships that once filled the area, have brought renewed energy to this downtown neighborhood. Living spaces range from inexpensive studios to penthouse condominiums from East to University avenues. Rochester Philharmonic Orchestra, Eastman School of Music, Blackfriars Theatre, Little Theatre and the Rochester Contemporary art gallery call the East End home.

Twelve Corners, with its pergola and retail shops, serves as the heart of Brighton (above). Wintertime in the Northeast brings creativity to the fore (right).

Ellwanger & Barry

www.ellwangerbarry.org

Ellwanger & Barry lies on rolling former nursery land just north of Highland Park, site of the annual Lilac Festival. The neighborhood's signature home style is the American Foursquare. Most homes here were built between 1900 and 1930, though some are older. Residents are close to the shops and restaurants of both the South Wedge and South Clinton Avenue.

Maplewood

www.rochestercityliving.com/neighborhoods/maplewood/maplewood.html

The grand homes of Maplewood, off Lake Avenue north of downtown, were built for early executives with Eastman Kodak Co. They are within walking distance of a 5,000-bloom rose garden in Maplewood Park, a part of the original plans for Seneca Park laid out by Frederick Law Olmsted. Most of the neighborhood's houses sprang up between 1890 and 1920 and represent a broad range of architectural styles and economic levels.

Al fresco dining turns the sidewalks of laid-back Park Avenue into patios during the summer (left). Along ArtWalk in the Neighborhood of the Arts nearby, sidewalks, benches, light poles and bus shelters are works of art (below).

premier preservation districts. These were the grand homes of the leaders who built Rochester.

South Wedge
www.swpc.org
One of the most ethnically diverse neighborhoods in the city is located just south of downtown on the east side of the Genesee. The South Wedge is popular with college students and young professionals who like the urban village atmosphere. (Abolitionist Frederick Douglass lived here too.) It has some of the more affordable housing in the city, primarily in homes built around the turn of the last century. South Avenue runs through the

Monroe Avenue
www.monroeavenue.com
If Monroe Avenue were a painting, it would be a Jackson Pollack or an Andy Warhol. Stretching from the Inner Loop to Culver Road, Monroe has a funky, eclectic style with roots in hippie culture. Monroe Avenue serves as "Main Street" for residents who live in the neighborhood. Urban energy is evident around the clock. Shops are open late on weekends, offering unusual clothing, shoes, poster art, jewelry, antiques and used books. Neighborhood streets have single- and multifamily dwellings built in the late 19th and early 20th centuries.

Neighborhood of the Arts
www.rochestercityliving.com/neighborhoods/arts
Converted factories here house apartments and studios for dancers and visual artists. Post-war apartment buildings, multifamily Victorians and cottages line the area's side streets. In the middle of it all is the Memorial Art Gallery, home of the Clothesline Arts Festival in September. Next door, actor Taye Diggs attended School of the Arts. ArtWalk features sidewalk imprints, artistic benches, tiled light poles, sculptures and bus shelters on University from MAG to George Eastman House. Village Gate Square is a converted factory housing restaurants, shops and offices. Next door at Anderson Alley Artists, studios are open to the public the second

Neighborhoods, up close

For an intimate look at the homes in some of Greater Rochester's coolest neighborhoods, check out the Landmark Society House and Garden Tour in June, the Inside Downtown Tour in September and the Corn Hill Holiday Tour in December. The Special Events section has details.

Saturday of the month. Writers & Books, a literary center, keeps a calendar jammed with readings and classes.

Park Avenue
www.park-avenue.org
Between Culver Road and Alexander Street, Park Avenue is a tree-shaded, residential neighborhood. Restaurants, salons and shops are tucked among Victorian homes on the mile-long route. Bistros and cafes make up the majority of Park Avenue businesses; the two biggest concentrations are near Berkeley and Goodman streets. Al fresco dining turns the sidewalks into patios during the summer. There are antique dealers, gift shops, wine shops, convenience stores and other village amenities. In this relaxed environment, you may forget you're in the city. Take a short stroll to see the mansions of East Avenue, one of the country's

heart of the Wedge; new restaurants are popping up all the time. The neighborhood is undergoing renewal, from the tip of the Wedge at Mt. Hope and South all the way down to the Ford Street Bridge. The South Wedge and surrounding areas have restaurants serving a wide range of cuisines, from southern barbecue to Indian.

Swillburg
www.rochestercityliving.com/neighborhoods/swillburg
The fact that Swillburg still stands today is testament to determined residents who put a stop to highway plans that would have split the neighborhood in two. Homes are modest and affordable. Close to downtown and highways, Swillburg is tucked conveniently between the commercial areas of South Clinton and Monroe avenues.

Places of *Worship*

When it was built in the 1890s, the soaring St. Michael's Church at 869 N. Clinton Ave. raised eyebrows in the diocese. The Irish bishop even reprimanded the parish's German priest for building such a showy church.

St. Michael's is all the more impressive given how it was built: The church's working-class parishioners, most of them immigrants, mortgaged their houses to pay for construction, says Cynthia Howk, architectural research coordinator for the Landmark Society of Western New York Inc. "These were not people of great wealth, yet they built that fantastic building."

St. Michael's is made of Lockport sandstone. Its spire, at 220 feet high, is the tallest in the region. With pointed arch windows and doors and Austrian stained-glass windows, the church still inspires awe. Located in Rochester's "forever immigrant neighborhood," the Gothic revival church is a monument to immigrant determination and respect for old-world craftsmanship. To visit, call 325-4040.

In downtown Rochester, most houses of worship date from the 1840s to the 1920s, Howk says. Few synagogues remain in the city's core, but churches are in abundance. A walking or driving tour of downtown and nearby neighborhoods reveals many in the Romanesque and Gothic Revival styles.

While the exteriors are readily evident, getting a peek at some amazing interiors might be more difficult, Howk warns. Access is often limited to protect against the theft of valuable sanctuary items. So if you'd like to see inside, call ahead, try the door—or attend a service.

WEST SIDE OF THE RIVER

St. Luke & St. Simon Cyrene Episcopal Church
17 S. Fitzhugh St.; 546-7730
Built circa 1823, this is the oldest public building in the city. "Nathaniel Rochester had it built when we were the village of Rochesterville," Howk says. "And if he walked in the doors today he'd still recognize the interior." The church also is one of the oldest examples of Gothic Revival in the Rochester region. In earlier years, the building sat right next to the Erie Canal, which now is Broad Street.

Downtown United Presbyterian Church
121 N. Fitzhugh St.; 325-4000
DUPC's claim to fame is its genuine Tiffany glass windows. The original church was designed in the Romanesque Revival style by famed architect A.J. Warner. After it burned in the early 20th century, his son, J. Foster Warner, redesigned it.

Hochstein School of Music & Dance
50 N. Plymouth Ave.; 454-4596
When it was Central Presbyterian Church, its sanctuary held the famous funeral services of abolitionist Frederick Douglass and women's suffragist Susan B. Anthony. It remained a church until the 1970s and today is a community music school. Hochstein has Romanesque Revival architecture.

Central Church of Christ
101 S. Plymouth Ave.; 325-6041
South of Main Street, across from the civic center, is another A.J. Warner church, built as First Presbyterian. It is constructed of limestone in a Gothic Revival design. It has the only pointed spire on a downtown church and a Tiffany-designed tile mosaic on the wall behind the altar.

St. Peter and Paul's Catholic Church
720 W. Main St.; 436-3110
This "amazing" church building, constructed circa 1910, is "right out of a catalog of northern Italian architecture," Howk says. "That is a real monumental religious building."

Memorial AME Zion Church
549 Clarissa St.; 546-5997
Memorial AME, now in a contemporary building, contains a historic window honoring Frederick Douglass. The famous abolitionist and Harriet Tubman were members.

EAST SIDE OF THE RIVER

Former Leopold Street Shul
30 Harrison St.; 232-5963
The oldest surviving synagogue building is downtown. It was built in the 1870s as Beth Israel Synagogue by Orthodox Jewish immigrants from Eastern Europe. In the 1970s, an African-American Jewish congregation acquired the building and opened the Church of God and Saints of

The grandeur of St. Michael's rises above Rochester's "forever immigrant" neighborhood in the North Clinton Avenue area. German immigrants financed its construction with second home mortgages.

Christ. Today it sits all by itself on the street; the bustling neighborhood that once surrounded it was razed in the 1960s.

Our Lady of Victory - St. Joseph's Church
210 Pleasant St.; 454-2244
Belgian Catholic parishioners built this church in the 1860s. It is a city-designated landmark and is listed in the National Register of Historic Places.

First Universalist Church of Rochester
150 S. Clinton Ave.; 546-2826
This is the most important remaining public building in Rochester designed by Claude Bragdon. It is listed in the National and State Registers of Historic Places. "The interior is pristine. This congregation has been a magnificent steward," Howk says. The style is Lombard Romanesque, a northern Italian design marked by rough, darker brick and ceramic tile on the building's exterior—"a real Arts and Crafts style," she says.
See inside: *Eastman School of Music holds Eastman at Washington Square concerts in the church sanctuary at noon on Thursdays during the academic year.*

Places of *Worship*

St. Mary's Church was built in 1835. Its eye-catching rose window was added in the 1920s.

St. Mary's Church

15 St. Mary's Place; 232-7140

Across Washington Square Park, this church and its rectory are what remain of a huge campus that once also included a school, convent and orphanage. The church dates from the mid-1800s. Its spectacular rose window was added in the 1920s and its bell tower circa 1940. The exterior of the church is Romanesque Revival. Inside, the church has been modernized, its elaborate walls painted white in a style more typical of Protestant churches.

See inside: *St. Mary's holds noon masses several days a week.*

Christ Church

141 East Ave.; 454-3878

At the corner of East and Scio is a French-influenced Gothic Revival church built in the 1890s. The original 1850s church, enclosed within, now serves as a chapel. The bell tower, added in the early 20th century, holds a chime of seven real bells. The landscaping in front was renovated by the developers of the new Sagamore on East condominiums across East Avenue.

Salem United Church of Christ

60 Bittner St.; 454-5973

Just north of Andrews Street and east of Clinton Avenue is a church with strong German roots. It was built in the 1870s in the Romanesque Revival style and is listed in the National Register of Historic Places. "It has very German-sounding names on the memorial windows," Howk says.

Community Bible Church

284 Andrews St.; 232-4575

This is the oldest originally Baptist church building in the city. Often overlooked, the tiny church was built in the Romanesque Revival architecture in the 1860s.

Lutheran Church of the Reformation

111 Chestnut St.; 454-3367

Near the Eastman School of Music is a Lutheran church that holds both German and English services. It is listed on the National Register of Historic Places. It, too, is Romanesque Revival.

Former Zion Lutheran Church

60 Grove St.

The building across from the Lutheran Church on Chestnut Street began as a German Lutheran congregation in the 1840s and was the site of the first Christmas tree in Rochester. Germany native George Ellwanger, a famed nurseryman who appears to have attended the church, started the tradition. "The public came to see this little tree all lit with candles," Howk says. The building later housed a Jewish-American war veterans chapter and an African-American congregation.

Bethel Christian Fellowship

321 East Ave.; 232-1136

Next to the Inner Loop is a huge church built of cut stone. A.J. Warner designed it in the late 1800s as Asbury Methodist Church (which moved in the 1950s to a new home farther out on East Avenue). This is Richardson Romanesque and is eligible for listing in the National Register of Historic Places.

See inside: *The church's clear glass doors allow a view of the sanctuary from the sidewalk.*

First Church of Christ, Scientist

440 East Ave.; 271-7503

From the 1880s to the mid-20th century, this church was Greek Orthodox. Its Classical Romanesque tradition is evident in the ornate ceiling—designed by the same architecture firm as the Eastman Theatre. "It's a fantastic building inside—pristine, just the way it was designed," Howk says.

Former Sacred Heart Academy Chapel

8 Prince St.; 647-6116

Tucked off East Avenue in a former school building is an 1890s chapel. The chapel was adapted for use as a dance studio in the 1970s. Today the school has become apartments and the chapel is again in use, with original pews found in storage and a new exterior entrance. A hot location for weddings, the non-denominational chapel is High Victorian Gothic, with cut medina stone, stained-glass windows from Europe and an "absolutely gorgeous interior," Howk says. "This is a chapel that's come back."

NOT DOWNTOWN BUT WORTH A VISIT...

First Unitarian Church of Rochester

220 S. Winton Road; 271-9070; www.rochesterunitarian.org/building.html

Architects and students from around the world regularly visit and study this famous church building. Renowned architect Louis Kahn designed it for the Unitarian congregation (Susan B. Anthony was a member) when its downtown location, built in the 1860s, was slated for demolition during the 1950s. The contemporary architecture is of poured concrete, brick and concrete block. Self-guided tour information is available at the church office.

The restored High Victorian Gothic chapel in the former Sacred Heart Academy (now Chapel Hill Apartments) is a favored setting for non-denominational weddings.

education

Education

Greater Rochester is a college town. Some of the most respected State University of New York campuses are located here, and our private liberal-arts colleges consistently rank among the best in the region and the country. Two major universities drive area high-tech and health care initiatives—one of them is Rochester's largest employer. All the campuses are expanding programs and facilities to accommodate demand. Some 80,000 students from every state and dozens of countries study in Rochester.

Colleges and universities

Nazareth College of Rochester is an independent, coed liberal arts and sciences college. Founded in 1924, the college emphasizes community service and experiential learning. It is known for its physical, music and art therapy programs. Thousands of area teachers and administrators have earned master's degrees at Nazareth. In the last decade, 22 students have been awarded Fulbright scholarships. Like virtually all colleges in the Rochester area, Nazareth is in the midst of growth. A recent purchase of 73 acres of property and buildings adjacent to its wooded Pittsford campus is launching a new era of expansion.
4245 East Ave., Pittsford *F13*; 389-2525; www.naz.edu

Listed as a "best value" in *U.S. News & World Report*, **Roberts Wesleyan College** is an independent Christian liberal arts college founded in 1866. It has more than 50 undergraduate programs, plus graduate programs in social work, education and

Roberts Wesleyan College (right) has expanded its graduate offerings in recent years, including programs in social work and management.

management. Some 1,800 students attend the campus in suburban North Chili. Roberts Cultural Life Center brings to Rochester's western suburbs a much-needed art gallery, theater and performance hall.
2301 Westside Drive, Chili *E9*; (800) 777-4RWC; www.roberts.edu

A technical university with strong ties to business, industry and government, **Rochester Institute of Technology** plays a key role in local

Some 18,000 students attend classes at Monroe Community College's Brighton campus (left) and downtown Damon Center.

Focused on your success.

St. John Fisher College Graduate Programs

Our graduate programs prepare students to stay ahead of the curve and be ready for whatever comes their way.

To learn more about our full-time, part-time, evening, and weekend programs, call (585) 385-8161 or visit www.sjfc.edu.

Fisher now offers the following master's degree programs:

- **Advanced Practice Nursing**
- **Business Administration**
- **Adolescence Education**
- **Childhood Education**
- **Educational Administration**
- **Human Resource Development**
- **Human Service Administration**

- **International Studies**
- **Literacy Education**
- **Mathematics/Science/ Technology Education**
- **Mental Health Counseling**
- **Special Education**

St. John Fisher College Graduate Programs.
The road to success starts here.

ST. JOHN
FISHER
COLLEGE

economic development efforts. Its eight colleges offer career preparation in a wide range of sciences and technology, arts, engineering and business. One of the colleges, National Technical Institute for the Deaf, offers a technical college curriculum to deaf students. RIT is recognized as one of the premier institutions for art, design, photography and crafts. The university's co-op program, launched in 1912, is one of the oldest and largest in the country. The Gordon Field House and Activities Center recently was added to broaden recreational opportunities for students, and the nationally ranked men's hockey team has moved into Division I.
1 Lomb Memorial Drive, Henrietta *F11*; 475-2411; www.rit.edu

Founded in 1948, **St. John Fisher College** in recent years has embarked on an ambitious expansion, adding 20 academic programs and new schools for education, business, pharmacy, and arts and sciences. A recent gift of $8 million from grocery chain magnate Robert Wegman will fund a new School of Nursing. The college has 2,500 full-time undergraduates and 1,000 part-time and graduate students. Athletic teams at Fisher are consistently competitive; the college also hosts the Buffalo Bills training camp every summer.
3690 East Ave., Pittsford *E14*; 385-8000; www.sjfc.edu

SUNY College at Brockport is a four-year university in a historic Erie Canal town. It has 21 distinguished faculty, the highest faculty ranking in the State University of New York system. SUNY Brockport offers liberal arts along with professional studies, including education, communications, criminal justice and physical education. The university has 40 undergraduate and 28 graduate programs. Teacher preparation is a major focus here, with certification in 18 areas, and its international education program is the largest in the SUNY system. Nearly 9,000 students attend the Brockport campus and the MetroCenter campus in downtown Rochester. SUNY Brockport is the birthplace of the internationally acclaimed Garth Fagan Dance Troupe.
350 New Campus Drive, Brockport *D7*; 395-2211; www.brockport.edu

Founded in 1867 as a teachers' college, **SUNY College at Geneseo** is widely regarded as one of the nation's most selective public colleges. The Honors College of the State University of New York system, SUNY Geneseo offers 54 degree programs in liberal arts and sciences. It has a strong focus on providing a core liberal-arts education. The campus serves as the cultural hub of Livingston County. The heart of the charming village of Geneseo, about 30 miles south of Rochester, is a National Historic Landmark.
1 College Circle, Geneseo *B20*; 245-5211; www.geneseo.edu

SUNY Empire State College, Genesee Valley, bills itself as the SUNY solution for the working adult. Emphasis is on individualized study with online coursework and one-on-one faculty interaction. SUNY Empire offers associate's degrees in arts and science, and bachelor's degrees in arts, science and professional studies.

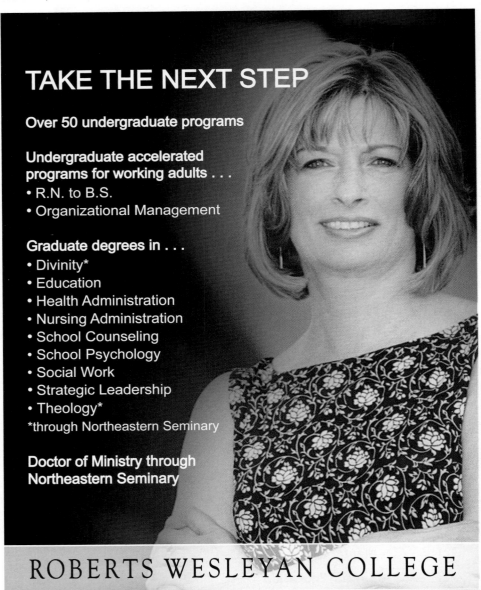

The co-op program at Rochester Institute of Technology is one of the oldest and most extensive in the country.

1475 N. Winton Road, Irondequoit *D13*; 224-3200; www.esc.edu

The **University of Rochester** brings researchers, medical professionals, top-ranked musicians and leading scholars from around the world. The private university, founded in 1850, recently passed Eastman Kodak Co. as the region's largest employer. On the River Campus, students work closely with faculty. A growing focus on entrepreneurship throughout its programs has earned UR recognition

from *Fortune Small Business* as one of the best colleges in the country for budding entrepreneurs. A major new building for biomedical engineering and optics collaboration taps research in an area of growing importance. UR's Eastman School of Music anchors the cultural district in the city's East End and is one of the top music schools in the world. The William E. Simon Graduate School of Business Administration consistently ranks among the best 30 in the nation. The Margaret Warner Graduate School of Education and Human Development is known for practical applications in education and recently launched an accelerated Ph.D. program. University of Rochester Medical Center faculty and students work in the School of Medicine and Dentistry, School of Nursing, Eastman Dental Center, Golisano Children's Hospital and Strong Memorial Hospital. Medical research into Alzheimer's, bird flu and AIDS has among the highest volunteer participation rates in the world.
Wilson Boulevard at Elmwood Avenue, Rochester *E12*; 275-2121; www.rochester.edu

Community colleges

Monroe Community College is one of only 20 community colleges chosen from among 1,200 in North America for membership in the League for Innovation in the Community College. Founded in 1962, MCC has a sprawling suburban campus with dorm rooms and a popular downtown campus that plans to move into a new city facility in coming years. 1000 E. Henrietta Road, Brighton *F12*; 292-2000; www.monroecc.edu

The nearly 5,000 students at **Finger Lakes Community College** study everything from horticulture to architectural design and drafting. The newly renovated Constellation Brands -

Marvin Sands Performing Arts Center is a popular venue for summer concerts. FLCC's 450-acre campus lies in the scenic Finger Lakes region, renowned for outdoor recreation opportunities and wineries.
4355 Lakeshore Drive, Canandaigua *B21*; 394-FLCC; www.fingerlakes.edu

Located in Batavia, **Genesee Community College** is an integral part of economic development in Genesee County. For the training and consulting it offers area businesses, it has received the Association of Community Colleges' National Best Practice Award for community economic development.

Thousands of area teachers and administrators have earned master's degrees at Nazareth College of Rochester.

GCC offers some 60 degree and certificate programs to roughly 6,000 full- and part-time students, including more than 100 from 27 other countries.
1 College Road, Batavia *B19*; 343-0055; www.genesee.edu

More college programs

Ryerson University in Toronto and **George Eastman House International Museum of Photography and Film** offer a joint master of arts degree in photographic preservation and collections management. **Ithaca College**'s physical therapy program has a Rochester Center adjacent to the University of Rochester and Strong Memorial Hospital. **Medaille College**'s Rochester campus in Brighton houses classrooms for the Buffalo college's accelerated learning program.

Specialty areas

DEAF EDUCATION

Rochester is home to a great number of deaf and hard-of-hearing people. The area has the largest population of deaf people per capita in the country and is considered highly deaf-accessible. **Rochester School for the Deaf** has been teaching deaf children and young adults for 125 years. The **National Technical Institute for the Deaf** at Rochester Institute of Technology is the nation's first and largest technical college for deaf and hard-of-hearing students. For hearing people who want to learn American Sign Language, virtually every college and many high schools offer ASL as a foreign-language option.

SEMINARIES

Bexley Hall Seminary, based in both Columbus, Ohio, and Rochester, is associated with the Episcopal Church and the Anglican Communion. It offers two degrees: a master of divinity and master of arts in pastoral theology.
26 Broadway, Rochester *CC6*; 546-2160; www.bexley.edu

The University of Rochester is a top research university with nationally ranked medical, business, science and music programs.

Colgate Rochester Crozer Divinity School offers a master of divinity, master of arts and doctor of ministry in transformative leadership. Personal enrichment and continuing-education courses also are available. Graduates include Martin Luther King Jr.
1100 S. Goodman St., Rochester *E4*; 271-1320; www.crcds.edu

Northeastern Seminary at Roberts Wesleyan College has master of arts and master of divinity degrees, plus a doctor of ministry degree. Students also can pursue a combined M.Div. and MSW degree.
2265 Westside Drive, Chili *E9*; 594-6802; www.nes.edu

At **St. Bernard's School of Theology and Ministry**, students can pursue a master of divinity, master of arts in theological studies or a master of arts in pastoral studies. St. Bernard's was one of the first Roman Catholic seminaries in the country to open its doors to laity. It has an extension campus in Albany, N.Y.
120 French Road, Brighton *F13*; 271-3657; www.stbernards.edu

Schools for the younger set

Rochester's high schools have national reputations for excellence. **Allendale Columbia School** is a coed college preparatory day school located close to the town line of Brighton and Pittsford. Nearly all of its graduates go on to four-year colleges. The city of Rochester's coed Catholic high school is **Aquinas Institute of Rochester**. Founded in 1902, Aquinas has added a fine-arts center and a sports complex in recent years. **Bishop Kearney High School** in Irondequoit also is Catholic and coed. Rochester millionaire Thomas Golisano and his wife, Heather, recently donated $3 million to the school. With no honor roll, the **Harley School** in Brighton fosters a spirit of non-competitiveness. It has 510 students in nursery school through 12th grade. **McQuaid Jesuit High School** is an all-male school in Brighton. Almost 99 percent of the class of 2005 went on to college.

Nazareth Schools comprise coed elementary and middle schools and an all-girls high school, **Nazareth Academy**. It has a joint program with RIT to prepare women for advanced study and careers in engineering. Like Bishop Kearney, **Our Lady of Mercy High School** recently received $3 million from the Golisanos. It is the largest all-women secondary school in the area. **School of the Arts** in the Rochester City School District specializes in theater, dance, music and art programs for city students. Actor Taye Diggs is a graduate. **Wilson Magnet High School** in Rochester is recognized among the top 1.5 percent of U.S. public schools in terms of academic challenges.

museu

Museums

Rochester-area museums tell many stories: the birth of the Mormon Church; the growth of photography and film; and the intimate life stories of movers and shakers like Frederick Douglass and Susan B. Anthony. Area museums focus on trains, toys, historic plants, dolls, Native American culture, sporting art and Jell-O. Don't miss a visit to one of Rochester's house museums; they recreate local life in the 19th century and are a direct result of the region's special focus on historic preservation.

Big Springs Museum and Historical Society
3095 Main St., Caledonia   *B20*
538-9880
Limited hours
On display are items chronicling the history of the Caledonia area, including clothing, farm machinery, kitchen utensils, toys and furniture. Personal collections comprise photographs, scrapbooks, newspaper clippings, greeting cards and war memorabilia.

Boynton House
16 East Blvd., Rochester   *D6*
Frank Lloyd Wright built this house for E.E. Boynton in 1908. You can't tour this private residence, but you can get a good look from the street. It is a well-preserved example of the architect's prairie style.

Campbell-Whittlesey House Museum
123 S. Fitzhugh St., Rochester   *C3*
546-7029; www.landmarksociety.org
One of the finest examples of Greek Revival architecture in America, this house represents the prosperity the Erie Canal brought to Rochester in the mid-1800s. Located in Corn Hill, Rochester's first residential neighborhood, the house features double parlors painted 12 tones and furniture decorated with gold stencils. Tours begin next door at the Landmark

Society of Western New York headquarters and gift shop, 133 S. Fitzhugh St.

Charlotte-Genesee Lighthouse and Keeper's Residence Museum
70 Lighthouse St., Rochester   *C12*
(behind church parking lot at 4492 Lake Ave.)
621-6179; www.frontiernet.net/~mikemay
Free admission; limited hours
The lighthouse once guarded Rochester's Lake Ontario shoreline. Visitors can climb the tower for one of the best views of the city. The museum displays memorabilia from Charlotte's (pronounced shar-LOT) heyday as a tourist attraction, along with local maritime history. Pick up a souvenir in the gift shop and pause for a picnic on the grounds.

George Eastman House International Museum of Photography & Film, a 50-room mansion on East Avenue, was the home of Kodak's founder and is a national historic landmark.

Fairport Historical Museum
18 Perrin St., Fairport   *F15*
223-3989;
www.angelfire.com/ny5/
fairporthistmuseum
Free admission
A huge mural by WPA artist Carl Peters can be found in the lobby of the museum, built as a library in 1937 as a WPA project. The museum houses the local history collections for the Perinton Historical Society and features a Victorian parlor and general store exhibit. Early property records, newspapers, scrapbooks, costumes and materials of interest to genealogists can be found here. Fairport owes its existence to the Erie Canal and the railroad, so much of the collection focuses on their role in the village's growth. After viewing the collections, stroll through the gift shop and gardens.

Ganondagan State Historic Site
1488 State Route 444, Victor   *B21*
742-1690; www.ganondagan.org
Ganondagan, designated a National Historic Landmark in 1964, marks a major 17th century Seneca town. Visitors can follow marked trails on Boughton Hill, where the town's burial grounds were, and on Fort Hill, site of the town's granary. Exhibits, videos and a reconstructed longhouse tell the centuries-old story of the Seneca Nation, one of six nations in the Haudenosaunee Confederacy.

Genesee Country Village & Museum
1410 Flint Hill Road, Mumford   *B20*
538-6822; www.gcv.org
One of the top three living-history museums in the country, Genesee Country Village features nearly 70 restored buildings dating from 1797 to 1870. Costumed interpreters go about the daily tasks of 19th-century life. Special events and classes bring visitors into activities. Four centuries of art are displayed in the John L. Wehle Gallery of Wildlife & Sporting Art. Five miles of interpreted trails in the Nature Center, open year-round, wind through woodlands and marshes. Two restaurants and three museum shops are on the grounds. (See story on page 47.)

George Eastman House International Museum of Photography & Film
900 East Ave., Rochester   *C5*
271-3361; www.eastmanhouse.org
An international leader in film preservation,

The Seneca Nation—a Native American community—flourished 300 years ago near today's Victor. Ganondagan State Historic Site marks the spot.

More room to play

Butterflies and books are coming to **Strong Museum** this summer as part of a $33 million growth spurt that will nearly double the museum's size to 280,000 square feet.

With the expansion, slated to open in July, Strong Museum becomes the second-largest children's museum in the country. Whimsical new architectural elements emphasize its focus on children and play.

A three-story, copper-colored aluminum tube—known as the caterpillar atrium—connects the original building with a new 40,000-square-foot wing. New exhibits will await in the addition and atrium:

Reading Adventureland will have hands-on activities that let guests step right into the pages of their favorite children's books. Inside nine enormous, interconnected cubes painted primary colors will be Field of Play, an exhibit on the importance of play in human development. Children will discover a play immersion theater and a giant walk-through kaleidoscope.

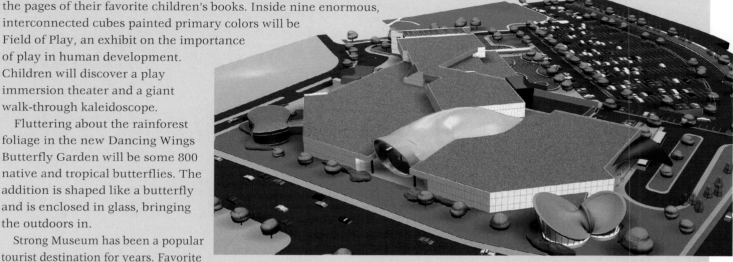

Fluttering about the rainforest foliage in the new Dancing Wings Butterfly Garden will be some 800 native and tropical butterflies. The addition is shaped like a butterfly and is enclosed in glass, bringing the outdoors in.

Strong Museum has been a popular tourist destination for years. Favorite exhibits include Sesame Street, One History Place, Super Kids Market, Kid to Kid and Making Radio Waves. In a trip down memory lane, its National Toy Hall of Fame inducts and showcases classic toys, like Raggedy Ann, the rocking horse, Play-Doh and Mr. Potato Head. The exhibit is being enlarged and renovated with a staircase entrance in the oval-windowed eye of the caterpillar tube.

Strong Museum will be closed from May 29 to July 13 in 2006 for final preparations. A grand opening of the expansion will be held July 14-16, 2006.

---

this National Historic Landmark collects and interprets images, films and equipment in photography and motion picture. Tour the 50-room Colonial Revival mansion and formal gardens of Eastman Kodak founder George Eastman. Take in exhibitions in nearly a dozen galleries. View classic and contemporary films in the Dryden Theatre. Create sunprints and more in the Discovery Room. The film archives hold one of the most extensive collections of silent films, as well as the personal film collections of Cecil B. DeMille, Martin Scorsese and Spike Lee.

Granger Homestead and Carriage Museum
295 N. Main St., Canandaigua   *B21*
394-1472; www.grangerhomestead.org
This was the retirement home of Gideon Granger, postmaster general under presidents Jefferson and Madison. The 1816 Federal-style mansion housed four generations of Grangers, as well as a private girls' academy and a ministers' retirement home. Today special events and tours show how the Grangers lived. The Carriage Museum displays nearly 50 19th- and 20th-century horse-drawn carriages. Carriage and sleigh rides are available; reservations are required. Also on the property is Hubbell Law Office, which once housed Walter

Hubbell and his law clerk, Stephen Douglas. One of just a handful of two-room law offices that remain in the state, it is open to visitors.

Hervey Ely House
11 Livingston Park at Troup St.,
Rochester   *C3*
Free admission; limited hours
Built in 1837, this Greek Revival features Doric

columns, elaborate plaster decorations and marble fireplaces. Hervey Ely was a prominent mill owner during Rochester's mid-19th-century boom. The house has been owned since the 1920s by the Irondequoit chapter of the Daughters of the American Revolution.

High Falls Museum
60 Browns Race, Rochester   *B3*
325-2030
Free admission
The museum is part of the High Falls Historic District along the Genesee River's west bank, where humming mills gave Rochester its first nickname, the Flour City. Through a simulated raceway, thundering falls and

Granger Homestead & Carriage Museum in Canandaigua displays nearly 50 horse-drawn carriages from the last two centuries.

From world-class art and photography to hands-on history, science, and technolog

Magnificent *Museums*

Genesee Country Village & Museum

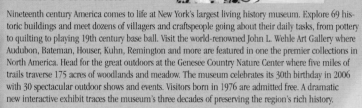

585-538-6822 • www.gcv.org
1410 Flint Hill Rd., Mumford, NY
20 miles SW of Rochester

Nineteenth century America comes to life at New York's largest living history museum. Explore 69 historic buildings and meet dozens of villagers and craftspeople going about their daily tasks, from pottery to quilting to playing 19th century base ball. Visit the world-renowned John L. Wehle Art Gallery where Audubon, Bateman, Houser, Kuhn, Remington and more are featured in one the premier collections in North America. Head for the great outdoors at the Genesee Country Nature Center where five miles of trails traverse 175 acres of woodlands and meadow. The museum celebrates its 30th birthday in 2006 with 30 spectacular outdoor shows and events. Visitors born in 1976 are admitted free. A dramatic new interactive exhibit traces the museum's three decades of preserving the region's rich history.

Special programming every day and major special events on weekends throughout the season.

Open May–October, with nature center and special programs year-round. Closed Mondays (except summer holidays). Hours: 10 a.m.–4 p.m., until 5 p.m. July–Labor Day.

2006 Calendar Highlights:

Log on to www.gcv.org for complete events listing.

May 2   Opening Day Happy Birthday! An interactive exhibition celebrating 30 years of assembling our region's extraordinary past.

June 3 & 4 Highland Gathering Scottish heritage celebration featuring dance, heavy athletics, tartan parade, bagpipe bands and Scottish goods.

June 24 & 25 War of 1812 Grand Tactical Explore period military encampments and witness hard-fought battles between American and British forces along the Niagara Frontier.

July 4   Independence Day Celebration
Pageants, parades and picnics.

July 15 & 16 Civil War Re-enactment Meet the soldiers and civilians on march through the camps. Battle re-enactments each day at 2 p.m.

August 11, 12 & 13 National Silver Ball Tournament Vintage base ball clubs from through the Northeast and Midwest compete for glory on three fields. Championship game on Sunday.

September 2 Fireworks Extravaganza
Old time country fair with livestock, farmer's market, and base ball season championship.

**September 30 & October 1
Agricultural Society Fair** A colorful country fair to celebrate the harvest.

**December
(Fridays–Sundays)
Yuletide in the Country**

George Eastman House

585-271-3361
www.eastmanhouse.org
900 East Avenue

More than you imagine!

This 12.5-acre estate in the heart of Rochester combines the world's leading museum of photography and film with the Colonial Revival mansion and gardens of Kodak founder George Eastman. Enjoy a variety of exhibitions on photography, film, and George Eastman; a hands-on learning center for children; the Museum Store and Café; plus an evening film program in the Dryden Theatre.

Call us or visit our Web site for information about weekly special events!

Open Tuesday–Saturday, 10 a.m.–5 p.m.; Thursday until 8 p.m.; Sunday, 1–5 p.m. Closed Mondays, Thanksgiving, and Christmas. Open holiday Mondays.

2006 Calendar Highlights:

Through Sept. 4, 2006   Picturing Eden
130 photographic works by 37 contemporary artists examine the garden as Paradise and a metaphor for good and evil.

April 22–Sept. 4, 2006   Seeing Ourselves: American Faces
Highlights from George Eastman House's photography collection, drawn from the exhibition *Seeing Ourselves*, which is being prepared to tour the United States.

Fall 2006   Why Look at Animals?
A celebration and exploration of the historic and contemporary roles of photography in helping us examine, idealize, and idolize animals.

November 15–December 14, 2006   Sweet Creations
This annual display of more than 60 gingerbread houses complements the turn-of-the-century holiday decorations throughout George Eastman's historic mansion.

February 13–25, 2007   Dutch Connection: George Eastman's Conservatory in Winter Bloom
This annual flower display includes hyacinths, tulips, freesias, and orchids provided by the Genesee Region Orchid Society.

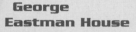

Memorial Art Galler

585-473-7720
TTY 585-473-6152
mag.rochester.edu
500 University Avenue

Journey through fifty centuries of humar creativity, from the treasures of antiquity 21st-century masterworks.

Considered "the best balanced collectio of any museum in the state outside of New York City," the Memorial Art Gall attracts more than 200,000 visitors ea year. Its permanent collection of 10,0 works spans 5,000 years of world ar includes masterworks by artists suc Monet, Cézanne, Matisse, Homer, (and O'Keeffe.

2006 Calendar Highligh
Italian Baroque Organ
North America's only full-size I Baroque organ, on permanent from the Eastman School of M For concert schedule, visit the Gallery's website.

So many worlds to discover at Rochester's outstanding, family-friendly museums!

Strong Museum
National Museum of Play®

585-263-2702 • www.strongmuseum.org
TTY 585-423-0746 • One Manhattan Square
Corner of Chestnut Street and Woodbury Blvd., Downtown

Beginning July 14, 2006, experience the bigger, even better Strong Museum—the National Museum of Play®. An astonishing $33 million expansion makes Strong the largest indoor family attraction in Western New York and the second largest children's museum in the nation. Discover two exciting new exhibits—*Field of Play* and *Reading Adventureland*—and walk among free-flying butterflies in *Dancing Wings* Butterfly Garden™. Step into *Sesame Street*, travel through *TimeLab*, and run a kid-sized supermarket in popular permanent exhibits. Visit the *National Toy Hall of Fame*® and a treasure trove of play-related collections including the world's most comprehensive collection of dolls and toys. Expanded food court, old-fashioned ice cream fountain, operating 1918 carousel, and indoor train. Two museum shops. Free parking.

Open Monday–Thursday, 10 a.m.–5 p.m., Friday, 10 a.m.–8 p.m., Saturday, 10 a.m.–5 p.m., Sunday, Noon–5 p.m.
Closed Thanksgiving and Christmas Day.

(Note: Due to construction, the museum will be closed from May 29 through July 13. Please call for special extended summer hours July 14 through Labor Day.)

Highlights of the Bigger, Even Better Strong Museum:
Reading Adventureland: A 12,000-square-foot exhibit about children's literature invites you to follow The Yellow Brick Road right into the pages of your favorite books. Visit the Wizard's Workshop, Adventure Island, the Upside-Down Nonsense House, Mystery Mansion, and Fairy Tale Forest.
Field of Play: See why play is so essential to learning and creativity at a multimedia presentation about play, and explore your playful side at several dynamic, interactive "play" stations including a giant walk-through kaleidoscope, a Jellyfish Jungle, a topsy-turvy house, and a kid-powered kinetic sculpture.
Dancing Wings Butterfly Garden™: The first and only butterfly conservatory in Upstate New York. This glass-enclosed structure is filled with lush tropical foliage and brightly-colored, free-flying tropical and native butterflies.
National Toy Hall of Fame®: Newly revamped and expanded, the prestigious hall annually inducts and showcases classic toys beloved by generations.
Expanded Food Court: Pizza Hut® Express, Taco Bell® Express, and Subway™ complement the existing Bill Gray's restaurant.

Rochester Museum & Science Center

585-271-4320 • www.rmsc.org
585-271-1880 (24-hr. recorded info)
657 East Avenue

Explore...Discover...Every Day!

Discover the fun of hands-on science at the RMSC's Museum and Planetarium, conveniently located on beautiful East Ave. Or share an outdoor adventure with your family at Cumming Nature Center near Naples, NY.

Museum & Science Center
Three floors of interactive exhibitions on science and technology, natural science, and our region's cultural heritage. Restaurant, gift shop, free parking. Museum hours: Monday–Saturday, 9 a.m.–5 p.m.; Sunday 12 noon–5 p.m.

Strasenburgh Planetarium
Spectacular giant-screen films, inspiring original star shows, or dazzling rock laser shows on the four-story dome. Call or check website for show times.

Cumming Nature Center
Located 40 mi. south of Rochester in the Bristol Hills. Hiking, cross country skiing, maple sugaring pancake breakfasts. Visitors center and ample free parking. Open weekends, January–October, 9 a.m.–5 p.m.

...tected
Eternity
...g-term, inte-
...ive exhibit for all
... that showcases a
... pair of lavishly deco-
...d ancient Egyptian coffins.

...e 18–September 10
...ond Rochester Biennial
...ional invitational featuring Carl
...urenza (photography), Sydney Licht
...nting), Michael Rogers (glass), Carol
...or (fiber), Allen Topolski (sculpture) and
...lia Yi (printmaking).

...tember 9 & 10
...T Bank Clothesline Festival
...hester's oldest and largest arts and crafts festival, now in its
... year, featuring original work by 550 artists from 27 counties.

...ober 1–December 31
...rgia O'Keeffe: Color and Conservation
...or new exhibition of rarely-seen works from all periods of O'Keeffe's
...igious career; one of only three national venues.

...ober 25–December 24
...America: Art from the Jewish Museum Collection, 1900-1955
...ks by 40 American Jewish artists in styles ranging from Social Realism to Modernism
...ostract Expressionism.

2006 Highlights

New Permanent Exhibition Now Open!
Expedition Earth: Glaciers & Giants
An amazing journey through millions of years exploring breathtaking changes in our region's environment. Glaciers, mastodons, and much more!

Opening April 14, 2006
New Riedman Gallery, featuring
K'NEX
Build cars, trucks, towers, or turtles—anything you can imagine—with this colorful construction toy.
How Things Work
Through hands-on investigation, find out how everyday devices (switches, thermostats, traffic lights and more) work!

Opening April 15, 2006
Amazing Journeys
A giant-screen film at Strasenburgh Planetarium. Travel with migrating birds, butterflies, whales, zebras, and more on their incredible journeys.

Opening June 18, 2006
Creation Station
A hands-on science showcase! Experiment with force and structure, light and images, and the fun effects of spinning!

October 7, 2006 – January 7, 2007
Dinosaurs!
Huge, robotic creatures invade the Riedman Gallery with awe-inspiring movement and sound effects.

other interactive exhibits, the museum shows how geology and technology shaped Rochester's industrial beginnings. At the nearby Triphammer Forge, view the layers of history at Brown's Race. The Pont de Rennes pedestrian bridge, particularly the eastern end, offers a spectacular view of the north-flowing river's High Falls.

Historic LeRoy House

23 E. Main St., LeRoy   *B20*
768-7433
Donated to LeRoy Historical Society in 1942, this was once the home of land agent Jacob LeRoy. Before the Civil War, Rev. Samuel Cox, a noted abolitionist, lived here. He also was chancellor of Ingham University, the first four-year university for women in the United States, located in LeRoy. A collection of local 19th-century redware from the Morganville Pottery is on permanent display in the home.

Hoyt-Potter House

133 S. Fitzhugh St., Rochester   *C3*
546-7029; www.landmarksociety.org
Free admission
This building was saved from demolition when the Landmark Society of Western New York chose it as its headquarters. The 1840 Greek Revival mansion also houses the Wenrich Memorial Library, a rich resource for information on local architecture, historic preservation, horticulture and decorative arts. Library research is by appointment.

Jell-O Gallery

23 E. Main St., LeRoy   *B20*
768-7433; www.jellomuseum.com
This gallery celebrates Jell-O, invented in 1897 right here in the village of LeRoy. Exhibits trace the history of the popular dessert. The gallery gift shop has dozens of products for collectors, from notecards and clocks to golf towels and Jell-O Barbie dolls.

Joseph Smith Farm

863 Stafford Road, Palmyra   *B21*
(315) 597-1671
Free admission
Though frequently associated with the Midwest and Salt Lake City, the Mormon Church was born in this area. The restored 1820s home of Joseph Smith, the charismatic religious leader who founded the Church of Jesus Christ of Latter-day Saints, is open for tours.

Landmark Society of Western New York

133 S. Fitzhugh St., Rochester   *C3*
546-7029; www.landmarksociety.org
In addition to maintaining house museums, the Landmark Society offers tours of historic neighborhoods. Its annual Corn Hill Holiday Tour of Homes happens the first Saturday of December. The tour takes visitors into beautifully restored historic homes in Corn Hill, the city's oldest residential district. The

Interactive science exhibits for children are a big focus in the Riedman Gallery at Rochester Museum and Science Center on East Avenue.

society's 36th annual House and Garden Tour visits Brighton in June 2006. Call the society for tickets and directions. The society also has maps for self-guided tours of historic neighborhoods, from downtown Rochester to outlying towns. See the Trails and Walking Tours section. You can also pick up a map from Downtown Guides at the Downtown Information Center, corner of Clinton Avenue and Main Street, 232-3420, or online at www.landmarksociety.org/tours/index.html.

Memorial Art Gallery

500 University Ave., Rochester   *C5*
473-7720; http://mag.rochester.edu
Founded in 1913 as a centerpiece for Rochester's growing interest in art, the gallery draws thousands of visitors a year from throughout the Northeast. More than two dozen works by Georgia O'Keeffe will be featured in a major exhibit this fall. Recent popular exhibitions featured Saint-Gaudens, Rembrandt, Corot, Kandinsky, Degas and Parrish. The museum's well-balanced art collection, dating to antiquity, includes the inner and outer coffins of Pa-debehu-Aset, an Egyptian official of the fourth century BCE. Craft installations, the Clothesline Festival and biannual Rochester-Finger Lakes Exhibition show off the region's many artists. The Gill Family Center offers activities for children and adults. There are school programs and classes for all ages, an art library, lectures and concerts. Admission to the museum shop and Cutler's restaurant is free.

Morgan-Manning House

151 Main St., Brockport   *D7*
637-3645
Free admission; tours by appointment
Dayton Morgan purchased the home in 1854, and it remained in his family for nearly 100 years. The Western Monroe Historical Society restored the house in 1965 after a damaging

fire, which also took the life of the last of the Morgan children, 96-year-old Sara Morgan Manning. Today the home looks much like it did during the 19th century.

The Rochester & Genesee Valley Railroad Museum

533-1431; www.rgvrrm.org

New York Museum of Transportation

533-1113; www.nymtmuseum.org
6393 East River Road, Rush   *G11*
(One mile north of Route 251)
Visitors can climb aboard and take photos of historic rail cars and vehicles, including freight and passenger cars, locomotives, cabooses, trolleys and more. In July 2006 the railroad museum marks the 50th anniversary of the end of subway service in Rochester with authentic trolley rides, slide talks and archival films of the subway's last days. The museums feature a restored 1909 Erie Railroad depot, a huge model railroad and photo displays of Genesee Valley transportation history. A track car shuttles visitors between the museums from mid-May to October. Souvenirs are available in the gift shop.

Rochester Museum and Science Center

657 East Ave., Rochester   *C5*
271-1880; www.rmsc.org
When RMSC opened in 1912 as Rochester's Municipal Museum, many of its founders likely had known longtime resident Frederick Douglass, who died in 1895. Today the museum pays tribute to the great abolitionist with an exhibit exploring his life. Other popular exhibits include Lake Ontario, K' Nex, How Things Work, personal and group identity, Rochester's Public Market in the early 1900s,

Thirty years of living in the past

Want to escape from the present?

Then check out Genesee Country Village & Museum in Mumford, 20 miles from downtown Rochester.

Genesee Country Village is the nation's third-largest living-history museum, behind Colonial Williamsburg in Virginia and Greenfield Village in Dearborn, Mich. This powerhouse trio leads a list of hundreds of U.S. living-history museums, says Judith Sheridan, secretary/treasurer of the Association for Living History, Farm and Agricultural Museums.

"Genesee Country Village & Museum is one of the pre-eminent historic sites in the U.S. Not only is it one of the largest, it's also one of the most professionally run establishments of its kind. They fully embody the purpose of living-history museums: to preserve our heritage and bring history to life."

The museum opened in 1976 during America's love affair with colonial history. Since that time it has grown to include 69 structures on 700 acres. The late John Wehle, a local businessman whose family founded Genesee Brewing Co., worked with architectural historian Stuart Bolger to acquire these buildings from around rural Western New York and assemble them as a replica 19th-century town of the region.

"We have a huge collection of buildings ranging from former private homes and churches to law offices and a boot and shoemaker's shop," says Katie DeTar, public relations manager. "These, along with our acres of heirloom gardens, enable guests to see exactly how people lived during the 19th century."

The museum purchased some structures, and others were donated.

While all the buildings have a unique story, visitor favorites include the Victorian Italianate Hamilton House from Campbell, Steuben County, built in 1870, and the hexagon-shaped Hyde House from Friendship in Allegany County. Other buildings of note are Romulus Female Seminary, Davis Opera House, Col. Nathaniel Rochester House and Hosmer's Inn.

Paid interpreters, some 120 of them, wear period garb and go about the daily tasks of life as weavers, farmers, tinsmiths, bakers, potters, gunsmiths and more. Volunteers help out as gardeners, painters, event assistants and gift shop clerks.

Nearly every weekend during the main season—May through October—is filled with special events, from Civil War re-enactments to musket-firing demonstrations to fiddlers' festivals. Visitors can sign up for Saturday-night Hearth Dinners or stroll the grounds and visit the complex's cadre of critters, including four oxen, six goats, five sheep and two pigs.

While the bulk of activity happens during the warmer months, museum grounds are busy during winter and early spring as well: cross-country skiing, snowshoeing and sugar maple tapping on 175 acres of woodlands and meadows.

The complex continues to expand. Opening in 2006 is a tailor shop, circa 1850.

The museum is known for keeping up with the times, Sheridan says.

"Genesee Country Village & Museum is constantly reinventing itself and leading the way among our country's living-history museums. It provides a marvelous service to visitors: encouraging what we hope will be a lifelong interest in American history."

Genesee Country Village & Museum
1410 Flint Hill Road, Mumford, 538-6822, www.gcv.org

1830s structure features handmade quilts, a beehive oven and furnishings of the period. Walking trails wind through a nature park on the grounds.

Valentown Museum

Route 96, across from EastView Mall, Victor   *B21*
924-4170; www.valentown.org
Built in 1879 as the first structure in a town that never materialized, Valentown houses a cobbler's shop, music school, country store and harness maker's shop. Important regional historical papers and artifacts are on display. In 1940, the late historian Sheldon Fisher bought the abandoned building and turned it into a museum. The town of Victor has grown explosively around it. The museum stands as a quiet reminder of the past in an area of busy commercial development.

Victorian scientific curiosities and more. Remains and a resin cast of a mastodon found south of Avon are on display. ExploraZone offers hands-on science exhibits through a partnership with San Francisco's Exploratorium. Strasenburgh Planetarium runs star shows, giant-screen nature films and late-night laser shows set to music. The museum's Cumming Nature Center (6472 Gulick Road, Naples) has six miles of walking trails and a visitor center in the Bristol Hills.

Sonnenberg Gardens and Mansion

151 Charlotte St., Canandaigua   *B21*
394-4922; www.sonnenberg.org
The summer home of Canandaigua benefactors Frederick Ferris Thompson and Mary Clark Thompson, Sonnenberg is a Victorian mansion and gardens. Frederick Thompson was a founder of the forerunner of Citibank. Sonnenberg has been named a state historic park. The 1885 Queen Anne-style mansion has 40 rooms. The gardens were designed and built in the early decades of the 20th century. You will find nine themed gardens and a reflecting pond, along with a conservatory complex that is considered one of the most significant residential greenhouse complexes in the country. The garden season for 2006 is from May 13 to Oct. 8. Finger Lakes Wine Center is on the grounds and accessible free of charge.

Stone-Tolan House Museum

2370 East Ave., Brighton   *E13*
442-4606; www.landmarksociety.org
546-7029, ext. 14, for group tours
Orringh Stone and his family managed their farm and rural tavern here from 1790 to 1820. One of Rochester's oldest houses, Stone-Tolan features furnishings, utensils and clothing of the period. Visitors will find an authentic representation of early 19th century landscape in the apple orchard, herb garden, privy, smokehouse and 200 varieties of plants.

Strong Museum

1 Manhattan Square, Rochester   *C4*
263-2700; www.strongmuseum.org
(Closed May 29 to July 13, 2006, for expansion)
Rated one of the top 10 children's museums in the country by Child *magazine, Strong Museum offers hands-on learning experiences and traveling exhibits. Kids can put on a play, produce a radio show, pilot a helicopter and play on "Sesame Street," an authentic reproduction of the TV show set. The National Toy Hall of Fame is located here. The museum also holds 500,000 objects collected by founder Margaret Woodbury Strong—including the world's most comprehensive collection of dolls. The museum is undergoing a $33 million expansion in 2006 that will nearly double its size. (See story on page 43.)*

Susan B. Anthony House

17 Madison St., Rochester   *C2*
235-6124; www.susanbanthonyhouse.org
The pioneer leader of the women's rights movement lived here with her sister Mary, writing and organizing, during the years she campaigned for woman suffrage. Anthony was arrested in this house for voting in 1872. She met with Frederick Douglass, Elizabeth Cady Stanton and other reformers in the parlor. The house, a National Historic Landmark, is filled with photos, memorabilia and much original furniture. The Education and Visitor Center next door at 19 Madison St., once the home of her sister Hannah, contains exhibits and a gift shop.

Tinker Homestead and Farm Museum

1585 Calkins Road, Henrietta   *F3*
359-7042
Free admission
Cobblestone buildings are rare, and Rochester is at the center of the largest concentration of this type of architecture. Tinker Homestead is a fine example of a home built in the style. The

Victorian Doll Museum and Chili Doll Hospital

4332 Buffalo Road, North Chili   *E10*
247-0130
View thousands of collector dolls in floor-to-ceiling glass cases. You'll find dolls of all kinds: bisque, china, wood, wax, metal, felt, ivory, papier mache, celluloid and paper. The museum also shows dolls representing famous personalities of comics, literature, movies, advertising, fashion and more. The doll hospital is not open for tours, but parts used for doll repairs are on view. The gift shop sells brand name and collector dolls.

Warner Castle at Rochester Civic Garden Center

5 Castle Park, corner of Mt. Hope Avenue and Reservoir Street, Rochester   *E3*
473-5130
Free admission
Designed in 1854 to resemble the ancestral castle of the Douglas clan, the former home of Horatio Gates Warner today houses a horticultural learning center, library and gift shop. Visitors also can tour gardens in back, including a sunken garden designed by famed landscape architect Alling DeForest.

Woodside: Rochester Historical Society

485 East Ave., Rochester   *C4*
271-2705; www.rochesterhistory.org
Rochester's finest address in the 1800s, today it is the home of the Rochester Historical Society. Founded in 1860 by Lewis Henry Morgan, the father of American anthropology, it is the city's oldest surviving museum. The library's 10,000 volumes and pamphlets are a rich resource for genealogists and history buffs. Original portraits of hundreds of area pioneers, including Nathaniel Rochester himself, are here.

parks & gardens

Parks

Ever since nurserymen George Ellwanger and Patrick Barry donated 20 acres for a city park in the 1880s, parks have been a quality-of-life priority in Rochester. Their donation formed the nucleus of Highland Park and launched the city's parks system.

Famed landscape architect Frederick Law Olmsted, who designed Central Park in New York City, was responsible for Rochester's anchor parks: North Park (now Maplewood and Seneca) and South Park (Genesee Valley). He sited them along the Genesee River, with trails that offer scenic views and wide lawns for both passive and active recreation.

Local residents today enjoy 21 parks on nearly 12,000 urban and suburban acres in Monroe County. Admission to all of them is free unless otherwise noted. Maps, trail descriptions and other park facts are available to download from the Monroe County Web site, www.monroecounty.gov. Follow the Parks link.

Most park trails are open to walkers, runners, horseback riders and cross-country skiers; check signs. Bicycles are not allowed on most trails, but there are exceptions. See the Trails and Walking Tours section on page 57 for details.

Lake Ontario meets Irondequoit Bay at the pier in Seabreeze.

to run, walk or bike along its paved path, a continuous stretch that connects Genesee Valley Park to the city center. Bridges provide access to paths and neighborhoods on the river's east side. The park has picnic tables, and at a bend in the river, its views of downtown are second to none.

Bausch & Lomb Riverside Park
Wilson Boulevard, Rochester *D3*

This city park follows the eastern bank of the Genesee River next to the University of Rochester. Calling it River Walk, Frederick Law Olmsted planned the three-quarter-mile stretch of 197 oak trees as part of the university campus. Most visitors use the park

Black Creek Park
Entrances on Union Street, Chili-Riga Town Line Road and Route 33A, Chili and Riga *F9*

Ride horseback in the fall or cross-country ski in the winter across Black Creek Park's more than 1,500 undeveloped acres. Non-fuel model airplane enthusiasts gather here to fly their

craft. Visitors also will find a playground, two ponds and picnic areas. Woodside Lodge and Pathfinder Shelter are available to rent.

Channing Philbrick Park
Linear Park Drive, off Route 441, Penfield *E14*

Irondequoit Creek tumbles 90 feet in one mile, giving the park's Falls Trail its name. Hikers like the route in all seasons; anglers abound during fishing season. There's a small playground, bathrooms, picnic tables and emergency phone.

Springdale Farm at Northampton Park is popular with children.

For something a little different

Green grass, softball fields and grills aren't the only attractions in area parks. Here are some unique offerings:

Black Creek Park—Fly your non-fuel model airplanes.

Churchville Park—Golf in the summer and skate in the winter.

Devil's Cove Park—The only way you can get here is on a boat.

Durand Eastman Park—A Robert Trent Jones golf course, arboretum and horseback riding

Ellison Park—Rochester's disc golf destination, plus horseback-riding trails

Genesee Valley Park—Two 18-hole golf courses, an indoor skating rink, canoe rentals, and both the Erie Canal and Genesee River

Highland Park—Breathe some spring air in the dead of winter at Lamberton Conservatory, and pay tribute to Vietnam veterans at the memorial.

Irondequoit Bay Marine Park—Take in Lake Ontario on the pier.

Maplewood Park—The sprawling rose garden comes alive in June.

Mendon Ponds Park—Ride a horse and feed the practically tame chickadees.

Northampton Park—Kids love Springdale Farm, as well as the kid-size slope for skiing and snowboarding. Make a day of it at Pulver House Museum and the remote-control flying field.

Ontario Beach Park—The restored 1905 Dentzel carousel and boardwalk beckon.

Powder Mills Park—In the summer, visit the historic fish hatchery. In the winter, learn to ski.

Seneca Park—Elephants and their like hang out here (at the zoo).

Webster Park—This is the only county park where you can camp or cabin overnight.

Churchville Park

Kendall Road and Main Street, Churchville *F8*
Located on Black Creek, Churchville Park offers fishing and boating. Though the park has no maintained trails, open spaces, lodges and shelters for picnics and relaxation abound. There's also a golf course and an outdoor skating rink.

Corbett's Glen Nature Park

Penfield Road south of North Landing Road, Brighton *E14*
Woods, meadows, wetlands and a waterfall on Allen's Creek fill the park's 17 acres. The creek is a spawning ground for salmon and trout.

Devil's Cove Park

Water access only from east shore of Irondequoit Bay, Webster *D13*
Curious boaters will find a natural and undeveloped spot for a quiet picnic in Devil's Cove.

Durand-Eastman Park

Lakeshore Boulevard, Culver Road and Kings Highway, Rochester *C13*
The park's 965 acres include 5,000 feet of Lake Ontario waterfront, trails for hiking, horseback riding and cross-country skiing, a Robert Trent Jones golf course, picnic shelters and playgrounds. Packed with mature trees and other plants, the park is an arboretum and a nature-lover's paradise.

Ellison Park

Blossom Road, Landing Road, Brighton *E14*
Irondequoit Creek winds through 447 acres of woods and wetlands here. The park has a disc golf course, tennis courts, softball fields, playground, shelters, lodges and trails for hiking, horseback riding and cross-country skiing.

Genesee Valley Park

Elmwood Avenue at Moore Road, and East River Road, Rochester *E12*
Landscape architect Frederick Law Olmsted designed the park, originally called South Park. Majestic trees, wide lawns and the Genesee River define the serene setting. The park is home to the Stonehurst Capital Invitational Regatta, which draws top-ranked collegiate rowing teams every October. Within the park, Genesee Valley Golf Club has two public, 18-hole golf courses.

Greece Canal Park

Elmgrove Road at Mellwood Road, Greece *D10*
The Barge Canal borders the southern edge of this 577-acre park. Woods, meadows and wetlands offer great hiking and biking; one of the trails is part of the New York State Canal Trail system. A playground, softball and soccer fields, picnic areas, lodges and shelters make the park a popular destination.

Highland Park

Reservoir Avenue at Goodman Street or South Avenue, Rochester *E3, 4*
Frederick Law Olmsted designed this park as an arboretum of trees, shrubs, azaleas, lilacs, rhododendron, horse chestnuts, Japanese maples, magnolias and more. The annual Lilac Festival is held here in May. Park highlights include a reservoir, Lamberton Conservatory, the Greater Rochester Vietnam Veterans Memorial, AIDS Remembrance Garden, Victims' Rights Memorial, Iris Friendship Garden and Warner Castle. Paved walking paths and sidewalks wind through woodlands and meadows.

Irondequoit Bay Park East

Empire Boulevard at Smith Road, Penfield *D14*
The park's undeveloped 182 acres provide fishing access on the bay's eastern shore in Irondequoit. Woodlands sloping down to shore are great for vigorous hiking.

Irondequoit Bay Park West

Empire Boulevard on south shore, Penfield *D13*
This park offers fishing spots on the bay, as well as forested hiking on 147 acres. A small undeveloped boat launch is available.

Irondequoit Bay Marine Park

I-590 and Culver Road, Irondequoit *C13*
The marine park provides fee-based boat access to Irondequoit Bay, which empties into Lake Ontario to the north. A pier is popular with anglers and a great place to watch boat activity. Hamburger stands and historic Seabreeze Amusement Park are close by.

Lehigh Valley Linear Trail Park

Rush-West Rush Road at Route 15A, Rush Plains Road at Junction Road, Mendon Route 251 at Route 64 (Pittsford-Mendon Center Road), Mendon *B20, 21*
The 15-mile linear park rolls through Monroe County's southern towns. Biking, hiking and

Aptly named Powder Mills Park draws hikers and cross-country skiers all winter (above). Corbett's Glen has acres of wetlands and woods, plus a waterfall on Allen's Creek (right).

Away from it all, in the city

In cities that understand the value of urban oases, parks designed by Frederick Law Olmsted are treasured. Some of the best examples of the famed landscape architect's work are right here in Rochester.

Rochester was the last of only five cities for which Olmsted designed a whole system of parks. (The others are Boston, Buffalo, Louisville and New York City. Additional cities hired him to design individual parks.) What makes Rochester's parks special is their largely intact design. Walking through them is to see Olmsted's vision realized in the alignment of walks, drives and trees, and in the magnificence of mature plantings.

"Olmsted changed how we saw our public open space and what we expected when we went to a park," says Joann Beck, senior landscape architect for the city. "These spaces bring value and commitment to the community. It's something that an emerging city could not acquire at any price."

And like no other system in his repertoire, Olmsted's parks in Rochester are distinct from one another. Genesee Valley has a pastoral quality, Highland is picturesque and Seneca is grand.

"You really have to see all three because each one is so distinctive," says Beck, who leads walking tours of the parks.

Highland, Seneca and parts of Maplewood are registered on the National Register of Historic Places. The remainder of Maplewood is part of the Maplewood Historic District.

Genesee Valley Park

Olmsted selected land that is rolling and meadowlike, with the wide, slow-moving Genesee meandering through. Here you'll find the classic English landscape adapted to the new world. "This is more like the landscape you see in Prospect Park and Central Park, with the big expansive views," Beck says.

Beck recommends: Walk or bike through the newly improved expanse between Elmwood Avenue and the Erie Canal. It has a restored carousel, a trail along the river and wide-open spaces anchored by massive oaks. Sheep once grazed here. For views of the canal, you'll find three picturesque footbridges added by Olmsted's sons. (The canal was rerouted from downtown in 1918 and intersects the river in the park.)

Tranquil Seneca Park is an oasis in the city.

Highland Park

Olmsted forged a rare 50-50 partnership with the city to develop and design this park, making Highland absolutely unique in his body of work. Sharing this responsibility is something he likely would have shunned earlier in his career.

Steep terrain was a design challenge. Olmsted made winding paths that took people up and down hills gradually, with vistas at every turn.

The horticultural displays that Highland is famed for—including its world-class collection of lilacs—were the city's priority, not Olmsted's, but he blended them into his vision with his signature finesse. The result is a nationally respected arboretum. Since 1892, the Lilac Festival has drawn hundreds of thousands every year for 10 days in May.

Beck recommends: In the pinetum (pie-nee-tum) along Reservoir Drive and Doctor's Road, mature conifers march up steep hills and reach to the sky, lending a cathedral effect.

Another visitor favorite is a stroll through the rhododendron valley. A paved path winds lazily through masses of century-old bushes bursting with blooms in early summer. Lamberton Conservatory on Reservoir Avenue is open year-round. The Lord & Burnham building was added after the park was developed but sited in consultation with Olmsted's firm. "It's a little jewel," Beck says.

Seneca Park

The original North Park is today two parks: Maplewood on the west side of the Genesee River and Seneca on the east. They are connected by a footbridge that offers extraordinary views of the river gorge.

Of the two, Seneca retains more of the Olmsted touches. Its 297 acres are the epitome of natural elegance and drama, with its towering trees, deep river gorge, and curvy roads and paths. The placid Trout Pond is the most noticeable Olmsted touch and still beautifully intact. Deep in this park, surrounded by forest, it's hard to imagine you are in the city.

Beck recommends: Take the park drive from its entrance on St. Paul Boulevard and watch vistas unfold as Olmsted

intended. The road winds down and around the Trout Pond, one of the most pristine and preserved Olmsted designs anywhere. Stop at any point to walk the trail along the gorge's edge, where rocky walls cascade to the river far below.

Maplewood Park

Maplewood is a point of pride for neighbors. Its annual festival in June draws thousands to the 5,000-bloom rose garden. Paths for walking and biking are popular; new signs, landscaping and art have been added in the last couple of years. (See the Trails & Walking Tours section for details on city trails.)

Beck recommends: This is the only Olmsted park where you'll find gorgeous close-up views of the Middle and Lower

Mirroring his designs of Prospect Park and Central Park in New York City, Olmsted gave Genesee Valley Park a pastoral quality reminiscent of the classic English landscape.

Falls. A sign marks Kelsey's Landing, where former slaves seeking freedom boarded ships bound for Canada. Through the trees to the gorge below near the Lower Falls, see if you can glimpse the remains of the Glen House, a popular dancing and dining establishment around the turn of the 20th century.

cross-country skiing are popular here.

Maplewood Park
See Maplewood Rose Garden, page 56.

Mendon Ponds Park
Multiple entrances on Route 65 (Clover Street) and Route 64 (Pittsford-Mendon Center Road), Pittsford and Mendon *G13*
The largest of the county's parks has 2,500 acres of woods, wetlands and water. It has 30 miles of trails. One-fifth of the park is a nature preserve filled with seven miles of wooded trails. It's a great place for hiking, horseback riding and cross-country skiing. The historic Cobblestone House, overlooking Hundred Acres Pond on Douglas Road, is available to the public for special events.

Mt. Hope Cemetery
791 Mt. Hope Ave., Rochester *E3*
461-3494; www.fomh.org
Dedicated in 1838, Mt. Hope was the first great Victorian cemetery developed by a municipality. Set on wooded, steeply rolling terrain, Mt. Hope holds mausoleums tucked into hillsides and abundant Victorian funerary art. It is the final resting place of American leaders in business and social reform, including Frederick Douglass, Susan B. Anthony, John Jacob Bausch, Henry Lomb, Frank E. Gannett and the city's founder, Col. Nathaniel Rochester. At the entrance, note the 1874 High Victorian Gothic gatehouse and the 1872 Moorish gazebo.

Northampton Park
Colby Street at either Hubbell Road or Salmon Creek Road, Sweden and Ogden *D8*
This 973-acre park in the towns of Ogden and Sweden features Springdale Farm, an educational attraction popular with families. Beginning skiers and snowboarders will find a rope tow, ski rental and a slope that's just the right size. The park has hiking trails, lodges and sports fields, along with the Pulver House Museum, operated by the Ogden Historical Society. A remote-control flying field is open to users with an AMA license.

Oatka Creek Park
Union Street and Stewart Road, Wheatland *D10*

In Oatka Creek's abundant waters, fly-casting anglers find trout. Roughly a mile of this waterway winds through the park's 461 undeveloped acres.

Ontario Beach Park
Beach Avenue at Lake Avenue, Charlotte *C12*
This is where the city of Rochester dips its toes into Lake Ontario. Along with a sandy beach with guarded swimming area, the park offers a playground, boat launch, fishing pier and boardwalk. The original 1905 Dentzel menagerie carousel and Roger Robach Community Center (the renovated former bathhouse) are reminders of Charlotte's days as the Coney Island of the West. Concerts by the Shore at the Performance Pavilion draw hundreds of music lovers on summer nights.

Powder Mills Park
Route 96 (Pittsford-Victor Road) at Park Road, Bushnell's Basin *G14*
A historic fish hatchery is the focal point, but Powder Mills Park offers plenty more: downhill skiing lessons, sand volleyball courts, trails for cross-country skiing and hiking, plus picnic shelters, fishing access and a playground.

Seneca Park
St. Paul Street north of Route 104, Rochester *D12*
A Frederick Law Olmsted park, Seneca hugs the Genesee River gorge on the east side, north of downtown. The park is home to the Seneca Park Zoo, established in 1894. Forested hiking trails, Trout Pond and dramatic views of the deep gorge are highlights of the park. Call 467-9453 for zoo hours and admission prices.

Tryon Park
North Winton Road at Tryon Park, Irondequoit *D13*
This little park (82 acres) along Irondequoit Bay's western shore is undeveloped and low-key. Nature lovers like the wooded trails and water views.

Webster Park
East Lake Road at Holt Road *C14*
Perched on a bluff overlooking Lake Ontario, the park has 550 rolling, treed acres. Groups use its lodges and shelters, including the spacious White House, a former residence. Sports fields, a playground, trails and picnic areas offer plenty to do. Venture out on the pier to catch a fish or a sunset. Cabins and a campground can be reserved from May to October.

Looking for a nearby state park? A dozen lie within a couple hours' drive of Rochester, all great camping, hiking and picnicking spots. Check out Easy Day Trips on page 92.
For more information on park trails, see the Trails and Walking Tours section on page 57.

Gardens

From grand Victorian gardens surrounding mansions to fields of roses and tulips in county parks, flowers are everywhere in Rochester. Some of the unique finds are an heirloom garden at a living-history museum, a sensory garden accessible to people with disabilities and two arboretums. In the winter, check out our conservatory, indoor gardens and flower shows. There is a charge for admission unless otherwise noted.

Ellwanger Garden
625 Mt. Hope Ave., Rochester *D3*
546-7029
Cultivated since 1867, this historic garden contains perennials, roses and trees in an English natural-garden style. George Ellwanger,

The Performance Pavilion at Ontario Beach Park is surrounded by music lovers during summer band concerts. In autumn, the park has a more tranquil feel.

Seneca Park Zoo

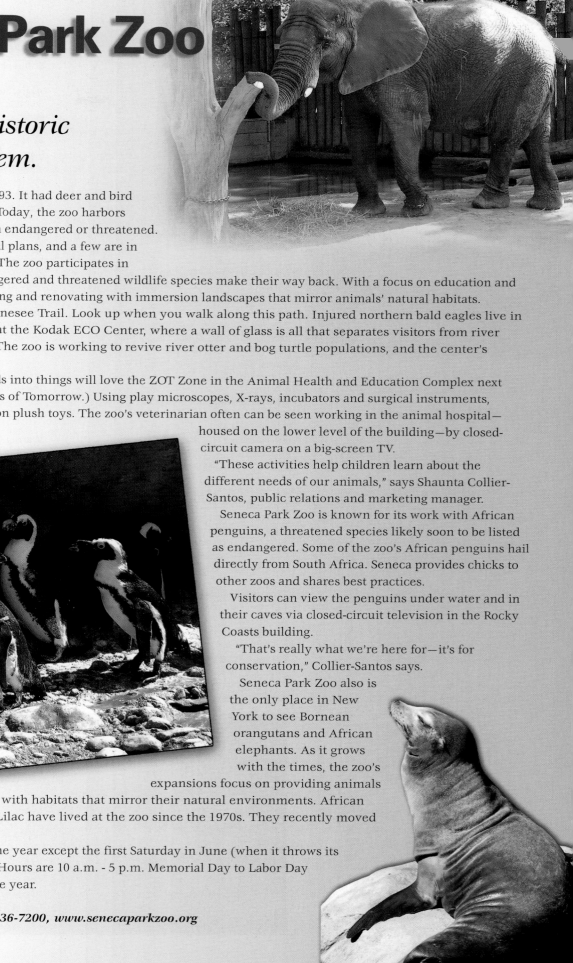

Tucked into one of Rochester's historic city parks is a gem.

Seneca Park Zoo opened in 1893. It had deer and bird displays and traveling exhibits. Today, the zoo harbors dozens of species, many of them endangered or threatened. At least 15 are in species survival plans, and a few are in population management plans. The zoo participates in worldwide efforts to help endangered and threatened wildlife species make their way back. With a focus on education and conservation, the zoo is expanding and renovating with immersion landscapes that mirror animals' natural habitats.

That's the idea behind the Genesee Trail. Look up when you walk along this path. Injured northern bald eagles live in the trees above. The trail ends at the Kodak ECO Center, where a wall of glass is all that separates visitors from river otters swimming under water. The zoo is working to revive river otter and bog turtle populations, and the center's exhibits tell the story.

Kids who like to get their hands into things will love the ZOT Zone in the Animal Health and Education Complex next door. ("ZOT" stands for Zoologists of Tomorrow.) Using play microscopes, X-rays, incubators and surgical instruments, children conduct examinations on plush toys. The zoo's veterinarian often can be seen working in the animal hospital—housed on the lower level of the building—by closed-circuit camera on a big-screen TV.

"These activities help children learn about the different needs of our animals," says Shaunta Collier-Santos, public relations and marketing manager.

Seneca Park Zoo is known for its work with African penguins, a threatened species likely soon to be listed as endangered. Some of the zoo's African penguins hail directly from South Africa. Seneca provides chicks to other zoos and shares best practices.

Visitors can view the penguins under water and in their caves via closed-circuit television in the Rocky Coasts building.

"That's really what we're here for—it's for conservation," Collier-Santos says.

Seneca Park Zoo also is the only place in New York to see Bornean orangutans and African elephants. As it grows with the times, the zoo's expansions focus on providing animals with habitats that mirror their natural environments. African elephants Genny C and Lilac have lived at the zoo since the 1970s. They recently moved into a new home on 2 1/2 acres.

The zoo is open every day of the year except the first Saturday in June (when it throws its annual fundraiser, Zoobilation). Hours are 10 a.m. - 5 p.m. Memorial Day to Labor Day and 10 a.m. - 4 p.m. the rest of the year.

Seneca Park Zoo,
2222 St. Paul St., Rochester, 336-7200, www.senecaparkzoo.org

one of Rochester's leading nurserymen, lived in a home adjacent to the garden.

Genesee Country Village & Museum
1410 Flint Hill Road, Mumford *B20*
538-6822; www.gcv.org
This historic village has a dozen heirloom gardens full of flowers, vegetables and herbs. Not just for show, their bounty is used by the museum's historical interpreters for meals, dyed fibers, decorations and crafts. Visitors will find medicinal, formal, cottage, children's and classical gardens, among others. Some gardens contain crops bred back to original types, such as Danvers half-long carrots and China rose radish.

George Eastman House Gardens
900 East Ave., Rochester *C5*
271-3361; www.eastman.org
George Eastman, who founded Eastman Kodak Co., grew up in a family immersed in horticulture. The formal gardens of his 50-room Colonial Revival mansion feature Italian, French and English landscapes. An English walled garden, a cutting garden and a terrace garden designed by Alling DeForest are among the sights. During the winter, tours of the mansion feature a plant-filled conservatory and magnificent flower arrangements.

Lamberton Conservatory
Highland Park
Reservoir Drive, Rochester *E3*
256-5878
Built in 1911 and open year-round, the conservatory shelters displays of tropical, desert and other exotic plantings, with clever educational markers to help visitors of all ages notice blooms and other plant activity. Be sure to see the Japanese fish in the center courtyard pond. Seasonal plant and flower displays are changed five times a year.

With nine gardens and a conservatory complex, something is always blooming at Sonnenberg Mansion and Gardens in Canandaigua (left and below).

Linwood
1912 York Road (off Route 36), York *B20*
584-3913
Established at the turn of the last century by a Buffalo industrialist as his family's country residence, this 325-acre property boasts eight acres of tree peony, water, Italian and sculpture gardens. Little known locally, the garden is renowned around the country, particularly for its tree peonies, cultivated here for 40 years. The private gardens are open to the public only during two Tree Peony Weekends in late May and early June.

Maplewood Rose Garden
Lake and Driving Park avenues, Rochester *A2*
Free admission
Part of an original Frederick Law Olmsted-designed city park, Maplewood Rose Garden boasts some 5,000 roses in hundreds of varieties. The annual Maplewood Rose Festival draws thousands every June. (It is taking a hiatus in 2006.)

Rochester Museum & Science Center
657 East Ave., Rochester *C5*
271-4552; www.rmsc.org
Free admission to gardens
The science museum's 12-acre landscaped campus holds three gardens: Garden of Fragrance is patterned after those planted by colonists. Mary E. Slifer Memorial Garden honors a conservationist with native ferns, wildflowers and exotic species in a shady setting. Kearns Family Garden features a bronze sculpture of young bears frolicking. Tulips in the spring and annuals in the summer encircle the garden.

Sharon's Sensory Garden
Nature Center, Mendon Ponds Park, Mendon *G13*
Free admission
Designed for full access by people with visual or physical disabilities, this informal garden emphasizes color, texture, fragrance and form. The layout lets visitors get close to the plants. Signs are in Braille and raised lettering. Graded

paths and raised flowerbeds allow full access for visitors in wheelchairs.

Sonnenberg Mansion and Gardens
151 Charlotte St., Canandaigua *B21*
Weekdays 394-4922; www.sonnenberg.org
At the former summer home of Canandaigua benefactors, nine themed gardens and a reflecting pond were designed and built in the early years of the 20th century. Among the gardens are a Japanese landscape, a formal Italian garden and individual themed gardens. The conservatory complex, ranked among the finest residential greenhouse complexes in the country, has the domed Palm House and tropical plants.

University of Rochester Arboretum
Elmwood Avenue at Wilson Boulevard, Rochester *E2*
273-5627; www.facilities.rochester.edu/arboretum
Free admission
In its 150-year history, the university has used trees as a central landscape design element. Frederick Law Olmsted Jr. served as designer and consultant to the architects during construction of the River Campus. In 1999, the university converted portions of the campus to an arboretum. Take a self-guided tour of more than 70 tree species and six gardens; the university's department of horticulture and grounds provides a detailed map.

Warner Castle
5 Castle Park, corner of Mt. Hope Avenue and Reservoir Street, Rochester *E3*
Free admission
The 22-room house, now home to the Rochester Civic Garden Center, was built for judge and publisher Horatio Gates Warner in 1854. The grounds in back include a sunken garden, a popular setting for wedding photographs. The garden was designed by landscape architect Alling DeForest.

Webster Sesquicentennial Arboretum
Irving Kent Park
1700 Schlegel Road, Webster *C15*
www.websterny.com/arboretum
Free admission
The arboretum is a 32.5-acre display of flowers, herbs, shrubs and mature woodland cultivated by the town of Webster and local volunteers. You'll find it in Irving Kent Park.

Trails & *Walking Tours*

The Best 100 Miles

When the Erie Canal opened as a trade route in 1825, commerce in Rochester reached a new level. Today this historic treasure and its towpath are part of a network of more than 260 miles of multi-use recreational trails and 524 miles of waterways across Upstate New York.

The New York State Canal System comprises the Erie and three other historic waterways: the Champlain, the Oswego and the Cayuga-Seneca Canals. The system links the Hudson River, Lake Champlain, Lake Ontario, the Finger Lakes and the Niagara River with communities rich in history and culture.

New York has one of the most extensive trail networks in the country, and it's still growing. Many of the trails follow the towpaths along the canals and connect to other trail systems throughout the state.

The towpath is a great place for cycling, hiking and running. An eight-day ride called Cycling the Erie Canal, held every summer, takes riders 400 miles from Buffalo to Albany. Rochester lies at the heart of that route, in the "Best 100 Miles" of the Erie Canal. Known as the Heritage Trail, this section provides a continuous bike and hike path from Lockport to Palmyra. Recent local improvements to the trail, between Long Pond Road in Greece and Lock 32 in Pittsford, added an asphalt surface, a centerline stripe and informational kiosks.

The Erie Canal traveled through downtown Rochester in the 1800s, crossing the Genesee River via an aqueduct. You can see the aqueduct below the Broad Street Bridge. It later was rerouted south of downtown, through Genesee Valley Park, where its intersection with the Genesee River remains one of the prettiest spots along either waterway.

Like the canals of Europe, the Erie Canal today is a recreational waterway for everything from pleasure craft to kayaks. From spring to fall, the canal is a parade of boats hailing from distant states and

Canada. Local marinas rent out self-skippered charter boats for canal cruises.

Near Rochester, you can find Erie Canal towpath entrance points in the villages of Brockport, Spencerport, Pittsford, Fairport and Bushnell's Basin. They have places to eat and shop—or just to sit and watch the ducks.

Other entrances, with parking areas and, in some cases, picnic tables and restrooms, can be found at:

■ Greece Canal Park on Elmgrove Road, south of Ridge Road in the town of Greece

■ Genesee Valley Park, entrance at Elmwood Avenue between Lattimore Road and Brooks Avenue in Rochester

■ Clinton Avenue between Westfall Road and Brighton-Henrietta Town Line Road in Brighton

■ Lock 32 off Clover Street (Route 65), between French Road and Jefferson Road.

www.canals.state.ny.us

Park trails

Monroe County's 21 county parks offer nearly 12,000 acres to cross-country ski, hike, horseback ride, bike, fish, picnic and play golf. See Parks and Gardens on page 49 for park descriptions and locations.

Most park trails are open to walkers, runners, horseback riders and cross-country skiers; check signs. Bicycles are not allowed on most trails.

Black Creek Park
Ridge: 1.4 miles, easy, rolling
Creek: 3.1 miles, moderate (due to length), rolling
Hickory: 1.4 miles, easy, flat
Bluebird: 1.2 miles, easy, flat
Wetland: 2.1 miles, easy, rolling

Durand-Eastman Park
Durand Lake: 1.2 miles, moderate, rolling hills
Trott Lake: 0.5 mile, easy, small hills
Eastman Lake: 1.5 miles, easy, gently rolling

Ellison Park
Coyote Den: 1.1 mile, easy, gradually uphill
Overlook Loop: 0.6 mile, moderate to difficult, one very steep section
Mill Race: 0.4 mile, easy, level
Indian Landing: 1.5 miles, easy, level
Butler's Gap: 0.7 mile, moderate, rolling (with one steep climb)

Genesee Valley Park
The county's recreational trail network converges in this park, linking nearly every town and many area parks. A paved trail leads runners, bikers and skaters past river views and over historic bridges on their way to the popular east-west Erie Canal path.

Greece Canal Park
Deer Run: 1.4 miles, easy, gently rolling
Canal: 0.9 mile, easy, gently rolling
Farm Artifact: 0.9 mile, easy, level
West: 0.4 mile, easy, level

Trails & *Walking Tours*

Highland Park
Paved walking paths wind up and down this hilly city park, through woodlands and meadows.

Irondequoit Bay Park East
Woodlands sloping down to shore are great for vigorous hiking.

Irondequoit Bay Park West
Forested hiking on 147 acres

Lehigh Valley Linear Trail Park
The 15-mile linear park rolls through Monroe County's southern towns. Biking, hiking and cross-country skiing are popular here.

Mendon Ponds Park
Bird Song/Swamp: 2 miles, moderate, hilly
Devil's Bathtub: 0.67 mile, easy, one steep climb
East Esker: 4.7 miles, challenging, hilly
Fern Valley: 1.4 miles, easy, gently rolling
Grasslands: 2 miles, easy, gently rolling
North Meadow: 1.8 miles, moderate, gently rolling
Pine Woods: 1 mile, easy, gently rolling
Quaker Pond Loop: 2.7 miles, easy, level
Southern Meadow: 3 miles, easy, gently rolling
West Esker: 1.5 miles, moderate, hilly

Northampton Park
Gardner: 1.8 miles, easy, level
Creek: 1.3 miles, easy, gently rolling
Fairview: 1.1 miles, easy, gently rolling
Loop: 0.4 mile, easy, level
Farm: 1.5 miles, easy to moderate, rolling

Powder Mills Park
Hatchery: 0.8 mile, moderate, rolling
Daffodil Meadow: 0.7 mile, easy, gently rolling
Ridge: 0.4 mile (one way), moderate, rolling
Trillium: 0.5 mile, easy (one way), level to gently rolling
Powder Horn: 0.6 mile, easy, gently rolling
Southern: Unmarked, moderate to challenging

Seneca Park
Olmsted North: 1 mile, easy to moderate, optional descents to river
Olmsted South: 0.7 mile, easy, gently rolling
Gorge Overlook: 0.1 mile, easy, level

Webster Park
Ridge: 1.4 miles, easy, gently rolling
West Loop: 1.6 miles, easy to moderate, some hills
Valley View: 0.6 mile, easy, gently rolling
Ryan's Point: 0.5 mile, moderate, hills
Orchard: 0.8 mile, easy to moderate, rolling

Walking tours

The Landmark Society of Western New York, one of the oldest and most active preservation organizations in the country, has put together walking tours of downtown and city neighborhoods to introduce you to Rochester's colorful past. We've chosen three to tell you about here, but you can download a tour guide commentary packed with many more details and a map. Just go to the Web site listed with each tour, or pick one up from the Downtown Guides Information Center at Clinton Avenue and Main Street, 232-3420. www.landmarksociety.org/tours/index.html

Center City: 4/5-mile loop
www.landmarksociety.org/tours/tour_pdf/1.pdf
This historic section of Rochester crosses and parallels the Genesee River. It features 24 sites along this tour, including two historic districts and 13 buildings listed in the National Register of Historic Places. As you walk, you will visit the places where Rochester began. Starting with the Genesee River and Main Street Bridge, the Erie Canal and its Broad Street aqueduct, and the location where world-renowned abolitionist Frederick Douglass published his anti-slavery publications, you'll absorb Rochester's fascinating local history.

Along this route you will see several examples of Rochester's best downtown architecture.

East End: 3/5-mile one way
www.landmarksociety.org/tours/tour_pdf/6.pdf
This tour begins at Rochester's famed Eastman Theatre and Eastman School of Music, which anchor the city's cultural district. The tour continues through Grove Place— downtown Rochester's tucked away, historic residential neighborhood—and ends at the Little Theatre. Grove Place, which two pioneer families settled in the 1840s, is a district on the National Register of Historic Places. It contains distinguished 19th century residential buildings, including the Ward House and the Gibbs Street townhouses. A decade of change shows in the classical architectural styles of the 1922 Eastman Theatre and the 1930s Art Deco facades of Hallman's Chevrolet (now Spot Coffee) and the Little Theatre.

High Falls/Brown's Race: 2/5 mile one way
www.landmarksociety.org/tours/tour_pdf/4.pdf
Welcome to Rochester's earliest industrial center. This urban cultural park highlights flour milling, Rochester's first industry. Brown's Race is a National Register Historic District and a city Preservation District. Your walking tour will be enhanced by grand views and interpretive markers. Be sure to stop at the Triphammer Forge, where you'll see a 25-foot waterwheel made of wood and iron. In the former Rochester Water Works is the Center at High Falls, a hands-on, interpretive museum that explores how High Falls flourished. There is very little in the Rochester area more historic than the Genesee River Gorge and its 96-foot High Falls. You can get a panoramic view from high above the gorge on the Pont de Rennes Bridge, a pedestrian and bike rider's enclave with benches.

Trail and tour resources

Footprint Press publishes trail guidebooks for the Rochester area. You can find them in bookstores or at www.footprintpress.com.

Rhoades Geologic Tours offers hiking, biking and bus tours of natural and local history in Upstate New York.
http://home.earthlink.net/~geologictours
Other helpful webs sites include:
■ www.bikerochester.com/clubs/off_road_trails/off_road_trail_list.htm
■ www.fingerlakestrail.org

Special Events

Inspired by the lakes, rivers and rolling terrain that surround our city, local artists create magic. You will discover that magic at the many festivals held here. Rochester has a deep and abiding interest in music, from classical to jazz to hip-hop?

The result? Festivals and concerts of all types, all year from military band concerts, played with a verve that will raise the hair on your arms, to a week of intimate shows by jazz artists from around the globe. Harvest festivals held in area towns celebrate wine, garlic, corn, apples and grapes—crops that grow here in abundance.

Don't forget winter. Rochester locals who don't like being stuck inside during the coldest months find their fun outdoors. Learn to ski or make maple syrup. Watch as ice sculptors chisel away to reveal their creations. Indoor boat, golf and RV shows held during our coldest months remind us that our warm-weather pursuits are just around the corner.

First held in 1892, the Lilac Festival in Frederick Law Olmsted-designed Highland Park is Rochester's oldest outdoor celebration. Attendees from around the country enjoy food, entertainment and, of course, lilac-sniffing.

May 2006

"Seeing Ourselves: Masterpieces from the George Eastman House Collection"
Through Aug. 13, 2006
George Eastman House
900 East Ave., Rochester   *C5*
www.eastmanhouse.org
Highlights from the House's photography collection are drawn from the exhibition "Seeing Ourselves," which is being prepared to tour the United States.

Kite Flight 2006
May 7, 2006 • 11 a.m. - 4 p.m.
Ontario Beach Park, Charlotte   *C12*
865-3320
Look for family entertainment and demonstrations by expert kite flyers at the beach. Bring a kite and watch the sky over the Lake Ontario shoreline fill with banners of all colors and construction.

Lilac Festival
May 12 - 21, 2006 • May 11 - 20, 2007
Highland Park
South and Highland avenues, Rochester   *E12*
Free admission
www.lilacfestival.com
The largest celebration of lilacs in North America launches Rochester's summer festival season. More than 1,200 lilac bushes in Frederick Law Olmsted-designed Highland Park are the main draw, but thousands flock to the park for over a week of musical entertainment, food, and arts and crafts vendors. Parking and shuttle at Monroe Community College, 1000 E. Henrietta Road, Brighton.

National Lake Trout Derby
May 27 - 29, 2006
Seneca Lake, Geneva   *B22*
(315) 781-2195 or (315) 789-8634
Held every Memorial Day, the derby is in its 42nd year. More than $29,000 in prizes will be handed out.

Rochester Memorial Day Parade
May 29, 2006 • 10:30 a.m.
East Avenue and Main Street,
downtown Rochester   *CC5*
The parade route starts on East at Alexander Street and proceeds to Main and then Plymouth Avenue.

June

J.P. Morgan Chase Corporate Challenge
June 1, 2006 • 7 p.m.
Rochester Institute of Technology,
Henrietta   *F11*
624-8245
www.jpmorganchasecc.com/
  events.php?city_id=3
This ritual of early summer is in its 16th year. The 10K Challenge is Rochester's largest road race; 8,663 entrants from 362 companies ran in 2005. Spectators are welcome to cheer on the racers and enjoy the party atmosphere.

East End Nightlife Festival
June 2, 2006 • 5 - 11 p.m.
East End District, Rochester   *CC6*
Rochester launches the summer with this favorite outdoor party in the East End. Area bars and street stages feature local and regional musical acts.

Fairport Canal Days
June 2 - 4, 2006
Main Street, Fairport   *F15*
Free admission
www.fairportcanaldays.com
This early-summer festival got its start in 1977.

The Wegmans Rochester LPGA, which annually features some of the biggest names in women's golf, this June will celebrate its 30th anniversary. Ten past champions are scheduled to compete in the Tournament of Champions on Tuesday, June 20.

Some 200,000 people attend the three-day event in the Erie Canal town of Fairport, an eastern Rochester suburb. More than 340 East Coast artisans display their work. Canal cruises are available on the Colonial Belle.

Highland Gathering
June 3 - 4, 2006
Genesee Country Village and Museum
1410 Flint Hill Road, Mumford   *B20*
538-6822
www.gcv.org
This weekend-long celebration of all things Scottish features pipe and drum bands, heavy athletics competition, tartans, food and dancing. Clans march in a parade of tartans and offer information on Scottish genealogy.

Landmark Society House and Garden Tour

June 3 - 4, 2006
Ambassador Drive, Brighton   E13
546-7029
www.landmarksociety.org
Rochester's preservation organization opens the doors to some of the region's finest historic homes in Brighton's stately Ambassador Drive neighborhood.

Wegmans Concerts by the Shore

Wednesdays, June 7 - Aug. 30, 2006
Ontario Beach Park, Charlotte   C12
865-3320
The lawn at Ontario Beach Park fills with blankets and chairs for these popular concerts. Local and regional bands set up in the Performance Pavilion for shows that take listeners from early evening into night. Everything from contemporary music to barbershop and old favorites is played here.

Party in the Park

Thursdays, June 8 - Aug. 10, 2006 • 5:30 p.m.
High Falls Festival Site
Browns Race, Rochester   B3
Free admission
428-6697
Bands, food and a party draw hundreds every Thursday evening to High Falls. In its third year at its new location, Party in the Park is a long-time celebration for the after-work crowd.

Rochester International Jazz Festival

June 9 - 17, 2006
15 venues, Rochester   CC6
www.rochesterjazz.com
The numbers talk: More than 300 musicians and more than 65,000 jazz enthusiasts from two dozen states and at least 15 countries came to the fourth annual festival in 2005. Some 100 concerts are scheduled this year. The European-style festival is known for bringing eclectic jazz performers from all over the world. The biggest names, too, have played sold-out shows, including Diane Reeves, Dave Brubeck, Norah Jones, John Hammond, Oscar Peterson, George Benson, Aretha Franklin, Al Jarreau, Sonny Rollins, John Mooney, the Carnegie Hall Jazz Band and Dr. John.

Peony Weekend at Ellwanger Garden

June 10 - 11, 2006 • 10 a.m. - 4 p.m.
625 Mt. Hope Ave., Rochester   D3
546-7029
www.landmarksociety.org
Eighty different kinds of perennials—featuring irises, peonies, hostas and roses—thrive in this garden established in 1867.

26th Annual Finger Lakes Carp Derby

June 11, 2006
People's Park on the Cayuga-Seneca Canal, Seneca Falls   B22
(315) 224-3994
www.carpderby.com
In a recent derby, 685 people took part on all the Finger Lakes and the Barge Canal, turning in 1,498 carp at a weigh-in at People's Park in Seneca Falls. The derby raises money for local charities.

Maplewood Rose Festival

June 17 - 18, 2006
Maplewood Rose Garden
28 Driving Park Ave., Rochester   A2
Free admission
428-6770
www.ggw.org/~mna/rose.htm
The festival centers on more than 5,000 blooms of 300 varieties in Maplewood Rose Garden high above the Genesee River Gorge's west bank. Take a tour of the river gorge and the Lower Falls through Maplewood Park. Or tour local grand, historic homes built in the late-19th and early-20th centuries. (The Maplewood Historic District is listed on the national and state Registers of Historic Places.) The three-day festival also features musical entertainment, about 100 arts and crafts vendors and food concessions.

Rochester Biennial

June 18 - Sept. 10, 2006
Memorial Art Gallery
500 University Ave., Rochester   C5
473-7720
mag.rochester.edu/look/exhibitions
This invitational exhibition of contemporary regional art includes photography, glass, painting, fiber, sculpture and printmaking.

Wegmans Rochester LPGA

June 19 - 25, 2006
Locust Hill Country Club
2000 Jefferson Road, Pittsford   F13
427-7100
www.rochesterlpga.com
The biggest names in women's golf compete for the $1.5 million purse at the Wegmans Rochester LPGA, now in its 30th year. It's one of the best-attended stops on the LPGA tour. Park at Monroe Community College and take the shuttle.

Rochester Harbor and Carousel Festival

June 23 - 25, 2006
Ontario Beach Park, Charlotte   C12
865-3320
Tens of thousands flock to the northern tip of the city for this festival, which features live entertainment, arts and crafts, food and children's activities.

Saturn Rochester Twilight Criterium

New York State Criterium Championships
June 24, 2006 • 3 - 11:30 p.m.
Downtown streets, Rochester:
Broad, Exchange, Irving,
Bausch & Lomb   DD3, 4, 5
www.rochestercrit.com
Free admission
Rochester is a big biking town. In only its third year, the criterium has made it onto the national racing calendar; 20,000 cow-bell racing fans are expected to attend. The world's top

In only its third year, the Saturn Rochester Twilight Criterium in June has made its mark on the national racing calendar. Top pro and amateur riders compete on a mile-long course on city streets.

pro and elite amateur riders race around a curvy, mile-long course on city streets. There also are kids' activities, food and beverages, a BMX freestyle show and a post-race party.

July

Rochester Jewish Film Festival

July 2006
Little Theatre
240 East Ave., Rochester   CC6
461-2000
www.rjff.org
One of a growing number of similar gatherings, the Rochester Jewish Film Festival screens feature-length films, documentaries and avant-garde short films that express the diverse Jewish experience. Visiting filmmakers, educational programs and family events round out the offerings.

Not-so-common market

It is best known for fresh produce and flowers, but **Rochester Public Market** hums all year with massive community garage sales, concerts and holiday celebrations. Here's a teaser of what's happening in 2006. See the calendar listings for details on some of these events.

Two entrances: *B5*
- 280 N. Union St. (three blocks north of East Main)
- At the end of Railroad Street, off East Main near Goodman Street

Open all year
Tuesday and Thursday 6 a.m. - 1 p.m.
Saturday 5 a.m. - 3 p.m.

Community Garage Sales and Super Fleas
Sundays, April 23 and 30; June 11, 18 and 25; July 9, 16, 23 and 30; Aug. 6, 13, 20 and 27; Sept. 10 and 17; Oct. 1, 8 and 15 • 8 a.m. - 2 p.m.

Chefs' Days
Saturdays, May 6 and 20; June 3 and 17; July 1 and 15; Aug. 5 and 19; Sept. 2 and 16; Oct. 7 • 10 a.m. - noon

Flower City Market Days
Sundays, May 7, 14, 21, 26, 28 and 29; and June 4 • 8 a.m. - 2 p.m.

Women United Health Fair
Saturday, May 13 • 9 a.m. - 1:30 p.m.

Youth Day
Saturday, June 10 • 10 a.m. - 1:30 p.m.

Artists' Row
Sundays, June 11 and Oct. 11 10 a.m. - 3 p.m.

Bands on the Bricks
Fridays, July 7, 21 and 28, and Aug. 4 • 6 -10 p.m.

Spanish International Festival
Sunday, Sept. 3 • noon - 8 p.m.

Savor Rochester Festival of Food
Monday, Sept. 18 • 5 - 8 p.m.

Harvest Jamboree and Country Fair
Sunday, Sept. 24 • 9 a.m. - 2 p.m.

Holidays at the Market
Sundays, Dec. 3, 10 and 17 9 a.m. - 2 p.m.

Sterling Renaissance Festival
July 1 - Aug. 13, 2006
Saturdays and Sundays, 10 a.m. - 7 p.m.
Route 104 to Route 104A, Sterling   *A23*
(800) 879-4446
www.sterlingfestival.com/renfest
The Elizabethan village of Warwick comes to life here every summer. Mingle with more than 800 professional actors and stagehands in 1585 attire. Soak in dozens of stage and street performances, dances, parades, food and revelry.

Why Look at Animals?
July 1, 2006 - Jan. 4, 2007
George Eastman House
900 East Ave., Rochester   *C5*
www.eastmanhouse.org
An historical and contemporary survey examining how animals have been depicted photographically, from daguerreotypes to digital images. Among the photographers represented are Edward Weston and William Wegman.

Independence Day Fireworks Celebration
July 4, 2006 • 10 p.m.
Downtown Rochester   *DD4, 5*
Free admission
The city of Rochester puts on a grand display of pyrotechnics to celebrate the Fourth of July. Bring a lawn chair and set up camp along the river south of I-490 (off Exchange Boulevard on the west or Mt. Hope Avenue on the east), but get there about an hour early for the best seat. (Listen closely: You can hear the blasts reverberating off downtown buildings.)

Noontime Concert Series
Wednesdays, July 5 - Aug. 2, 2006 • Noon
Aqueduct Park,
downtown Rochester   *CC3*
Free admission

Bands on the Bricks
Four Fridays, July 7, 21, 28 and Aug. 4, 2006
6 - 10 p.m.
Rochester Public Market
280 N. Union St., Rochester   *B5*
Milestones Music Room and the city of Rochester present four evenings of blues, rock

GardenScape, featuring elaborate horticultural displays with innovative landscape designs, is considered one of the finest garden shows in the Northeast.

and country music at the Public Market, along with a beer garden and food for sale. Vendors will be selling clothing, jewelry and novelties.

Corn Hill Arts Festival
July 8 - 9, 2006
Saturday, 10 a.m. - 6 p.m.
Sunday, 10 a.m. - 5 p.m.
Exchange Boulevard and Plymouth Avenue, Rochester   *EE2*
Free admission
262-3142
www.cornhill.org/festival.html
Five hundred artists and craftspeople converge on Rochester's oldest neighborhood. Homes in Corn Hill are among the most historic in the city. Some 200,000 people shop, enjoy the music and sample treats. Parking on area streets and in temporary lots.

Monroe County Fair
July 12 - 16, 2006
County Fairgrounds, 2695 E. Henrietta Road, Henrietta   *F12*
334-4000
www.mcfair.com
First held in 1823, the county fair features a space education center, demolition derby and other entertainment, music, agricultural exhibits, plenty of rides and, of course, as much cotton candy and caramel corn as you can eat.

East End Nightlife Festival
July 14, 2006 • 5 - 11 p.m.
East End District, Rochester   *CC6*
The East End closes its streets to traffic for its monthly summer happy hour. Area bars and street stages feature local and regional bands.

Finger Lakes Wine Festival
July 14 - 16, 2006
Watkins Glen International
2790 County Route 16, Watkins Glen   *C22*
(866) 461-7223
www.flwinefest.com
More than 70 Finger Lakes wineries set up tasting counters to share their bounty. Arts, crafts and gourmet foods are for sale. Enjoy jazz and blues entertainment, wine seminars and pace car rides on the Watkins Glen International road course.

Hill Cumorah Pageant
July 14, 15, 18 - 22, 2006 • 9:15 p.m.
Route 21, two miles north of
NYS Thruway Exit 43 near Palmyra   *B21*
Free admission
(315) 597-5851
www.hillcumorah.com/Pageant/program.htm
The Church of Jesus Christ of Latter-day Saints has mounted this large-scale, outdoor pageant for more than 60 years. Thousands of visitors from around the world attend each night. Held at Hill Cumorah, birthplace of the Mormon Church, the pageant features sophisticated sound and lighting technology.

September's Clothesline Festival is marking its 50th year in 2006. It is Rochester's longest-running arts festival and the Memorial Art Gallery's biggest fundraiser.

Strong Museum expansion
Grand Opening
July 14 - 16, 2006
1 Manhattan Square, Rochester   *C4*
263-2700
www.strongmuseum.org
The expansion of this children's museum will nearly double its size, adding two exhibits, "Reading Adventureland" and "Field of Play," indoor and outdoor butterfly gardens, a food court and expanded shops.

Casey Jones Day
July 15 - 16, 2006
New York Museum of Transportation
6393 E. River Road, Rush   *G11*
533-1113
www.nymtmuseum.org
All aboard! Annual demonstration runs of the museum's Rochester subway track speeder will be included this year in a commemoration of the 50th anniversary of the abandonment of the Rochester subway. This is the only place for miles where you can take a trolley ride.

New York Derby
July 15, 2006
Finger Lakes Gaming & Racetrack
Route 96, Farmington   *B21*
581-4898
www.fingerlakesracetrack.com
The focal point of the track's schedule is the 35th running of the New York Derby, with a $150,000 purse. This is the second leg of the Big Apple Triple for New York-bred 3-year-olds. (The other legs are the Mike Lee Stakes at Belmont Park and the Albany Stakes at Saratoga.)

Rochester MusicFest
July 15 - 16, 2006
Frontier Field, Rochester
428-6690
www.rochestermusicfest.com
Frontier Field near High Falls is the setting for the original Rochester music festival, now in its 13th year. Relax to the sounds of national R&B artists, including Earth, Wind & Fire, the Isley Brothers, George Clinton and Rochester native Tweet.

Cosequin Stuart Horse Trials

July 20 - 23, 2006
1707 Murray Road, Victor   *B21*
924-2514
www.stuarthorsetrials.org
In this Olympic-style competition, horse and rider are tested in three diverse disciplines: dressage, cross-country and stadium jumping. Begun 16 years ago, the event draws top international riders and their horses and is part of the Gold Cup Series.

GrassRoots Festival of Music and Dance

July 20 - 23, 2006
Route 96, Trumansburg   *C23*
(607) 387-5098
www.grassrootsfest.org
Traditional and contemporary roots musicians— bluegrass, folk, zydeco, Cajun and more—are in high gear at this annual jam session. More than 60 bands from around the world play on four outdoor stages in the beautiful Finger Lakes region. The festival has garnered a national reputation since its start in the early 1990s. Proceeds benefit local non-profits.

Spencerport Canal Days

July 29 - 30, 2006 • 10 a.m. - 5 p.m.
Events throughout village of Spencerport   *D9*
Free admission
349-1331
www.ogdenny.com/Canaldays
The Erie Canal has long made a stop in this suburban village, a fact Spencerport celebrates with this mid-summer community event. A classic

Children and adults alike enjoy the Mendon Ponds Winterfest, featuring opportunities to sled, ice fish, snowshoe and ski.

car show, canoe races on the canal, a 10K race and creative activities for children join traditional arts and crafts booths and food vendors.

August

Clarissa Street Reunion

August 2006
Clarissa Street, between Troup Street and Bronson Avenue   *EE1*
Free admission
234-4177
Now in its 11th year, this event is a happy tradition of great live music, kids' activities, historic displays and delicious food. Historic displays recall the days before urban renewal plowed through the area, which is one of Rochester's oldest neighborhoods. The crowds grow every year, but it's still the place to feel Rochester's vibe.

Park Ave. Summer Art Fest

Aug. 5 - 6, 2006 • 10 a.m. - 6 p.m.
Park Avenue from Alexander Street to Culver Road   *C5*
Free admission
473-4482
www.park-avenue.org/events.html
The Park Ave. neighborhood has held this outdoor arts, crafts and music festival for 30 years. More than 250,000 visitors browse the booths of 300 artists and craftspeople from 21 states and Canada. The festival showcases roughly 60 musical acts at stages along the avenue.

East End Nightlife Festival

Aug. 11, 2006 • 5 - 11 p.m.
East End District, Rochester   *CC6*
At the East End's favorite outdoor party, area bars and street stages feature local and regional musical acts.

Puerto Rican Festival

Aug. 11 - 13, 2006
Civic Center Plaza, Rochester   *CC4*
234-7660
www.prfestival.com
Rochester's Puerto Rican community throws this colorful festival of food, music and dance every year.

Nextel Cup at the Glen

Aug. 11 - 13, 2006
Watkins Glen International
2790 County Route 16, Watkins Glen   *C22*
(607) 535-2481
www.theglen.com
AutoWeek has called this one of three NASCAR "races you absolutely can't miss." Multiple left

and right turns plus elevation changes make this Nextel Cup race a test of technical skill.

Avon Corn Festival
Aug. 12, 2006
Genesee Street, Avon   *B20*
Free admission
226-8195
The corn harvest earns a celebration of its own in this Livingston County town, about 20 miles south of Rochester. Games, arts and crafts vendors, barbecue and other foods lead to an outdoor concert in the evening.

Brockport Summer Art Festival
Aug. 12 - 13, 2006
Saturday, 10 a.m. - 6 p.m.
Sunday, 10 a.m. - 5 p.m.
Main Street, Brockport   *D7*
473-4482
www.rochesterevents.com/brockport.html
This town on the Erie Canal offers boat races and a duck derby during its summer bash. Along Main Street, more than 100 artists and craftspeople display and sell their creations. Grab a snack from a vendor and listen to live music or just stroll through town for some people-watching.

Carifest
Aug. 12, 2006
High Falls Festival site
Commercial Street at
Browns Race, Rochester   *BB2*
254-7569
Carifest brings the Caribbean to Rochester every August with a morning parade down Main Street. Food and music fill the afternoon and evening festival at High Falls Festival site.

Walnut Hill Farm
Carriage Driving Competition
Aug. 16 - 20, 2006
397 W. Bloomfield Road, Pittsford   *G13*
385-2555
www.walnuthillfarm.com
Now in its 35th year, Walnut Hill is the largest carriage-driving show in the world and the

Featuring 300 artists and craftspeople from 21 states and Canada, Park Ave. Summer Art Fest draws more than 250,000 people on the first weekend in August.

premier event of this type in North America. The gathering celebrates the art and sport of traditional horse and carriage driving in a late-19th-century country fair setting. View carriages exhibited by more than 250 competitors from 20 states, Canada and Europe.

Seneca Lake Whale Watch Festival
Aug. 18 - 19, 2006
Lakeshore Park, Routes 5 & 20, Geneva   *B22*
www.senecalakewhalewatch.com
You'll be waiting forever if you hope to see a whale in this land-bound lake! Instead, take in the music acts on two stages, cardboard boat race, fireworks and lighted boat parade, kids' games and amusement rides, antique boat display, arts and crafts sales, and New York wine and cheese garden.

Diesel Days
Aug. 19 - 20, 2006
Rochester & Genesee Valley Railroad Museum
533-1431
New York Museum of Transportation
533-1113
East River Road, one mile
north of Route 251, Rush   *G11*
More than 1,000 train buffs turned out for last year's celebration of the diesel locomotive. The museums have six operating diesels, from a small 45-ton switcher to large 1,000- and 1,200-horsepower road switchers. Take a ride on a locomotive or caboose.

New York State Fair
Aug. 24 - Sept. 4, 2006
New York State Fairgrounds
State Fair Boulevard,
Geddes   *A24*
(800) 475-3247
www.nysfair.org/
state_fair/2006

Louise Brooks Exhibit
Aug. 26, 2006 - Feb. 5, 2007
George Eastman House
900 East Ave.,
Rochester   *C5*
www.eastmanhouse.org
A photography exhibition celebrating famed silent-film star Louise Brooks, who had a close relationship with George Eastman House, marks the 100th anniversary

National R&B artists such as Ciara take the stage each July at the Rochester MusicFest, now in its 13th year.

of her birth. Moves to the International Center of Photography in New York City in 2007.

September

Rochester River Challenge
International Paddling Festival
September 2006
South Wedge Landing
Mt. Hope Avenue at Alexander Street,
Rochester   *D3*
256-1740, ext. 101
Rochester's first outrigger canoe race, now in its ninth year, is a popular, inclusive event that celebrates city living. A 5K road race and other activities also are held.

New York State Festival of Balloons
Sept. 1 - 3, 2006
Dansville   *C20*
www.nysfob.com/index.html
Celebrate the 24th anniversary of this colorful festival with early-morning and evening launches. The valley also is filled with arts and crafts vendors, food purveyors and entertainment, including a lumberjack show, children's rides and amusements and a car show.

International Spanish Festival
Sept. 3, 2006 • Noon - 8 p.m.
Rochester Public Market
280 N. Union St., Rochester   *B5*
325-6650
Experience the food, music and cultures of 20 Spanish-speaking countries.

Labor Day Parade
Sept. 4, 2006 • 11 a.m.
Downtown Rochester   *CC4*
263-2650
The parade honors the workers who built Rochester and the nation. The route runs down East Avenue at Alexander Street to Plymouth Avenue via Main Street.

New York Breeders' Futurity
& New York Oaks
Sept. 4, 2006
Finger Lakes Gaming & Racetrack
Route 96, Farmington   *B21*
581-4898
www.fingerlakesracetrack.com

Rochester Irish Festival
Sept. 8 - 10, 2006
Camp Eastman
Lakeshore Boulevard, Irondequoit   *C13*
www.rochesteririshfestival.org
Music and refreshments take center stage at the 12th annual festival dedicated to all things Irish. At an on-site "Celtic College," participants can learn Gaelic, learn to dance and play musical instruments, and trace their Irish roots. Gift vendors will be on hand.

The Festival of Food at the Rochester Public Market is a showcase for the region's fine restaurants, breweries and wineries. Proceeds benefit local food cupboards.

Clothesline Festival
Sept. 9 - 10, 2006
Saturday, 10 a.m. - 6 p.m.
Sunday, 10 a.m. - 5 p.m.
Memorial Art Gallery
500 University Ave., Rochester   *C5*
473-7720
mag.rochester.edu/visit/clothesline
Marking its 50th year, Clothesline is Rochester's longest-running arts festival and the Memorial Art Gallery's biggest fundraiser. Six hundred artists and craftspeople from Upstate New York show and sell original work in all media. Dance and music performances and food concessions offer a break from browsing.

Oktoberfest in Irondequoit
Sept. 15 - 17 and 22 - 24, 2006
Camp Eastman
Lakeshore Boulevard, Irondequoit   *C13*
336-6070
www.irondequoit.org/events/oktober.htm
Nearly a quarter of Rochesterians have German roots, and many of them come to Oktoberfest to celebrate. Bands from Germany and Austria perform in two tents on two stages, offering visitors their choice of entertainment for dancing and singing. Traditional German food, drink and imported wares are available.

11th Annual Finger Lakes Fiber Arts Festival
Sept. 16 - 17, 2006
Saturday, 10 a.m. - 5 p.m.
Sunday, 10 a.m. - 4 p.m.
Hemlock Fairgrounds, South Main Street
(Route 15A), Hemlock   *B20*
Watch sheep shearing, yarn spinning and other fiber arts demonstrations, visit vendors' booths and take a wagon ride. See sheep, llamas, alpacas, goats and rabbits.

Palmyra Canaltown Days
Sept. 16 - 17, 2006
Palmyra   *B21*
(315) 597-6700
This Finger Lakes town is in the midst of renewal. Palmyra notes its place on the historic Erie Canal with this annual festival. Visit downtown's antique shops and museums while you're there.

ArtWalk Alive
Mid-September 2006 • Noon - 4 p.m.
University Avenue between Atlantic and Elton Streets, Rochester   *C5*
www.rochesterartwalk.org
University Avenue turns into a giant artists' studio every September. The music you'll hear runs the gamut from Appalachian and blues to funk, jazz and improv. Spoken word artists perform freestyle "slam" poetry and avant garde scatting. See African, modern and belly dancing, and watch visual artists create on the spot.

Rochester Marathon
Sept. 17, 2006 • 8 a.m.
Frontier Field
1 Morrie Silver Way, Rochester   *BB1*
www.rochestermarathon.com
The marathon's first year saw some 1,700 runners. The second annual run will feature full- and half-marathons and a four-person team relay. A health and fitness expo will be held Sept. 15 and 16.

Festival of Food
Sept. 18, 2006 • 6 - 10 p.m.
Rochester Public Market
280 N. Union St., Rochester   *B5*
Free admission; charge for tasting tickets
328-3380, ext. 142
www.festivaloffood.org
Rochester's fine restaurants, breweries and wineries offer food and beverages to sample in this fundraiser for local food cupboards. Specialty small food processors and farmers also are on hand.

Naples Grape Festival
Sept. 23 - 24, 2006 • 10 a.m. - 5 p.m.
Memorial Town Park, Route 21, Naples   *C21*
Free admission
374-2240
www.naplesvalleyny.com/
  GrapeFestivalIntro.htm
This fall festival takes visitors to the hills of Naples during prime "leaf-peeping" season. Held in the heart of the Finger Lakes wine region, the festival celebrates everything grape. Visitors can take winery tours and horse-drawn wagon rides—or watch their feet turn purple in the grape-stomping contest. Don't leave without a grape pie.

Harvest Jamboree and Country Fair
Sept. 24, 2006 • Noon - 6 p.m.
Rochester Public Market
280 N. Union St., Rochester   *B5*
428-6770
A favorite fall pastime is picking out pumpkins, eating doughnuts and drinking cider. Take pony and hayrides, or try line-dancing lessons. Watch butter churning and cider pressing. You'll also find plenty of fresh produce, including organics, plus activities for the kids.

Inside Downtown Tour
Sept. 29 - 30, 2006
Friday, 5:30 - 8:30 p.m.
Saturday, 11 a.m. - 4 p.m.
Downtown Rochester   *C3, 4*
546-7029
www.landmarksociety.org
Get a look at new luxury condos, hip loft apartments, and skyscraper vistas during the third annual tour of downtown living, sponsored by Rochester's preservation group.

Hilton Apple Fest
Sept. 30 - Oct. 1, 2006
Route 18 (West Avenue)
Between Heinz and Henry streets, Hilton   *B9*
Free admission
234-3378
www.hiltonapplefest.org
Apple orchards surround Greater Rochester's northern borders, which makes the region a leading producer of apples and related products. Hilton's annual tribute, approaching its silver anniversary, celebrates the harvest with a photo contest, arts and craft exhibitors, food vendors, an auto show and a 5-mile run.

Roots of local festivals

They celebrate corn, garlic, wine, apples, grapes; roses and lilacs; maple syrup and winter; jazz and R&B.

Here's how a handful of Rochester's biggest festivals began.

Lilac Festival

Horticulturist John Dunbar started Highland Park's lilac collection in 1892. Some of the 20 varieties were descendants of flowers native to the Balkan Mountains.

The Lilac Festival began in 1898, six years after Dunbar planted those first lilacs at the corner of Highland Avenue and Goodman Street. Three thousand people showed up on a Sunday in May to see and smell the blooms. A decade later, the number of visitors had blossomed into 25,000.

These days, Highland Park staff cultivate more than 1,200 lilac bushes in shades from white to deep purple. The festival, now a 10-day event in mid-May, draws more than 500,000 people and is the largest such event in North America. Many visitors continue to make the lilacs the main focus of their attention. But today's Lilac Festival offers plenty else to distract: arts and crafts vendors, food and entertainment.

Corn Hill Arts Festival

Corn Hill is one of the oldest residential areas in the city. A mix of towering Victorians and simple cottages, the neighborhood boomed when the Erie Canal brought business to Rochester. After World War II, city residents fled to the suburbs, and Corn Hill fell into decline. Construction of I-490 and the Civic Center during the 1960s wiped out one-of-a-kind mansions and other landmarks.

To save what was left, the Landmark Society of Western New York stepped in, persuading city officials to conserve historic properties as part of its urban renewal efforts. The society saved the Hoyt-Potter House, now its headquarters, and got to work raising support for the neighborhood's architecture.

The Corn Hill Arts Festival was born in 1968 as a way to build awareness. Nearly 40 years later, it is one of the most highly respected festivals of its kind in the United States, drawing more than 300,000 visitors each July. And with artists' booths set up on streets, the festival is a great way to view the architecture it was created to save.

Clothesline Festival

The Memorial Art Gallery's first Clothesline Festival blew in on the winds of Hurricane Audrey. The year was 1957, and 2,000 determined art lovers and 101 exhibitors braved the elements to launch what would become one of the region's premier arts and crafts shows. It wasn't the last time bad weather would roar in, but showgoers have learned to adapt. Clothesline has become MAG's biggest annual fundraiser. Today it brings in hundreds of artists for a weekend in September. Their booths fill the gallery's 17-acre campus.

October

Georgia O'Keeffe: Color and Conservation
Oct. 1 - Dec. 31, 2006
Memorial Art Gallery
500 University Ave., Rochester   *C5*
473-7720
http://mag.rochester.edu
The show is the first to focus on American master Georgia O'Keeffe's choice of color and her involvement in conservation issues. It will include 25 rarely seen oils and two pastels. It's the first time O'Keeffe's work has been exhibited in Rochester.

ImageOut
Oct. 6 - 15, 2006
Area theaters
271-2640
www.imageout.org
Rochester's lesbian and gay film and video festival is the largest event of its kind in Upstate New York. Some 50 programs offer screenings of feature-length films, short cinema, international fare and documentaries.

Rochester River Romance
Oct. 6 - 8, 2006
Various locations along the Genesee River
428-6770
www.cityofrochester.gov
Rochester's earliest growth can be tied directly to the Genesee River, where settlers produced flour in mills built along its shores. During Romance weekend, fall foliage is in peak color. Take a guided hike or bike ride deep into the river gorge, or a boat ride on the river and the Erie Canal. The Stonehurst Capital Invitational Regatta, a premier event on the fall collegiate racing schedule, headlines this annual city event.

Ghost Walk
Oct. 20 - 21 and 27 - 28, 2006
Third Presbyterian Church, Rochester
and neighboring streets   *C4*
546-7029
www.landmarksociety.org
This Halloween favorite chills audiences with true, gory tales from Rochester's past told by "recently returned" Rochesterians in period costumes.

November

National Toy Hall of Fame
Induction Celebration
November 2006
Strong Museum
1 Manhattan Square, Rochester   *DD6*
263-2700
www.strongmuseum.org
Among the more than 30 toys already in the Hall of Fame are the rocking horse, Monopoly, Barbie, Play-Doh, the teddy bear, Scrabble and Crayola crayons. The Hall inducts its newest members during this annual celebration, amid strolling toys and other entertainment.

High Falls Film Festival
Nov. 8 - 13, 2006
Dryden Theatre at George Eastman House and Little Theatre, Rochester   *C5, CC6*
258-0481
www.highfallsfilmfestival.com
Rochester is the birthplace of women's rights and motion picture film. This festival brings them together by showcasing the work of women in the film and video industry. Recent festivals have drawn movies from around the world, along with film fans from a dozen countries and nearly half the states. Panels, workshops, parties and awards (including the "Failure Is Impossible" Award in honor of Susan B. Anthony) round out the week.

Fifth Annual Fine Craft Show
Nov. 10 - 12, 2006
Memorial Art Gallery
500 University Ave., Rochester   *C5*
473-7720
mag.rochester.edu
Juried show and sale showcases works by 40 master craft artists from around the country.

Now in its 35th year, the Walnut Hill Farm Carriage Driving Competition is the largest carriage-driving show in the world and the premier event of this type in North America.

Sweet Creations: Gingerbread House Display

Nov. 15 - Dec. 14, 2006
George Eastman House
900 East Ave., Rochester   *C5*
www.eastmanhouse.org
On view in Rochester's grandest house museum: more than 60 intricately designed gingerbread houses. Created by professional bakers, Scout troops, families and others in the community, the houses are sold in a silent auction that benefits future restoration projects at the Eastman House. It's a great time to see the museum decked out in holiday finery too.

Holiday Festival of Crafts

Thanksgiving
Weekend 2006
The Harley School
1981 Clover St.,
Brighton   *E13*
554-3539
www.rfag.org/
    index.htm
The Rochester Folk Art Guild sells beautifully crafted items its members make at their Finger Lakes working farm: furniture, fiber arts, glass, pottery and handmade paper.

The High Falls Film Festival showcases the work of women in the film and video industry. Attendees have previewed films such as "Transamerica," starring Felicity Huffman (left).

December

Kwanzaa Celebration

All month
Memorial Art Gallery
500 University Ave., Rochester   *C5*
473-7720
mag.rochester.edu
The gallery hosts family events all month to mark Kwanzaa, the African-American and Pan-African holiday that celebrates family, community and culture.

Corn Hill Holiday Tour

Dec. 2, 2006
Landmark Society of Western New York
Hoyt Potter House
133 S. Fitzhugh St., Rochester   *EE3*
546-7029
www.landmarksociety.org
Visit charming cottages, newer condos and towering mansions decked out for the holidays in Rochester's well-preserved, 19th-century residential neighborhood.

Freezeroo Winter Racing Series

Six races, December 2006 - February 2007
Rochester-area parks
Hosted by Greater Rochester Track Club
www.grtconline.org
Now in its 28th year, this winter racing series for Rochester's hardcore runners is one of the oldest in the Northeast.

January 2007

Recreational Vehicles Show

Early January 2007
Minett Hall at the Dome Center
East Henrietta and Calkins Roads,
Henrietta   *F12*

Mendon Ponds Winterfest

Late January 2007
Entrances at Clover Street and
Pittsford-Mendon Center Road,
Pittsford and Mendon   *G13*
www.mendonpondswinterfest.org
Hundreds of winter enthusiasts take over Monroe County's largest park with sledding, ice fishing, snowshoeing and skiing. Learn about geocaching, birding, telescopes, iceboating, orienteering, curling and more.

Psychic Festival

Late January 2007
Clarion Riverside Hotel,
120 E. Main St., Rochester   *CC4*
586-8537
More than 35 readers give readings at this 26th annual event. See what the tarot, crystals and auras can tell you. Books and jewelry are for sale.

Rochester Boat Show

Late January 2007
Rochester Riverside Convention Center
123 E. Main St., Rochester   *C3*
More than 300 boats, more than 18 dealers and 20 boating accessories dealers.

February

Many Black History Month activities are held throughout the month. Check local listings.

Rochester-Finger Lakes Region Scholastic Art Awards Exhibition

Early February 2007
Bevier Gallery, Rochester Institute of Technology
James E. Booth Building,
73 Lomb Memorial Drive, Henrietta   *F11*
Art work by junior and senior high school students from Central and Western New York is displayed.

Walk the Walk: Encounters with Rochester's African-American Ancestors

Early February 2007 • 12:15 p.m.
Hochstein Performance Hall
50 N. Plymouth Ave., Rochester   *CC2*
454-4596
Free admission
Frederick Douglass, Austin Steward, Anna Murray, Captain Sunfish and others from Rochester's past are portrayed by local actors in this popular annual event.

Lakeside Winter Celebration

Feb. 4, 2007
Ontario Beach Park, Charlotte   *C12*
Free admission
865-3320
As long as it's cold and snowy, why not embrace it? Rochester flocks to the lakefront for a chili cook-off, snow sculpture competitions, a polar bear plunge, a winter golf tournament and ice sculpture demonstrations.

Susan B. Anthony Birthday Luncheon
Early February 2007
Rochester Riverside Convention Center
123 E. Main St., Rochester   *C3*
279-7490
www.susanbanthonyhouse.org
Past speakers for this fundraiser have included Cokie Roberts, Helen Thomas and Ken Burns.

Groundhog Day Festival
Feb. 2, 2007
Greece Canal Park, Greece   *D10*
Enjoy the park and the Erie Canal with ice fishing, snow bowling and Frisbee golf. Native American storytelling, demonstrations of birds of prey and chainsaw woodcarving are also featured.

Susan B. Anthony Day
Feb. 15, 2007
Susan B. Anthony House
17 Madison St., Rochester   *C3*
235-6124
www.susanbanthonyhouse.org
The famous suffragist's birthday is celebrated at her home in Rochester.

Rochester Golf Show
Mid-February 2007
Rochester Riverside
Convention Center
123 E. Main St., Rochester   *CC4*
Rochester is one of the most avid golf communities in the country. We have some 80 courses to choose from and host major PGA and LPGA tournaments. But winter is a cold reality. Come shake off the chill and check out the latest golf equipment, clothing, travel ideas, clinics, seminars and a putting contest.

**The Dutch Connection:
George Eastman's
Conservatory in Winter Bloom**
Mid- to late February 2007
George Eastman House
900 East Ave., Rochester   *C5*
www.eastmanhouse.org
The historic house is decorated for winter the way George Eastman preferred, filling the conservatory with thousands of tulips, hyacinths and freesia.

Home Fair Expo
Late February 2007
Dome Center
2695 E. Henrietta Road, Henrietta   *F12*
338-3600

March

**Greater Rochester
International Auto Show**
Early March 2007
Rochester Riverside Convention Center
123 E. Main St., Rochester   *CC4*
(843) 686-5640
The 22nd annual car show will feature shiny new

models—and sneak previews of select 2008 models. See the latest convertibles, concept cars, SUVs and hybrids. If you know they make bras for cars, this is the place for you.

GardenScape
Mid-March 2007
The Dome Center
2695 E. Henrietta Road, Henrietta   *F12*
265-9018
www.rochesterflowershow.com
GardenScape is considered one of the finest garden shows in the Northeast. Elaborate horticultural displays feature innovative landscape designs. Get ideas from the experts in workshops. Also featured: a children's interactive garden and a marketplace crammed with all things gardening.

SIMCON Gaming Convention
Mid-March 2007
Douglass Dining Center,
University of Rochester River Campus,
Wilson Boulevard, Rochester   *E2*
www.simcon.org
For more than 25 years, this four-day convention has drawn gaming enthusiasts from around the country. Sanctioned tournaments center on games of all kinds, including role-playing, historical miniatures, board games and war games. Developers are on hand for panel discussions and workshops.

St. Patrick's Day Parade
March 17, 2007 • 12:30 p.m.
East Avenue between Alexander Street and Liberty Pole Way, Rochester   *CC5, 6, 7*
234-5167
www.rochesterparade.com

Sap, Syrup and Sugar Festival
Two weekends in mid-March 2007
Genesee Country Village and Museum
1410 Flint Hill Road, Mumford   *B20*
538-6822
www.geneseecountryvillage.org
Try tapping a tree and taste one of the delights of living in the North at the maple syrup festival. Take a guided walk among the sugarbush, and watch 19th-century maple sugaring and modern-day syrup-making techniques at this living-history museum.

The 10K J.P. Morgan Chase Corporate Challenge is Rochester's largest road race. Last year, more than 8,600 runners took part.

April

Rochester Red Wings Opening Day
Early April 2007
Frontier Field
1 Morrie Silver Way, Rochester   *BB1*
423-WING
www.redwingsbaseball.com

**Skin & Steel Motorcycle
and Tattoo Extravaganza**
Early April 2007
Rochester Riverside Convention Center
123 E. Main St., Rochester   *CC4*
www.skinandsteel.com
The region's biggest event is a midwinter boost for tattoo and motorcycle fans. Thousands take in the trophy motorcycle show (judged by pros from the Rats Hole Chopper Show), live music and more than 100 vendors, including tattoo artists and bike dealers.

sports & recreation

Sports

Pro sports

Rochester Americans: From October to early spring, the International Hockey League franchise of the Buffalo Sabres plays in the Blue Cross Arena downtown. 1 War Memorial Square, Rochester *DD3*; 454-5335; www.amerks.com

Rochester Knighthawks: Rochester's National Lacrosse League Central Division team plays box lacrosse in the Blue Cross Arena from December to April. 1 War Memorial Square, Rochester *DD3*; 454-5335; www.knighthawks.net

Rochester Rattlers: With its origins in Native American culture, lacrosse is popular in the Northeast. Rochester's Major League Lacrosse team plays outdoor matches against Boston, Baltimore and other teams from June to August. 460 Oak St., Rochester *B2*; 454-5425; www.rochesterrattlers.com

Rochester RazorSharks: This new American Basketball Association team brings pro hoops back to Rochester after a 20-year hiatus. The RazorSharks are in a league with teams from New York, Canada, Maryland and Pennsylvania. Home games are held in Blue Cross Arena. 1 War Memorial Square, Rochester *DD3*; 232-9190; www.razorsharks.com

Rochester Red Wings: The Triple-A ball club has a new major league affiliation with the Minnesota Twins organization. The 118-year-old club plays more than 70 home games a year at Frontier Field, next to Eastman Kodak Co. headquarters. 1 Morrie Silver Way, Rochester *BB1*; 423-9464; www.redwingsbaseball.com

Rochester Rhinos: Rochesterians love their soccer, and Rhinos fans are among the most loyal in the country. An average of 10,000 attend each men's game. In 2006, the Rhinos added a women's team by the same name. Formerly the Ravens, the USL W-League has been playing teams from across the continent since 1996. The teams will move into their new stadium, PaeTec Park, in June 2006. 460 Oak St, Rochester *B2*; 454-KICK; www.rhinossoccer.com

Buffalo Bills: This NFL team holds its preseason training camp at St. John Fisher College in the Rochester suburb of Pittsford. Admission is free. Come watch rookies and veterans battle it out for playing spots from late July to mid-August. 3349 Monroe Ave., Pittsford Plaza, Pittsford *E14*; 387-0740 (Rochester office); www.buffalobills.com

Frontier Field (above), next door to Eastman Kodak Co. headquarters, is home to the Rochester Red Wings (right) and, until June 2006, the Rochester Rhinos soccer team.

Sports halls of fame

WITHIN A 4-HOUR DRIVE

DIRT Motorsports Hall of Fame and Classic Car Museum: Closed January to March. One mile from I-90, Route 31, Weedsport; http://dirtmotorsports.com/DirtNE/OLD/Museum/Dirt%20Museum.html

Hockey Hall of Fame: BCE Place, 30 Yonge St., Toronto, Ontario, Canada; (416) 360-7735; www.hhof.com

International Boxing Hall of Fame: 1 Hall of Fame Drive, Canastota; (315) 697-7095; www.ibhof.com

National Baseball Hall of Fame and Museum: 25 Main St., Cooperstown; (888) HALL-OF-FAME; www.baseballhalloffame.org

National Soccer Hall of Fame and Museum:
Wright Soccer Campus, 18 Stadium Circle, Oneonta; (607) 432-3351; www.soccerhall.org

UNDER 7 HOURS

Naismith Memorial Basketball Hall of Fame:
1000 W. Columbus Ave., Springfield, Mass.; (877) 4HOOPLA; www.hoophall.com

Pro Football Hall of Fame: 2122 George Halas Drive N.W., Canton, Ohio; (330) 456-8207; www.profootballhof.com

Major sports venues in the area

Blue Cross Arena at the War Memorial:
Home ice for Rochester Americans hockey team and arena for concerts and events. 1 War Memorial Square, Rochester *DD3*

Frontier Field: Home of Rochester Red Wings baseball team. 1 Morrie Silver Way, Rochester *BB1*

Oak Hill Country Club: Hosts PGA Championship, U.S. Open, Ryder Cup. 353 Kilbourn Road, Pittsford *E13*

Locust Hill Country Club: Hosts annual Wegmans Rochester LPGA. 2000 Jefferson Road, Pittsford *F13*

PaeTec Park: New home of Rochester Rhinos and Rochester Rattlers. 460 Oak St., Rochester *B2*

University of Rochester Fauver Stadium:
Division III football and soccer, plus high school playoffs. Wilson Boulevard, Rochester *E12*

St. John Fisher College Growney Stadium:
Hosts Buffalo Bills training camp. 3690 East Ave., Pittsford *E14*

Rochester Institute of Technology:
Home of J.P. Morgan Chase Corporate Challenge race. 1 Lomb Memorial Drive (off Jefferson Road), Henrietta *F1*

Seabreeze Amusement Park, in Irondequoit near Lake Ontario, features a scream-inducing spinning roller coaster.

Recreation
Amusement parks

Roseland Water Park: The 56-acre, Victorian-style park opened in 2001. It features a giant wave pool, water playgrounds, extreme tube slides, raft ride and more. 250 Eastern Blvd., Canandaigua *B21*; 396-2000; www.roselandwaterpark.com

Seabreeze: At more than 125 years old, Seabreeze is the fourth-oldest amusement park in the country. A fifth-generation family business, the park has grown to 70 attractions, including a water park, four roller coasters, a wave pool and thrill rides. New in 2004: a spinning roller coaster, only the second in the country. 4600 Culver Road, Rochester *C13*; (800) 395-2500; www.seabreeze.com

Six Flags Darien Lake: Less than an hour west of Rochester, Darien Lake features five roller coasters, including Superman Ride of Steel, which climbs 208 feet and goes over 70 miles per hour. Rides, restaurants, shops, live shows, a water park, and camping and hotel accommodations are available. 9993 Allegheny Road, Darien Center *B19*; 599-4641; www.sixflags.com/darienlake

Boating

Rochester was the nation's first boomtown, thanks to the historic Erie Canal, whose mule-drawn boats transported goods to distant points. Rochester is surrounded by water; the canal meanders gently through countryside and towns with names like Fairport and Spencerport. The north-flowing Genesee River intersects the canal and spills into Lake Ontario. The Finger Lakes lie a short, scenic drive away. If you like being out on the water, you'll find plenty to make you happy here. Bring your own boat or rent one, take a cruise, or just enjoy the sunset from shore.

Take a cruise on Rochester's waterways

Tours run from late spring to autumn:

Canandaigua Lady: Narrated tours of Canandaigua Lake from the north shore on a paddlewheel steamboat. Steamboat Landing restaurant and banquet hall on shore. 205 Lakeshore Drive, Canandaigua *B21*; 396-7350

Colonial Belle: Largest Erie Canal tour boat holds 246 passengers. Narrated tours, meals, bar. Public cruises Tuesday through Sunday, May - October. 400 Packett's Landing, Fairport *F15*; 223-9470; www.colonialbelle.com

Harbor Town Belle: Authentic 80-foot paddle wheeler offers cruises of Lake Ontario, Genesee River and Irondequoit Bay. Meals, special and charter events available. Marina Drive, Rochester *C12*; (800) 836-8930

Mary Jemison: Heads south, upstream, from the newly constructed Corn Hill Landing past the University of Rochester and through Genesee Valley Park, to the picturesque junction of the Erie Canal and Genesee River. Daily excursions May – October. Corn Hill Landing, 290 Exchange Blvd., Rochester *EE4*, 262-5661

Sam Patch: Narrated excursions of the Erie Canal aboard a replica 19th-century canal packet boat. Meals and desserts available. Daily excursions May – October. Schoen Place, Pittsford *F14*; 262-5661

Spirit of Rochester: Accommodates more than 535 passengers on cruises of Lake Ontario, plus fall foliage tours up the Genesee River gorge. Meals available. 18 Petten St. Extension, Rochester *C12*; 865-4930

The Sam Patch replica packet boat carries passengers on the Erie Canal between the village of Pittsford and Lock 32 at Clover Street.

Irondequoit Bay, with Lake Ontario in the background, is a boating playground in the summer.

BOATING CLUBS

Genesee Yacht Club: Tuesday-night races, Saturday regattas and Sunday-morning Sunfish races, plus a sailing school in cooperation with Rochester Yacht Club. Marina Drive, Rochester; 266-9796; www.geneseeyc.org

Rochester Canoe Club: Informal family club involved in sailing and racing, with a special focus on one-design sailboat racing. 2050 Bay Shore Blvd., Irondequoit; 288-2380; www.rochestercc.org

Rochester Offshore Powerboat Association: Runs and regattas for powerboat enthusiasts in July and August; www.rochesteroffshore.com

Rochester Power Squadron: Cruises, sail races, navigation contests and education for sail and power boaters. 987-8989; www.usps.org/localusps/rochester/start.htm

Rochester Yacht Club: A 125-year-old, private club that hosts national and international regattas and sponsors club-level sailboat racing. 5555 St. Paul Blvd., Irondequoit; 342-5511; www.rochesteryc.com

BOATING LESSONS AND RENTALS

Bayside Boat & Tackle: Fishing and pedal boats, canoes and kayaks. 1300 Empire Blvd., Penfield; 224-8289; www.baysideboatandtackle.com

Braddock Bay Bait & Tackle: Fishing boats and canoes. 372 Manitou Road, Hilton; 392-6600

City Pier Ice Cream & Rentals: Paddle boats and canoes. City Pier, Canandaigua; 396-9080

Jansen Marina Inc.: Fishing, skiing and pontoon boats. 7099 State Route 21, Naples; 374-2384; 5750 E. Lake Road, Conesus; 346-2060

Leisure Time Marina of Conesus: Pontoon, power and fishing boats, and jet skis. 5364 E. Lake Road, Conesus; 346-2260

Oak Orchard Canoe & Kayak Experts: Canoes, kayaks. 1350 Empire Blvd., Penfield; 288-5550

MARINAS AND BOAT LAUNCHES

There are dozens of marinas and boat launches in the area. The New York State Department of Environmental Conservation lists them all, from car-top launches to full-service marinas, on its Web sites:

- www.dec.state.ny.us/website/dfwmr/fish/marinas.html
- www.dec.state.ny.us/website/dfwmr/fish/foe4cbl1.html

Climbing

Rochester Rock, Ice and Snow Climbing Club: Information on local ice-climbing areas and camaraderie for like-minded climbers. www.frontiernet.net/~lilgamin/rriscc.htm

Genesee Valley Chapter of Adirondack Mountain Club: Club for outdoor enthusiasts who hike, canoe and ski in the Adirondack Mountains of northern New York. Holds frequent hikes and workshops in the Rochester area. 987-1717; www.gvc-adk.org

Rock Ventures: Large indoor climbing, ropes course and fitness center for experienced and beginning individuals and classes, parties, team building. 1044 University Ave., Rochester C6; HI-CLIMB (442-5462); www.frontiernet.net/~rockvtr

Cycling

Information on all things cycling in Rochester, the Genesee Valley and the Finger Lakes: www.bikerochester.com

CLUBS

City of Rochester Department of Parks & Recreation: The parks department leads biweekly, leisurely rides on the Genesee Riverway Trail and Erie Canal. Cyclists will travel through historic parks and city neighborhoods. Rides begin at 6:15 p.m. roughly every other week from May 30 to Sept. 5. Additional tours are held on one weekend a month from July to October; 428-6770; www.bikerochester.com/clubs/city_roch_cal/city_of_rochester_rides.htm

Finger Lakes Cycling Club: Based in Ithaca, the club hosts rides daily (except Friday) in the Finger Lakes region; www.flcycling.org

Genesee Valley Cycling Club: Bicycle-racing club takes training rides from April to September, races on Tuesday nights and holds time trial training nights on Thursdays. http://gvcc.11net.com

Huggers Ski Club – Pedal Power: Recreational riding club. www.huggersskiclub.org

Rochester Area Recumbent Enthusiasts: Group rides for recumbent cyclists every weekend from May to October. 461-5084; http://home.rochester.rr.com/rare

Rochester Bicycling Club: Road and mountain

With thousands of acres of parkland and converted railbeds, Greater Rochester offers cyclists plenty of opportunities to go off-road.

A favorite stop on the Tour

Past LPGA champions return to Rochester for 30th blast

The Wegmans Rochester LPGA, at Locust Hill Country Club in Pittsford, is one of the most popular stops on the Tour. It's known for drawing large crowds of knowledgeable golf fans and the biggest names in the sport. This year's field will compete for a $1.8 million purse.

To mark the tournament's 30th year, 10 past winners of the Wegmans Rochester LPGA will compete in a Tournament of Champions on Tuesday, June 20. The $50,000 purse still beats what many Rochester LPGA winners received in the earliest years: First place in 1977 garnered just $11,000.

Scheduled to appear are Nancy Lopez, Patty Sheehan, Pat Bradley, Kathy Whitworth, Deb Richard, Judy Dickinson, Tammie Green, Sandra Haynie and Lisa Kiggens.

On Tuesday night, a first-ever opening ceremony will pay tribute to the winners. They'll be joined by other past champions—Rosie Jones, Meg Mallon, Karrie Webb, Laura Davies, Rachel Hetherington, Kim Saiki and Lorena Ochoa—on the 18th green at 8 p.m. The ceremony will be open to the public, with music, food and drinks, and a fireworks display.

The Wegmans Rochester LPGA is held the week before the Women's U.S. Open. Planning to appear in this year's competition are Paula Creamer, Christina Kim, Natalie Gublis and Morgan Pressel. The winner in 2005 was Lorena Ochoa. It was her first victory at Rochester.

Ticket prices will remain at 2005 levels and are offered at three levels. Hall of Fame passes buy admission to the course, the clubhouse and the champions' pavilion all week for $65. A daily pass for $20 and a tournament pass for $35 also are on sale.

As always, tournament proceeds will benefit Camp Haccamo and Rochester Rotary Sunshine Campus. To date, more than $6.6 million has been generated for these children's summer camps.

Wegmans Rochester LPGA, June 19 - 25, 2006, 427-7100,
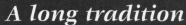
www.rochesterlpga.com

A long tradition

Greater Rochester has hosted the U.S. Open, the PGA Championship, the Ryder Cup and other big tournaments. Five area courses were designed and built by Donald Ross, including Oak Hill Country Club, site of the 1995 Ryder Cup matches and the 2003 PGA Championship. Onetime Rochesterian Robert Trent Jones designed Durand Eastman Golf Course and five other local courses. Golf legend Walter Hagen was born here in 1892. PGA players Jeff Sluman and Dudley Hart are native Rochesterians and part owners of Lake Shore Country Club in Greece.

If the LPGA isn't enough golf watching, the PGA Nationwide Tour comes to Rochester in 2006 with the Xerox Classic Nationwide Golf Tournament. Bring your camera to catch the pros practicing on Monday and Tuesday. Youth and adult clinics and a long-drive contest also are in the mix on Tuesday. The tournament, which carries a $575,000 purse, will be televised live on the Golf Channel.

Xerox Classic Nationwide Golf Tournament: Aug. 7 - 13, 2006
Official Pro-Am: Aug. 9, 2006
Irondequoit Country Club, 4045 East Ave., Pittsford, 325-7760, ext. 3226

biking club hosts rides from "slow and easy" rides to 200-plus-mile treks. www.rochesterbicyclingclub.com

RIDES AND RACES

Tour de Cure: June 11, 2006. Mendon Ponds Park, Mendon *G13*

Saturn Rochester Twilight Criterium: June 24, 2006, 3 - 11:30 p.m. Free admission. A USA Cycling race. Downtown streets, Rochester: Broad, Exchange, Irving, Bausch & Lomb *DD3*; www.rochestercrit.com

Golf

More than 80 public and private golf facilities lie within a half-hour drive of the city, making Rochester one of the most golf-rich areas of New York State. Genesee Valley Golf Course, a public facility in the city's Genesee Valley Park, is closest to downtown hotels. Visitors staying in suburban hotels will find many courses within a short drive.

PUBLIC AND SEMI-PRIVATE GOLF COURSES

Arrowhead Golf Club: 655 Gallup Road, Spencerport *D9*; 352-5500

Batavia Country Club: 7909 Batavia-Byron Road, Batavia *B19*; (800) 343-7600

The Belfry International Golf Club of Rochester: 1233 Lehigh Station Road, Henrietta *G12*; 334-4540

Drop-in yoga classes are held at Breathe Yoga and Juice Bar in Pittsford.

Braemar Country Club: 4704 W. Ridge Road, Greece *D10*; 352-5360

Bristol Harbour Resort: 5410 Seneca Point Road, Canandaigua *B21*; 396-2200

Brockport Country Club: 3739 Monroe Orleans County Line Road, Brockport *D7*; 638-5334

Caledonia Country Club: 303 Park Place, Caledonia *B20*; 538-9956

Centerpointe Country Club: 2231 Brickyard Road, Canandaigua *B21*; 924-5346

Chili Country Club: 760 Scottsville-Chili Road, Chili *F10*; 889-9325

Conesus Golf Club: 1 Pine Alley, Conesus *C20*; 346-2100

Cragie Brae Golf Club: 4391 Union St., Scottsville *G9*; 889-1440

Davis' Countryside Meadows: 11070 Perry Road, Pavilion *B19*; 584-8390

Deerfield Country Club: 100 Craig Hill Drive, Brockport *C8*; 392-8080

Durand Eastman Golf Course: 1200 Kings Highway North, Rochester *C13*; 266-0110

Eagle Vale Golf Course: 4344 Nine Mile Point Road, Fairport *E15*; 377-5200

FarView Golf Club: 2419 Avon-Geneseo Road, Avon *B20*; 226-8210

Genesee Valley Golf Course: 1000 E. River Road, Rochester *F12*; 424-2920

Greystone Golf Club: 1400 Atlantic Ave., Walworth *A22*; (800) 810-2325

Lake Shore Country Club: 1165 Greenleaf Road, Greece *C12*; 663-9100

LeRoy Country Club: 7759 E. Main Road, LeRoy *B20*; 768-7330

Livingston Country Club: Lakeville Road, Geneseo *B20*; 243-4430

Mill Creek Golf Course: 670 Hosmer Road, Churchville *G9*; 889-4110

Ozzie's Corner Golf Course: 1147 Moscow Road, Hamlin *A7*; 964-5440

Parkview Fairways Public Golf Course: 7100 Boughton Road, Victor *B21*; 657-7539

Pinewood Country Club: 1189 Ogden-Parma Town Line Road, Spencerport *B9*; 352-5314

Ravenwood Golf Club: 929 Lynaugh Road, Victor *B21*; 924-5100

Riverton Golf Club: Scottsville-West Henrietta Road, Henrietta *G10*; 334-6196

Salmon Creek Country Club: 355 Washington St., Spencerport *D9*; 352-4300

Shadow Lake Golf & Racquet Club: 1850 Five Mile Line Road, Penfield *E12*; 385-2010

Shadow Pines Golf Club: 600 Whalen Road, Penfield *E12*; 385-8550

St. John Fisher Golf Course: 3690 East Ave., Rochester *E14*; 385-8458

Terry Hills Golf Course: 5122 Clinton St. Road, Batavia *B20*; (800) 825-8633

Twin Hills Golf Course: 5719 Ridge Road, Spencerport *C9*; 352-4800

Webster Golf Club: 440 Salt Road, Webster *C15*; *East* 265-1201; *West* 265-1307

Wild Wood Country Club: Rush-West Rush Road, Rush *B20*; 334-5860

Winged Pheasant Golf Links: 1475 Sand Hill Road, Farmington *B21*; 289-8846

Woodcliff: 199 Woodcliff Drive, Perinton *G14*; 248-4880

EXECUTIVE/PAR 3 COURSES

Buttonwood: 600 Trimmer Road, Spencerport *C9*; 352-4720

Executive South Family Golf Center: 3850 E. Henrietta Road, Henrietta *G12*; 334-1300

Lake Shore Executive Golf Course: 1150 Greenleaf Road, Greece *C12*; 621-1030

Winding Creek: 6392 Plastermill Road, Victor *B21*; 924-0280

A historic route for Rochester marathoners

In 2005, its inaugural year, the Preferred Care Rochester Marathon featured John Bingham—better known as "the Penguin" for his popular *Runner's World* column—and temperatures in the 60s. Nearly 1,800 runners hit the streets.

Organizers are hoping for similar weather and at least 2,500 to run this year's race, slated for Sept. 17. Planners have improved the route to avoid last year's traffic snarls.

Full- and half-marathon and four-person team relay runners start downtown and head east. The marathon and relay route goes to Fairport and hops on the Erie Canal towpath westbound in Perinton Park. Full-marathon runners will cover nearly half the route on this historic path. Half-marathoners converge on the canal path in Brighton, and all race to Genesee Valley Park, where they turn north and follow the Genesee River up to downtown. The start and finish are once again at Frontier Field on State Street.

The best places to watch are Schoen Place in Pittsford; Embankment Park (off Marsh Road some two miles from Schoen Place); on the east side of the river in Genesee Valley Park; along Plymouth Avenue in Corn Hill; and, naturally, at the finish line at Frontier Field.

The Preferred Care Rochester Marathon benefits the Arthritis Foundation. Lynn Doescher, development director of the Arthritis Foundation, said organizers expect the half-marathon to attain Rochester Runner of the Year classification. The 13-mile race also might be in the grand prix race series of USA Track and Field.

Crowne Plaza Rochester is hosting racers this year. A health fair and expo will be held at the hotel Friday, Sept. 15, from 10 a.m. to 7 p.m., and Saturday, Sept. 16, 9 a.m. to 4 p.m. The race starts at 8 a.m., Sunday, at Frontier Field. *www.rochestermarathon.com*

GOLF PRACTICE RANGES

Auburn Creek Golf Range: 7331 Victor-Mendon Road, Victor *B21*; 924-7570
Big Oak Driving Range & Golf Shop: 441 N. Washington Ave., East Rochester *E14*; 586-0614
Dyer Straights: 1012 Route 15A, Honeoye Falls *B20*; 624-5360
Eagle Vale Golf Club & Learning Center: 4344 Nine Mile Point Road, Fairport *E15*; 377-5200
Golf Rite Practice Facility: 4154 Buffalo Road, Chili *F10*; 594-8150
The Golf Tee Family Fun-Tastic: 1039 Ridge Road, Webster *D14*; 872-1390
The Links at Black Creek: 420 Ballantyne Road, Chili *F10*; 889-2000

Metalwood Driving Range: 4706 W. Ridge Road, Spencerport *D10*; 352-1016
Mill Creek Golf: 670 Hosmer Road, Churchville *G9*; 889-4110
Parkview Fairways Public Golf Course: 7100 Boughton Road, Victor *B21*; 657-7539
Ravenwood Golf Club: 929 Lynaugh Road, Victor *B21*; 924-5100
Rochester Sports Dome: 4618 W. Ridge Road, Spencerport *D10*; 352-5300
Southern Meadows Golf Course: 1025 Rush-Scottsville Road, Rush *B20*; 533-2440
Twin Hills Golf Course: 5719 W. Ridge Road, Spencerport *D9*; 352-4800
Webster Golf Club: 440 Salt Road, Webster *C15*; 265-1307

Horseback riding

Black North Farm Inc.: 707 Gillett Road, Spencerport *D9*; 352-6937
Copper Creek Farm: 5041 Shortsville Road, Shortsville *B21*; 289-4441
Heberle Stables: 751 Browncroft Blvd., Penfield *E14*; 482-1290
Rocking Horse Equestrian Center: 1319 Penfield Center Road, Penfield *E15*; 872-7417
Wolcott Farms 4 Seasons of Fun: 3820 Hermitage Road, Warsaw *C19*; 786-3504; www.wolcottfarm.com
Woodruff Training Stables: 4919 S. Livonia Road, Livonia *B20*; 346-3843

Ice skating

ESL Sports Centre: Indoor. Call for hours and fees. Monroe Community College campus, 2700 Brighton-Henrietta Town Line Road, Brighton *F12*; 424-GOAL
Frank Ritter Memorial Ice Arena: Call for hours and fees. Rochester Institute of Technology campus, 51 Lomb Memorial Drive, Henrietta *F11*; 475-2614
Genesee Valley Ice Rink: Indoor. Call for hours and fees. 145 Elmwood Ave., Rochester *F11*; 235-6684
Highland Park pond: Outdoor. Free skating, warming hut, open to public. Next to James P.B. Duffy School No. 12, 999 South Ave., Rochester *E3*
Lakeshore Hockey Arena: Call for hours and

Manhattan Square Park Ice Rink is the place to skate downtown.

fees. 123 Ling Road, Greece *C12*; 865-2801, 865-2800 (recording)

Manhattan Square Park Ice Rink: Outdoor. Undergoing renovation; call for hours and fees. 353 Court St., downtown Rochester *C4*; 428-7541

Thomas Creek Ice Arena: Indoor. Call for hours and fees. 80 Lyndon Road, Fairport *F15*; 223-2160

Webster Ice Arena: Indoor. Call for hours and fees. 865 Publishers Parkway, Webster *C14*; 787-3530

Webster Recreation Center Ice Rink: 530 Webster Ave., Rochester *D13*; 654-8900

Racing

Batavia Downs: Standard-bred harness races around a half-mile oval take place July to December. The also track has 586 video gambling machines, a restaurant and a special-events room. Batavia Downs is the oldest lighted track of its kind in North America. 8315 Park Road, Batavia *B19*; 343-3750; www.batavia-downs.com

Cayuga County Fair Speedway: Since 1955, this track (formerly known as Weedsport Speedway) has held stock car races on a 3/8-mile, high-banked oval track. It's the headquarters of DIRT (Drivers Independent Race Tracks) Motorsports Inc., as well as the sport's hall of fame and classic car museum. County Fairgrounds on Route 31, Weedsport *B23*; (315) 834-6606; www.dirtmotorsports.com/CCFS

Finger Lakes Gaming & Racetrack: Thoroughbred racing has been bringing fans to this track for over 40 years. Gambling fans like the 1,000 Las Vegas-style video lottery terminals added in 2004. Finger Lakes has hosted more than 60,000 races and entertained 18 million fans. 5857 Route 96, Farmington *B21*; 924-3232; www.fingerlakesracetrack.com

Watkins Glen International: Features auto racing on a 2.45-mile road course and a 3.37-mile Grand Prix course. The Glen hosts a NASCAR Nextel Cup Series race in August. 2790 County Road 16, Watkins Glen *C22*; (607) 535-2486; www.theglen.com

Spencer Speedway: This half-mile oval track marked its 50th year in 2004. Spencer runs

IndyCar racing returns to the Glen

The Watkins Glen Indy Grand Prix moves to June this year, giving fans the first opportunity to see the newly crowned 2006 Indy 500 champion. Sahlen's Six Hours of the Glen, featuring the Grand American Rolex Sports Car Series, is scheduled for June 3. The Menards Infiniti Pro Series and the IRL IndyCar Series take to the historic long course on June 4. Danika Patrick, 2005 rookie of the year, is slated to compete.

Watkins Glen Indy Grand Prix: June 2-4, 2006. Watkins Glen *C22*; www.theglen.com

three classes: Street Stocks, Grand American Modifieds and NASCAR Modifieds. The NASCAR Dodge Weekly Racing Series is a popular event. 3011 Ridge Road (Route 104), Williamson *A22*; (315) 589-3018; www.spencer-speedway.com

Rowing, kayaking & canoeing

CLUBS

Brighton Crew: 328-3960, www.brightoncrew.org

Finger Lakes-Ontario Watershed (FLOW) Paddlers Club: www.flowpaddlers.org

Pittsford Crew: Clover Street, Pittsford; 234-7463 (hotline), 381-9560 (boathouse)

Rochester Rowing Club: www.geneseewaterways.org

RETAILERS / INSTRUCTORS / GUIDES / RENTALS

BayCreek Paddling Center: 1099 Empire Blvd., Penfield *D13*; 288-2830; www.baycreek.com

Braddock Bay Paddlesports: 416 Manitou Road, Greece *B10*;. 392-2628; www.paddlingny.com

Genesee Waterways Center: Elaine P. Wilson Boathouse, 149 Elmwood Ave., Rochester *E2*; Lock 32 Whitewater Park, Clover Street, Pittsford *F13*; 328-3960; www.geneseewaterways.org

Oak Orchard Canoe and Kayak Experts: 2133 Waterport Road, Waterport, Orleans County *A19* and 1350 Empire Blvd., Penfield *F13*; 682-4849 or 288-5550; www.oakorchardcanoe.com

Pack, Paddle, Ski: Outdoor adventure. South Lima *B20*; 346-5597; www.packpaddleski.com

Running

With great routes, active clubs and some of the oldest races in the Northeast, Rochester is a runner's town.

CLUBS

Cats Athletic Club: Running club for all levels. Info on local races. Holds the PolarCat series of winter races at various locations. www.catspage.com

Genesee Valley Harriers: Member of the USA Track & Field Association's Niagara District and host of the 2005 National Club Cross Country Championships. Info on local races. www.gvh.net

Greater Rochester Track Club: Info on races, routes, track facilities and running groups. Hosts the Freezeroo winter racing series. www.grtconline.org

Rochester Area Triathletes: 10-year-old group that offers high-level training for experienced triathletes/duathletes and support for newcomers. http://rochestertriathletes.com

Rochester NY Frontrunners: Gay and lesbian running club for all fitness levels. Park Avenue

Paddlers find an almost mystical world of creeks and wetlands off the southern end of Irondequoit Bay.

A stadium of their own

Once again, Rochester soccer fans have something to celebrate

It's a new place to watch the game. Professional soccer in Rochester now has its own home, PaeTec Park, not far from the city's High Falls Entertainment District.

The Rochester Rhinos, a United Soccer League first division team, have been sharing space with the Triple-A Rochester Red Wings at nearby Frontier Field. The new stadium is soccer-specific, with seating for 17,500, 20 private suites and a state-of-the-art synthetic playing field.

The Rhinos will unveil PaeTec Park at a grand opening Saturday, June 3, 2006, with a game against the Virginia Beach Mariners and special entertainment.

Rochesterians love their soccer—it's played at every level, by children and adults, and leagues abound. The Rhinos have enjoyed a large and loyal following since the franchise began in 1996. Game attendance consistently exceeds that of much larger markets, averaging 10,000 per game.

"This is soccer town USA. The fans are very knowledgeable of the game," says Frank DuRoss, Rhinos president. "They expect a fun night out and they expect a winning tradition—which the Rhinos have always delivered. We've won four championships in 10 years."

"Get your tickets here!"

PaeTec Park has more than 3,000 seats priced at $9, compared with 1,000 seats priced at $12 at Frontier Field. Game-day ticket pricing ranges from $25 in the Club level to $9 in the end zone. Children 12 and under can take advantage of $8 end zone seats.

The park is an eight-minute walk to the High Falls Entertainment District. Parking also is available at the stadium and on nearby streets.

PaeTec Park gives fans better sightlines than Frontier Field, where seating is best suited for watching baseball. The stadium scoreboard is 90 feet high and 50 feet wide. Twenty portable and five permanent concessions sell the usual stadium fare plus food unique to Rochester.

Rhinos games are marked by lots of fan interaction: Marketing staff toss team T-shirts into the stands. Youth teams are enlisted to greet the Rhinos when they take the field. Giveaways are announced all through the game.

"It's high energy; it's not your typical soccer event," DuRoss says. "There's a lot going on prior to the game, fireworks after the game, bands playing pregame—a very festive atmosphere."

PaeTec Park houses a number of spinoff soccer franchises that carry the Rhinos name, including a women's team in the USL W-

League (formerly the Rochester Ravens) and the Rochester Junior Rhinos.

Besides soccer, the stadium serves as the home of the Rochester Rattlers of Major League Lacrosse. Other likely events include Buffalo Bills controlled scrimmages and high school and collegiate games in a variety of sports. Down the line, look for drum and bugle competitions, concerts and community events.

HOK Sports Facility Group of Kansas City, Mo., designed the park. HOK has worked with nearly all major-league football and baseball teams. The firm recently designed soccer stadiums in Australia and New Zealand.

PaeTec Park, 460 Oak St., Rochester B2;
www.rhinossoccer.com

neighborhood runs held three times a week. www.frontrunners.org/clubs/rochester

RACES

Run for the Young: May 13, 2006, 9:30 a.m., 5K/1 mile, 1000 North Greece Road, Greece

Apple Blossom 5K and 10K: May 20, 2006, 10 a.m., Williamson

Rochester Spring Classic Duathlon: May 20, 2006, 8:30 a.m., Formula 1, super sprint, Stewart Lodge, Mendon Ponds Park, Mendon

Medved Lilac 10K and 5K Family Fun Run: May 21, 2006, 10 kilometers, 9 a.m.; 5 kilometers, 8 a.m., Highland Park, Rochester

J.P. Morgan Chase Corporate Challenge: June 1, 2006, 7 p.m., 3.5 miles, Rochester Institute of Technology, Henrietta; 624-8245; www.jpmorganchasecc.com/events.php?city_id=3 **F11**

Temple Beth El 90th Anniversary 5K: June 4, 2006, 8:15 a.m., 139 S. Winton Road, Rochester

PowerBar Trail Race: June 10, 2006, 9 a.m., 9 miles and 4.5 miles, Beach Lot, Mendon Ponds Park, Mendon

Fleet Feet Sports Firecracker Five Mile: July 4, 2006, 8:30 a.m., 5 miles, Perinton Park, Fairport

Shoreline Triathlon: July 30, 2006, 8:30 a.m., sprint distance, Hamlin Beach State Park Area 4, Hamlin

Sodus Point Triathlon: Aug. 20, 2006, time TBA, sprint distance, Sodus Point

Greece Police Athletic League 5K and 1 Mile: Aug. 26, 2006, time TBA, 5K and 1 mile, Greece

Oak Tree Half Marathon and 5K: Sept. 3, 2006, time TBA, 13.1 miles and 5K, Geneseo

Bristol Mountain Winter Resort has the highest vertical rise of any ski area between the Catskills and the Rocky Mountains.

Dorschel MADD Dash 10K: Sept. 10, 2006, 8:30 a.m., 10K and 2-mile walk, Rush-Henrietta High School, 2034 Lehigh Station Road, Henrietta

Finger Lakes Triathlon: Sept. 10, 2006, 7:30, 8 and 11 a.m., Olympic, sprint and kids' tri, Kershaw Park, Canandaigua

Susan B. Anthony 5K: Sept. 24, 2006, time TBA, 5K, Rochester

Rochester Autumn Classic Duathlon: Oct. 1, 2006, time TBA, Formula 1 and super sprint, Stewart Lodge, Mendon Ponds Park, Mendon

34th Webster Turkey Trot: Nov. 23, 2006, time TBA, 4.4 mile and 2.5 mile fun run, Parkview Lodge, Webster

Johnny's Runnin' o' the Green: Mid-March 2007, 10:30 a.m., 5 miles, Blue Cross Arena at Rochester War Memorial, Rochester

Skiing & tubing

Western New York Snow Phone: (800) 367-9691

Rochester Nordic Ski Club: www.rochesternordic.org

Cross-country ski trails are abundant in area parks. For details, see the Trails category on page 57 and the Parks and Gardens section on page 49.

Brantling Ski and Snowboard Center: 10 trails, skiing, racing, snowboarding and snowmobiling. 4016 Fishfarm Road, Sodus **A22**; (315) 331-2365; www.brantling.com

Bristol Mountain Winter Resort: 1,200-foot vertical rise, 32 slopes and trails, 45 minutes from Rochester. 5662 Route 64, Canandaigua **C21**; 374-6000; www.bristolmt.com

Holiday Valley Resort: 52 slopes, 750-foot vertical drop, 13 lifts. Route 219, Ellicottville **D18**; (716) 699-2345; www.holidayvalley.com

Polar Wave Snowtubing Park: Snow tubing with chutes for slow, medium and fast rides. Rope-tow returns riders to the top. 3500 Harloff Road, Batavia **D19**; (888) 727-2794; www.polarwavesnowtubing.com

Swain Ski and Snowboard Center: 21 trails, snowboarding and tubing, one hour from Rochester. County Route 24, Swain **C20**; 234-SNOW; www.swain.com

Tennis

PUBLIC CITY COURTS

Cobbs Hill Park: Culver Road and Norris Drive **C5**

Genesee Valley Park (East): 200 Elmwood Ave. **F12**

Maplewood Park: Maplewood Drive at Seneca Parkway **A2**

Tryon Park (West): Tryon Park at Loudisa Drive **D13**

PRIVATE CLUBS

Brighton Tennis Club: 3195 Brighton-Henrietta Town Line Road, Brighton **F13**; 427-8701

Barb and Jeff Franks Tennis Academy: 260 Hogan Road, Fairport **F15**; 223-0575

Manhattan Square Tennis Club: 8 Manhattan Square Drive, Rochester **DD5**; 325-3219

Mid-Town Athletic Club: 200 E. Highland Drive, Brighton **E13**; 461-2300

Tennis Club of Rochester: 1 Dort Cameron Drive, Pittsford **G14**; 248-8980

The Tennis Club of Webster: 701 Phillips Road, Webster **C15**; 265-1800

Rural *Rochester*

On the Farm

If you picture the New York City skyline whenever you hear "New York," this fact might surprise you: Agriculture is the No. 1 business in the state. Twenty-five percent of the state's land area, roughly 7.6 million acres, is farmland.

The "cream" of the crop is milk and dairy. The state ranks third in production in the nation; nearby Wyoming County is the top-producing county in the state.

The big crops grown around Rochester are apples, cabbage, sweet corn and grapes. A short drive to the surrounding countryside

makes this quickly apparent. You'll see rows of corn and fields of cabbage in the Genesee Valley, acres of apple orchards near Lake Ontario and rolling vineyards in the Finger Lakes region. A growing number of farmers raise organic produce and range-fed chickens, cows, sheep, bison, ostrich and other animals. All of which makes the area's weekly farm markets busy places.

Rochester's horticultural history is evident in an abundance of plant nurseries and garden centers, some more than a century old. In the winter, there are maple syrup tapping and winery events that will warm your toes. For details, see the Special Events and Wineries sections.

Attractions

COMMUNITY FARMERS MARKETS

Brockport: Mid-June to late October. Saturdays, 8 a.m. - 1 p.m. Market Street, Brockport *D7*; 637-5300, ext. 19

East Rochester: Early May to mid-November. Sundays, 8 a.m. - noon. Techniplex Plaza, 300 Main St., East Rochester *E14*; 387-3553

Fairport: Early May to mid-November. Saturdays, 7 a.m. - noon. 9 Lift Bridge Lane East, Fairport *F15*; 223-6795

Greece: Greece Ridge Center Farmers Market - Early July to late October. Thursdays and Saturdays, 9 a.m. - 3 p.m. 271 Greece Ridge Center Drive, Greece *D11*; 225-1140

Irondequoit: Early June to late October. Thursdays, 4 - 8 p.m. Medley Centre northwest parking lot, 285 Medley Centre Drive, Irondequoit *D13*; 336-6070

North Chili: Early July to late October. Saturdays, 8 a.m. - 1 p.m. United Methodist Church of North Chili, 2200 Westside Drive, Chili *E9*; 594-9111

Pittsford: Early June to late October. Tuesdays and Saturdays, 8:30 a.m. - 2:30 p.m. Pittsford Plaza, 3349 Monroe Ave., Pittsford *F13*; 424-6220

Rochester Foodlink: Location and time TBA; 328-3380

Rochester Main Street: Early November to mid-June, Wednesdays and Fridays, 11 a.m. - 2 p.m. Mid-June to late October, Fridays, 11 a.m. to 2 p.m. Sibley Centre atrium, 220 E. Main St., Rochester *CC5*; 546-1711

Rochester Public Market: Year-round. Tuesdays and Thursdays, 6 a.m. - 1 p.m., and Saturdays, 5 a.m. - 3 p.m. Rochester Public Market, 280 N. Union St., Rochester *B5*; 428-6770

Rush: Mid-June to late October. Rush United Methodist Church, 6200 Rush-Lima Road (Route 15A), Rush *B20*; 533-2475

Scottsville: Late June to early October. Sundays, 9 a.m. - 1 p.m. Scottsville Ice Arena, 1800 Scottsville-Chili Road, Wheatland *B20*; 889-1810, ext. 7

Webster: Mid-July to late October. Webster Village Hall, 28 W. Main St., Webster *A21*; 872-4648

U-PICK FARMS AND FARM MARKETS

Aman's Farm & Market: Plants, gardening supplies, gift shop, beer. 2458 E. Ridge Road, Irondequoit; 544-8360

Bauman's Farm Market & Cider Mill: Fruit, cider, seasonal events. 1340 Five Mile Line Road, Webster; 671-2820

"Oh, give me a home..."

If you're tooling around the byways of Wayne County, pull over to watch the bison roam in the pastures of **Bison Hill Farm** near Newark. The best views are on Bauer Van Wyckle Road, off Pulver Road.

Rural
Rochester

Take a Drive

Here are some routes that will take you out into the country:

Ontario State Parkway runs along the southern shore of Lake Ontario, the easternmost of the Great Lakes. Spectacular views of the lake, apple orchards and farms unfold along 35 miles in Monroe and Orleans counties. Where the parkway ends near Lakeside Beach, a left turn takes you to **Route 18**. Both are chains in a link known as the Seaway Trail, a designated National Scenic Byway, which runs 500 miles from Massena, N.Y., to Erie, Pa. (Read more about the Seaway Trail on page 96.)

Before Interstate 90 was built, Route 20 was the main thoroughfare from Boston to Oregon. In Central New York, Route 20 coincides with Route 5 between Avon and Auburn. With its start as a Seneca Nation trail, it later became a military supply route. Locals call this historic corridor simply "5 and 20" (www.routes5and20.com) and know it as a great place to find antiques. In the historic towns along the way you'll find local art, crafts and gifts too. Restaurants serve regional favorites and comfort food.

Route 15 begins in the city of Rochester at 1 Mt. Hope Ave., where it intersects with South Avenue. It travels south through the city and Brighton before opening up to farm country in southern Henrietta and Rush. And then it just keeps going. See flea markets, farm stands and small-town America—if you want, all the way to South Carolina, 800 miles away.

The **wine trails** around the Finger Lakes in central New York follow roads that offer splendid views of the lakes and surrounding vineyards: Route 21, Canandaigua Lake; Routes 54A and 54, Keuka Lake; Routes 14, 96A and 414, Seneca Lake; and Routes 89 and 90, Cayuga Lake. (See the Wineries section for maps.)

Good routes for **antiquing** include Routes 5 & 20 in Bloomfield (www.bloomfieldantiquemile.com), Lima, Avon and Caledonia; Route 332 in Farmington; Route 20 in Madison; and Route 104 in Genesee, Monroe and Wayne counties.

Macedon: (315) 986-4202

Maier's Mud Acres: Produce, pies, honey, festivals. 1040 Canandaigua Road, Macedon; (315) 986-2551

Patch of Paradise: U-pick flowers. 4509 Christian Road, Dansville; 335-9871

Powers Farm Market: Produce, pumpkins, fall festivities. 161 Marsh Road, Pittsford; 586-4631

Red Jacket Orchards: Cider, juices, farm market, gift boxes. 957 Routes 5 & 20 West, Geneva; (315) 781-2749

Schmidt's Farm Market: 845 Manitou Road, Hilton; 392-6845

Sodoma's Farm Market: 4490 Sweden Walker Road, Brockport; 637-8751

Whittier Fruit Farm: U-pick apples, farm market, cider, gifts, events. 219 Whittier Road, Ogden; 594-9054

Wickham Farms: Farm market, events. 1821 Route 250, Penfield; 377-3276

FARM ANIMALS AND WILDLIFE
See Sports and Recreation for horseback riding.

Lollypop Farm: Petting zoo of rescued farm animals. 99 Victor Road, Fairport *F15;* www.lollypopfarm.org

Mendon Ponds Park: Hand feed the chickadees. Multiple entrances on Route 65 (Clover Street) and Route 64 (Pittsford-Mendon Center Road), Pittsford and Mendon *G13;* www.monroecounty.gov

Seneca Park Zoo: Wildlife in the city. St. Paul Blvd., Rochester *D12;* www.senecaparkzoo.org

Springdale Farm: Petting zoo, farm activities, corn maze, sheep shearing. Colby Street at either Hubbell Road or Salmon Creek Road, Sweden and Ogden *D8;* www.springdalefarm.org

Bergen Farm Market: Routes 33 and 19, Bergen; 494-1320

Brown's Berry Patch: Fruit, ice cream, deli, activities. 14264 Route 18, Waterport; 682-5569

Cobble Creek Farm: Produce, hay rides, garden center, petting zoo. 5161 W. Ridge Road, Spencerport; 352-8484

Colby Homestead Farms: Dairy, produce. 263 Colby Road, Spencerport; 352-3830

DeConinck Farm Market: 1532 Maiden Lane, Greece; 227-4198

Fraser's Garlic Farm: Organic garlic, pumpkins. 1379 Johnson Road, Churchville; 350-8295

Freshlink Farms: Hydroponic produce. 1345 Penfield Center Road, Penfield; 872-7303

Gentle's Farm Market: Roadside produce. 1092 Penfield Road, Penfield; 586-2506

Green Acre Fruit Farms: U-pick fruit and pumpkins, farm tours, hayrides. 3460 Latta Road, Greece; 225-5926

Gro-Moore Farms: Farm market, hayrides, U-pick strawberries. 2811 E. Henrietta Road, Henrietta; 359-3310

Herman's Farm Market and Cider Mill: Apples, farm market, cider. 741 Five Mile Line Road, Webster; 671-1246

Hurd Orchards: Fruit, flowers, baked goods, gift shop, events. 17260 Ridge Road, Holley; 638-8838

Kelly's Farm Market: 611 Wilder Road, Hilton; 392-8102

Kirby's Farm Market: Farm market, U-pick apples, cider, events. 9739 W. Ridge Road, Brockport; 637-2600

Kyle Farms: All-natural lamb. 5837 E. Henrietta Road, Rush; 202-7768

Long Acre Farms: Farm market, ice cream, corn maze, activities. 1342 Eddy Road,

wineries

Wineries

For a taste of old-world winemaking, visit the Finger Lakes southeast of Rochester.

Well-marked routes wind around Canandaigua, Keuka, Seneca and Cayuga lakes. Some 80 wineries are tucked into gentle hills that slope down to the lakes—providing the ideal climate for growing the grapes used in chardonnay, Riesling, pinot noir, cabernet franc, and French-American and native varietals.

Finger Lakes wines are winning competitions at the international level. You can sample the latest vintages year-round. Wineries are busiest with visitors during the summer and fall, so if you'd like to linger over the latest vintages (perhaps with the winemakers themselves), go in the winter or spring. Food-and-wine pairings, holiday gatherings and other special events are held all year. The Finger Lakes boasts a growing number of restaurants that serve New York cuisine (signature dishes made with fresh, local ingredients), and inns provide overnight accommodations. Call or check winery and wine trail Web sites for details.

Tasting rooms

NYStateWine.com: Tasting room and wine gallery; gift baskets; wine accessories. 29 N. Franklin St., Watkins Glen *C22*; (607) 535-2944; www.nystatewine.com

Area wine and liquor shops hold free wine tastings and classes. Here's a sampling:

Century Wines and Liquors: Canadians flock to this store for its deep discounts. 630 W. Ridge Road, Greece *D11*; 621-4210

Marketview Liquor: At 14,000 square feet, it has one of the largest selections in the area. 1100 Jefferson Road, Henrietta *F12*; 427-2480

Pittsford Wine & Spirits: 654 Schoen Place, Pittsford *F14*; 218-0200

Schuber Liquor Store: A Schuber family business since 1945, this is a neighborhood fixture. 373 Park Ave., Rochester *C5*; 473-1937

Wine Sense: This wine-only shop has knowledgeable staff and weekly tastings. 749 Park Ave., Rochester *D5*; 271-0590; www.wedefinewine.com/winesense/default.htm

Canandaigua Wine Trail and Northern Wineries

(877) FUN-IN-NY; www.canandaiguawinetrailonline.com

1. **Arbor Hill Grapery** 6461 Route 64, Naples; (800) 554-2406; www.thegrapery.com

2. **Casa Larga Vineyards** 2287 Turk Hill Road, Fairport; 223-4210; www.casalarga.com

3. **Finger Lakes Wine Center at Sonnenberg Gardens** 151 Charlotte St., Canandaigua; 394-9016

4. **Widmer's Wine Cellars Inc.** 1 Lake Niagara Lane, Naples; (800) 836-5253

Deer Run Winery 3772 W. Lake Road, Geneseo; 346-0850; www.deerrunwinery.com *(not mapped)*

Eagle Crest Vineyards Inc. 7107 Vineyard Road, Conesus; 346-2321 *(not mapped)*

Lamoreaux Landing Wine Cellars, in Lodi on Seneca Lake, is a member of the Finger Lakes Wine Guild, wineries in the region that produce world-class wines from European grape varieties.

Keuka Lake Wine Trail

2375 Route 14A, Penn Yan; (800) 440-4898; www.keukawinetrail.com

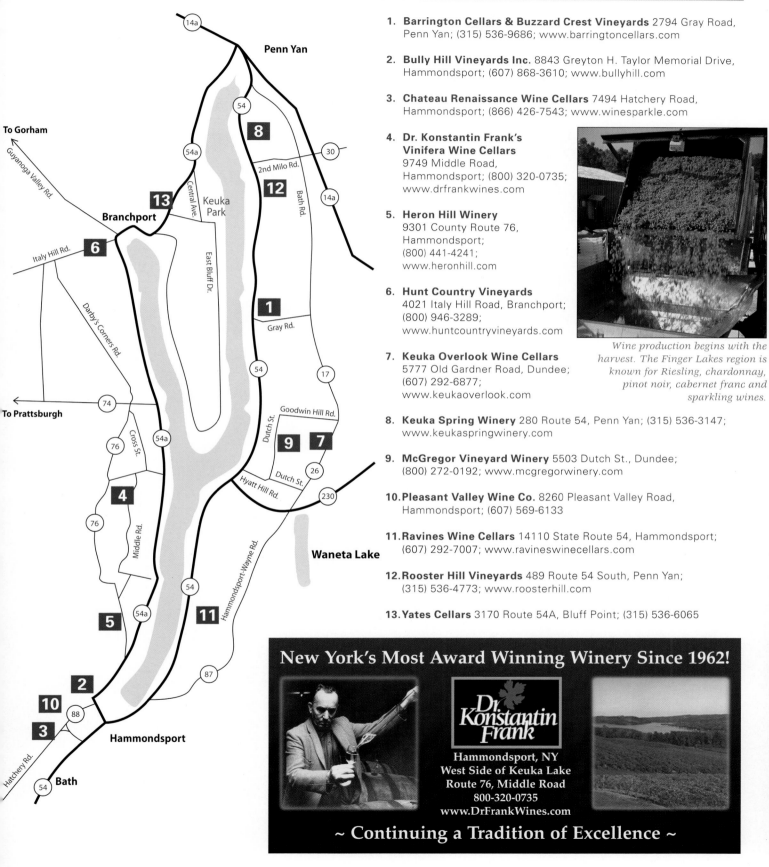

1. **Barrington Cellars & Buzzard Crest Vineyards** 2794 Gray Road, Penn Yan; (315) 536-9686; www.barringtoncellars.com

2. **Bully Hill Vineyards Inc.** 8843 Greyton H. Taylor Memorial Drive, Hammondsport; (607) 868-3610; www.bullyhill.com

3. **Chateau Renaissance Wine Cellars** 7494 Hatchery Road, Hammondsport; (866) 426-7543; www.winesparkle.com

4. **Dr. Konstantin Frank's Vinifera Wine Cellars** 9749 Middle Road, Hammondsport; (800) 320-0735; www.drfrankwines.com

5. **Heron Hill Winery** 9301 County Route 76, Hammondsport; (800) 441-4241; www.heronhill.com

6. **Hunt Country Vineyards** 4021 Italy Hill Road, Branchport; (800) 946-3289; www.huntcountryvineyards.com

7. **Keuka Overlook Wine Cellars** 5777 Old Gardner Road, Dundee; (607) 292-6877; www.keukaoverlook.com

8. **Keuka Spring Winery** 280 Route 54, Penn Yan; (315) 536-3147; www.keukaspringwinery.com

9. **McGregor Vineyard Winery** 5503 Dutch St., Dundee; (800) 272-0192; www.mcgregorwinery.com

10. **Pleasant Valley Wine Co.** 8260 Pleasant Valley Road, Hammondsport; (607) 569-6133

11. **Ravines Wine Cellars** 14110 State Route 54, Hammondsport; (607) 292-7007; www.ravineswinecellars.com

12. **Rooster Hill Vineyards** 489 Route 54 South, Penn Yan; (315) 536-4773; www.roosterhill.com

13. **Yates Cellars** 3170 Route 54A, Bluff Point; (315) 536-6065

Wine production begins with the harvest. The Finger Lakes region is known for Riesling, chardonnay, pinot noir, cabernet franc and sparkling wines.

A place to enjoy New York's bounty

If you savor the fresh taste of locally cultivated food and wine, put the New York Wine and Culinary Center at the top of your list of places to visit.

The center, on the shores of Canandaigua Lake, spotlights New York's agricultural, wine and culinary strengths. It comes to fruition in the summer of 2006.

The Adirondack-style structure is billed as a one-of-a-kind learning center for foodies and wine lovers. New York is home to some 200 wineries, and agriculture is the state's No. 1 business. With the growth of the Slow Food movement and increasing interest in organic foods, the center is opening at a good time.

"It's unique in the world. It really is," says Jim Trezise, president of the New York Wine & Grape Foundation, one of the organizers. "When I did my research in California and other places, there are wine-tasting rooms and there are restaurants. But there is nothing that brings

everything together under one roof."

The center will have a large tasting room where visitors can sample wines from each of the state's wine regions: Niagara, the Finger Lakes, the Hudson Valley and Long Island. Upstairs, a tapas bar will serve samples of true New York cuisine—food made with agricultural ingredients grown throughout the state—paired with New York wines.

"You can learn about wine, and wine with food, and agriculture. You can learn how to cook. You can watch, in many cases, famous chefs do demonstrations," Trezise says. "It's basically from the farm to the table all in one place."

Chefs will ply their trade in a theater-style demonstration kitchen. Cooking classes will be held in a hands-on kitchen equipped with 18 Viking ranges. There will be a demonstration garden, lecture and lab space, health and nutrition information, and a gift shop selling wine, specialty foods and culinary tools. A private dining room will be available for small parties and corporate events.

Visitors will leave the center knowing where their food comes from: Permanent and rotating exhibits will tell about the agricultural products "grown, caught and raised" in New York, Executive Director Alexa Gifford says.

The New York center stands out from similar places—such as Copia in the Napa Valley—for its range of programming, education and training, Trezise says. Besides celebrity chef cooking demonstrations, public events will include lectures, concerts and a summer culinary camp. The center also will be a base for training in the hospitality and health and nutrition industries.

Several big players in food, wine and education, all based in the region, came together to make the center happen: Constellation Brands Inc., Wegmans Food Markets Inc., Rochester Institute of Technology and the New York Wine & Grape Foundation. The center's grand opening is slated for mid-June 2006.

800 S. Main St., Canandaigua; 394-7070; www.nywcc.com

Seneca Lake Wine Trail

Seneca Lake Winery Association; 100 N. Franklin St., Watkins Glen; (877) 536-2717; www.senecalakewine.com

West side of Seneca Lake

1. **Amberg Wine Cellars**
   2200 Routes 5 & 20, Flint;
   (585) 526-6742; www.ambergwine.com

2. **Anthony Road Wine Co.**
   1020 Anthony Road, Penn Yan;
   (315) 536-7524; www.anthonyroadwine.com

3. **Arcadian Estate Winery**
   4184 Route 14, Rock Stream;
   (800) 298-1346; www.arcadianwine.com

4. **Belhurst Winery** 4069 Route 14, Geneva;
   (315) 781-0201; www.belhurst.com

5. **Billsboro Winery** 4760 W. Lake Road,
   Geneva; (315) 789-9538;
   www.billsboro.com

6. **Cascata Winery at the Professors' Inn**
   3651 State Route 14, Watkins Glen;
   (607) 535-8000; www.cascatawinery.com

7. **Castel Grisch Estate Winery**
   3380 County Route 28, Watkins Glen;
   (607) 535-9614;
   www.fingerlakes-ny.com/castelgrich.htm

8. **Chateau D'Esperance** 29 N. Franklin St., Watkins Glen; (607) 535-2944;
   www.nystatewine.com

9. **Earle Estates Winery & Meadery** 2770 Route 14, Penn Yan; (315) 536-6755;
   www.meadery.com

10. **Four Chimneys Farm Winery** 211 Hall Road, Himrod; (607) 243-7502;
    www.fourchimneysorganicwines.com

11. **Fox Run Vineyards Inc.** 670 Route 14, Penn Yan; (800) 636-9786;
    www.foxrunvineyards.com

12. **Fulkerson Winery** 5576 Route 14, Dundee; (607) 243-7883;
    www.fulkersonwinery.com

13. **Glenora Wine Cellars Inc.** 5435 Route 14, Dundee; (800) 243-5513;
    www.glenora.com

14. **Hermann J. Wiemer Vineyard Inc.** 3962 Route 14, Dundee; (800) 371-7971.
    www.wiemer.com

15. **Hickory Hollow Wine Cellars** 5289 Route 14, Dundee; (607) 243-9114;
    www.hickoryhollowwine.com

16. **Lakewood Vineyards Inc.** 4024 State Route 14, Watkins Glen; (607) 535-9252.
    www.lakewoodvineyards.com

17. **Miles Wine Cellars** 168 Randall Crossing Road, Himrod; (607) 243-7742;
    www.mileswinecellars.com

18. **Prejean Winery** 2634 Route 14, Penn Yan; (315) 536-7524;
    www.prejeanwinery.com

19. **Seneca Shore Wine Cellars** Route 14 and Davy Road, Penn Yan;
    (800) 588-8466

20. **Torrey Ridge Winery** 2770 Route 14, Penn Yan; (315) 536-1210;
    www.torreyridgewinery.com

21. **Villa Bellangelo** 150 Poplar Point Road, Dundee; (607) 243-8602;
    www.bellangelo.com

22. **Woodbury Vineyards Gift and Tastings Shop** 4141 Route 14, Dundee;
    (866) 331-9463; www.woodburyvineyards.com

Rock Stream Vineyards 162 Fir Tree Point Road, Rock Stream; (607) 243-8322
(not mapped)

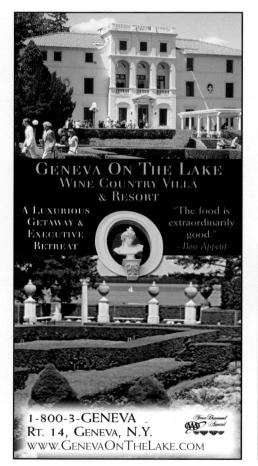

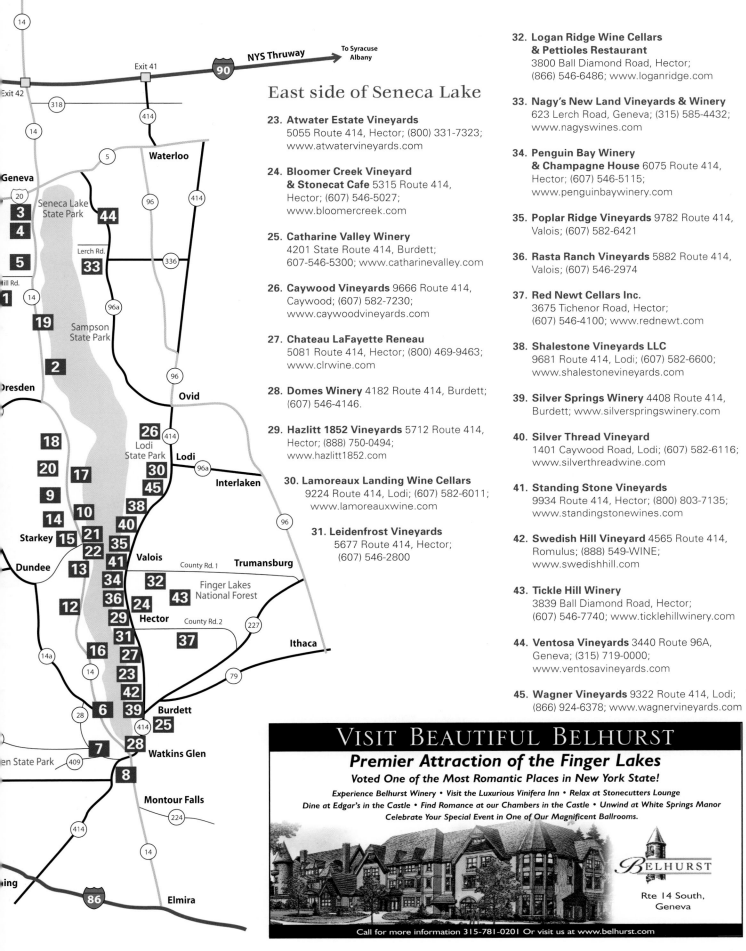

East side of Seneca Lake

23. Atwater Estate Vineyards
5055 Route 414, Hector; (800) 331-7323;
www.atwatervineyards.com

**24. Bloomer Creek Vineyard
& Stonecat Cafe** 5315 Route 414,
Hector; (607) 546-5027;
www.bloomercreek.com

25. Catharine Valley Winery
4201 State Route 414, Burdett;
607-546-5300; www.catharinevalley.com

26. Caywood Vineyards 9666 Route 414,
Caywood; (607) 582-7230;
www.caywoodvineyards.com

27. Chateau LaFayette Reneau
5081 Route 414, Hector; (800) 469-9463;
www.clrwine.com

28. Domes Winery 4182 Route 414, Burdett;
(607) 546-4146.

29. Hazlitt 1852 Vineyards 5712 Route 414,
Hector; (888) 750-0494;
www.hazlitt1852.com

30. Lamoreaux Landing Wine Cellars
9224 Route 414, Lodi; (607) 582-6011;
www.lamoreauxwine.com

31. Leidenfrost Vineyards
5677 Route 414, Hector;
(607) 546-2800

**32. Logan Ridge Wine Cellars
& Pettioles Restaurant**
3800 Ball Diamond Road, Hector;
(866) 546-6486; www.loganridge.com

33. Nagy's New Land Vineyards & Winery
623 Lerch Road, Geneva; (315) 585-4432;
www.nagyswines.com

**34. Penguin Bay Winery
& Champagne House** 6075 Route 414,
Hector; (607) 546-5115;
www.penguinbaywinery.com

35. Poplar Ridge Vineyards 9782 Route 414,
Valois; (607) 582-6421

36. Rasta Ranch Vineyards 5882 Route 414,
Valois; (607) 546-2974

37. Red Newt Cellars Inc.
3675 Tichenor Road, Hector;
(607) 546-4100; www.rednewt.com

38. Shalestone Vineyards LLC
9681 Route 414, Lodi; (607) 582-6600;
www.shalestonevineyards.com

39. Silver Springs Winery 4408 Route 414,
Burdett; www.silverspringswinery.com

40. Silver Thread Vineyard
1401 Caywood Road, Lodi; (607) 582-6116;
www.silverthreadwine.com

41. Standing Stone Vineyards
9934 Route 414, Hector; (800) 803-7135;
www.standingstonewines.com

42. Swedish Hill Vineyard 4565 Route 414,
Romulus; (888) 549-WINE;
www.swedishhill.com

43. Tickle Hill Winery
3839 Ball Diamond Road, Hector;
(607) 546-7740; www.ticklehillwinery.com

44. Ventosa Vineyards 3440 Route 96A,
Geneva; (315) 719-0000;
www.ventosavineyards.com

45. Wagner Vineyards 9322 Route 414, Lodi;
(866) 924-6378; www.wagnervineyards.com

Cayuga Lake Wine Trail

P.O. Box 123, Fayette; (800) 684-5217; www.cayugawinetrail.com

1. **Americana Vineyards Winery**
4367 E. Covert Road, Interlaken; (607) 387-6801;
www.americanavineyards.com

2. **Bellwether Hard Cider** 9070 Route 89, Trumansburg;
(888) 862-4337; www.cidery.com

3. **Buttonwood Grove Winery** 5986 Route 89, Romulus;
(607) 869-9760; www.buttonwoodgrove.com

4. **Cayuga Ridge Estate Winery** 6800 Route 89, Ovid;
(607) 869-5158; www.cayugaridgewinery.com

5. **CJS Vineyards** 6900 Fosterville Road, Auburn; (315) 730-4619;
www.cjsvineyards.com

6. **Cobblestone Farm Winery** 5102 State Route 89, Romulus;
(315) 549-8797; www.cobblestonefarmwinery.com

7. **Frontenac Point Vineyard** 9501 Route 89, Trumansburg;
(607) 387-9619; www.frontenacpoint.com

8. **Glenhaven Farm Winery** 6121 Sirrine Road, Trumansburg;
(607) 387-9031; www.glenhavenfarm.com

9. **Goose Watch Winery** 5480 Route 89, Romulus; (315) 549-2599;
www.goosewatch.com

10. **Hosmer Winery** 6999 Route 89, Ovid; (888) 467-9463;
www.hosmerwinery.com

11. **King Ferry Winery Inc. (Treleaven)** 658 Lake Road,
King Ferry; (800) 439-5271; www.treleavenwines.com

12. **Knapp Winery & Restaurant** 2770 County Road 128 (Ernsberger Road), Romulus;
(800) 869-9271; www.knappwine.com

13. **Lakeshore Winery** 5132 Route 89, Romulus; (315) 549-7075; www.lakeshorewinery.com

14. **Long Point Winery** 1485 Lake Road, Aurora; (315) 364-6990; www.longpointwinery.com

15. **Lucas Vineyards** 3862 County Road 150, Interlaken; (800) 682-9463;
www.lucasvineyards.com

16. **Montezuma Winery** 2981 Auburn Road,
Seneca Falls; (315) 568-8190;
www.montezumawinery.com

17. **Sheldrake Point Vineyard & Cafe**
7448 County Road 153, Ovid; (866) 743-5372;
www.sheldrakepoint.com

18. **Six Mile Creek Vineyard** 1551 Slaterville Road,
Ithaca; (800) 260-0612; www.sixmilecreek.com

19. **Swedish Hill Vineyard** 4565 Route 414,
Romulus; (888) 549-9463; www.swedishhill.com

20. **Thirsty Owl Wine Co.** 6799 Elm Beach Road,
Ovid; (866) 869-5805; www.thirstyowl.com

Chateau Dusseau 5292 Erron Hill Road, Locke;
(607) 351-3818; *(not mapped)*

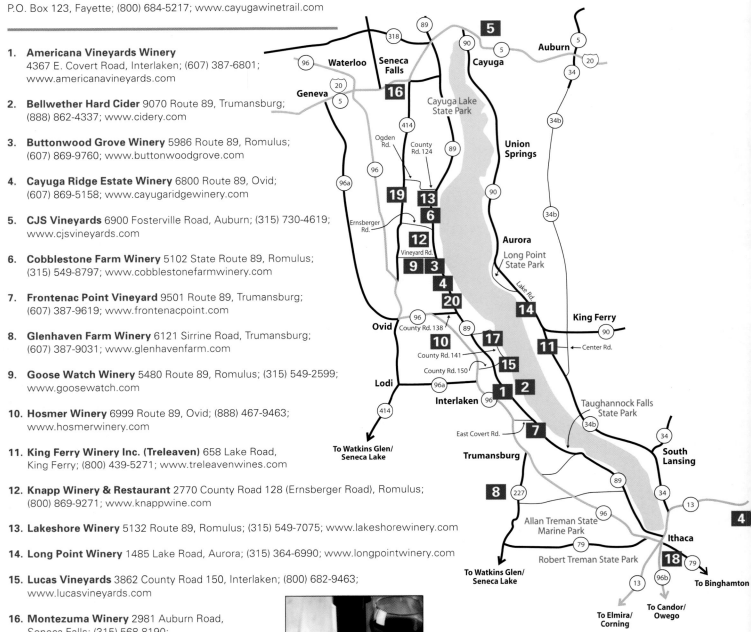

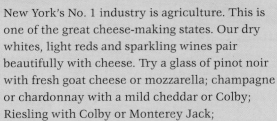

A loaf of bread, a bottle of wine and thou

New York's No. 1 industry is agriculture. This is one of the great cheese-making states. Our dry whites, light reds and sparkling wines pair beautifully with cheese. Try a glass of pinot noir with fresh goat cheese or mozzarella; champagne or chardonnay with a mild cheddar or Colby; Riesling with Colby or Monterey Jack; gewurztraminer with Swiss. Add locally grown pears, apples or grapes and a loaf of homemade bread and you have a true New York experience. Says wine expert Dan Berger: "You don't have to have the gourmet food experience of your life as long as you have a good bottle of wine and a good cheese."

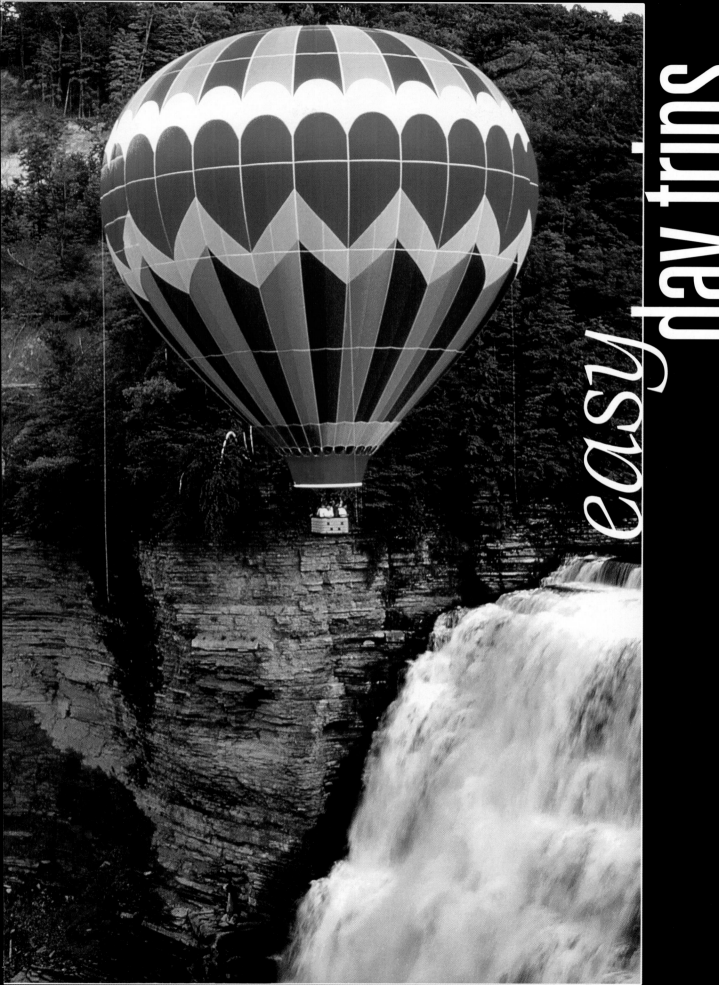

easy day trips

Easy Day Trips

Championship Division I basketball and Frank Lloyd Wright architecture are a short drive away when you're visiting Rochester. Our region is home to the picturesque Finger Lakes, some 80 wineries and communities along the Genesee River, Lake Ontario and the "Best 100 Miles" of the world-famous Erie Canal. Here is where two hours or less will take you:

The Abbey of the Genesee   B20
www.geneseeabbey.org
Rochesterians seeking a meditative place to reflect and regroup have found a destination in the Abbey of the Genesee. It is located in Piffard, a small town south of Geneseo in Livingston County. Visitors can join the community's Trappist monks for liturgical prayer in the Abbey Church or take a more solitary path. Stay for a day or a week; individual and group retreats are available. Be of a quiet mind; long periods of serious silence await. The grounds and wooded areas are perfect for walks and contemplation. The brothers have made delicious Monks' Bread in their bakery (not open for tours) since 1951. They also bake date-and-nut loaves, brownies and fruitcakes. All are available for sale at the abbey and at stores in Rochester. Buy some goodies fresh from the oven before you leave.

Buffalo   A17, 18; B17, 18
www.buffalocvb.org/home.html
Fans of chicken wings and sports have always found a home in Buffalo, but there's much more to love about this city. The region boasts historic architecture, renowned art museums and one of the great wonders of the world, Niagara Falls. Buildings designed by Frank Lloyd Wright, Louis Sullivan and H.H. Richardson are set amid an elaborate parks system created by landscape architect Frederick Law Olmsted. There are numerous galleries and other attractions, including the Albright-Knox Art Gallery, known for its significant collection of 20th-century paintings and sculpture. Niagara Falls is the nation's oldest state park and a sight to behold in any season.

Chautauqua Institution   B18
www.ciweb.org
Chautauqua is a historic educational center on the shores of Chautauqua Lake in

The steep, jagged formations at Chimney Bluffs State Park—geologists say they are chopped-off drumlins—lie only an hour's drive east of Rochester along the shore of Lake Ontario. The undeveloped park is a great place for a hike.

southwestern New York. Thousands visit every year for intellectual and spiritual growth and renewal. Founded in 1874 by an Ohio businessman and a Methodist minister, Chautauqua has a rich history of encouraging the open discussion of politics, religion, literature and science. The arts are alive here too, in the form of a symphony orchestra, ballet, conservatory theater and opera company. Come here during the nine-week summer season to study or to take in a performance in the amphitheater. Or just stroll around the peaceful, 750-acre campus; its Victorian buildings, along with charming old rooming houses and inns, comprise a national historic district.

Chimney Bluffs   A22
Some 45 miles east of Rochester, along the shores of Lake Ontario, you'll find Chimney Bluffs, an undeveloped state park. Geologists say the steep bluffs, towering over the lake's edge, are chopped-off

Thousands of people visit the Chautauqua Institution annually during its nine-week summer season.

Corning   *D22*

www.corningny.com

Home of the international company that shares its name, the city of Corning draws visitors from all over the world to Corning Museum of Glass. You'll see live glass-blowing demonstrations, exhibitions of art glass and other attractions that delve into the science, history and art of glass. The Rockwell Museum of Western Art explores American Western and Native American art in a mix of traditional and contemporary exhibits. Take a leisurely drive to antique shops and wineries, or visit three nearby aviation museums. (British Airways calls Route 54A one of the top 15 scenic drives in the world.) Stretch your legs on a walking

drumlins. They look like waves of chocolate icing whipped up to a point. Relentless Great Lakes winds chisel away at the rocks, but they are highly resistant to erosion, accounting for their vertical shapes. This is a great place to see Rochester's seafaring side. Take Route 104 east to Lake Bluff Road north, which turns into Garner Road. Pass the state park entrance and continue to East Bay Road, turning north. You can park in a lot by the road.

Cooperstown

www.cooperstownchamber.org

Cooperstown is best known, of course, for the National Baseball Hall of Fame & Museum. That is reason enough to visit. But it has many more things to see and do, from opera to microbreweries. The Farmers' Museum is a hands-on history museum devoted to agriculture and rural life. Glimmerglass Opera, performing during the summer, collaborates with the New York City Opera. The area's natural beauty draws hikers and campers. The town itself, with well-kept Victorian homes and tidy shops, sits on the shores of Otsego Lake; James Fenimore Cooper waxed eloquent about the lake's "glimmerglass" quality in "Leather-stocking Tales."

Cooperstown boasts attractions like the Farmers' Museum and Glimmerglass Opera. But the biggest draw is the National Baseball Hall of Fame & Museum. Doubleday Field is home to the Hall of Fame game every summer.

You can bet on it

Got the urge to try Lady Luck? Three casinos lie within a two-hour drive of Rochester.

Turning Stone Casino Resort in Central New York is run by the Oneida Indian Nation. You'll find what seems like acres of table games plus keno, bingo and the Oneida Nation's patented Instant Multi-Game machines. In the tradition of card clubs, the poker room features four different poker games. (If you need to brush up on your game, free lessons are given daily.)

Two other casinos are a convenient stop if you plan to visit Niagara Falls while you're here. Seneca Niagara Casino opened New Year's Eve 2002 in the previous home of the Niagara Falls Convention Center on the American side of the falls. In addition to gambling, the casino offers a free membership, live shows in Bear's Den Theater, restaurants and bars. The Seneca Nation of Indians runs the complex. Niagara Fallsview Casino Resort is the largest provincial investment ever made in the Niagara region. It went up in 2004. Overlooking Horseshoe Falls, the 2.5 million-square-foot complex holds 3,000 slot machines, 150 table games, a five-star hotel, restaurants, health spa, meeting rooms and a 1,500-seat theater.

Turning Stone Casino Resort, www.turning-stone.com

Seneca Niagara Casino, www.snfgc.com *A17*

Niagara Fallsview Casino Resort, www.fallsviewcasinoresort.com *A17*

Skaneateles is a charming place to visit any time of year, but especially in August when it hosts a month-long chamber music festival featuring top-flight musicians such as violinist Hilary Hahn.

tour of town, and then stop for a bite to eat on historic Market Street.

East Aurora   B18

www.eanycc.com/visit.asp

It was here that Elbert Hubbard fashioned an American version of William Morris' English crafts complex. The Roycrofters—artisans who worked on leather crafts, furniture, copperware and fine books in the Roycroft community here—made a significant mark on the arts and crafts movement in this country. The stock market crash of 1929 and the Depression closed the campus before renewed interest in the Roycrofters brought it back to life. You can visit the restored 14-building campus, now a national historic landmark, and dine or stay overnight at the Roycroft Inn across the street. Millard Fillmore House, built by the 13th president, and the Roycroft Museum, in a Craftsman bungalow, are open for tours.

Finger Lakes   B21 – C23

www.fingerlakes.org

This hilly lake region of Central New York is a popular weekend getaway destination. If you like to shop for antiques and crafts, sample world-class wines, or just get outdoors, spend a day or two in the Finger Lakes. Best known for its 60 wineries, the area also has a growing number of restaurants and inns. At the southern end of Cayuga Lake, visit the campuses of Ithaca College and Cornell University in Ithaca. Watch a NASCAR race at Watkins Glen International. Stop at the birthplace of women's rights in Seneca Falls; a national park marks the spot. If you love the outdoors, state parks dot the region, with plenty of places to fish, ski, hike, bike, row and camp. On Keuka Lake, the village of Hammondsport offers restaurants and antique and crafts shops. See the Wineries section for more details.

Ithaca   C23

www.visitithaca.com

What can you expect from a city that has its own currency? Ithaca is unique. Home of Cornell University and Ithaca College, Ithaca is known for its deep gorges, waterfalls, culture and activist zeal. You'll find organic, healthy restaurants (including the famed Moosewood), shops that sell artwork and crafts, and numerous bed-and-breakfasts. Wineries of the Finger Lakes are a scenic drive up Cayuga Lake. Great places for hiking include Cornell Plantations, an arboretum and botanical garden; Buttermilk Falls State Park; and Taughannock Falls State Park. Pick up fresh fruit and vegetables at Ithaca Farmers Market and Cornell Orchards, a research and teaching orchard and sales room.

A trip through time

The Seaway Trail, which hugs the shorelines of two lakes—Erie and Ontario—and the St. Lawrence and Niagara rivers, has been called the Great American road trip. The entire route stretches some 500 miles.

Experience the nation's northern coast with a scenic drive along local roads.

The Seaway Trail winds along this coast from northwestern Pennsylvania to east of Massena in St. Lawrence County. It hugs the shorelines of lakes Erie and Ontario and the St. Lawrence and Niagara rivers.

It's been called a Great American road trip. And for good reason: It passes through small towns and big cities, past lake vistas, farmland and rolling vineyards. Along the way are reminders of the battles fought for control of North America and, ultimately, for U.S. independence.

The Seaway Trail follows the local roads closest to shore, from Route 5 in Chautauqua and Erie counties to Routes 12 and 37 in the North Country. At roughly the midway point of the 500-mile route, Rochester is a great starting point for a weekend—or longer—jaunt.

Battles

The Seaway Trail is a designated National Scenic Byway for, among other things, its historic role in the emergence of the United States as a nation.

Sites on the route mark the 250th anniversary of the French and Indian War, fought from 1754 to 1763. France had a major presence in this area at that time, an influence that remains—particularly in French-speaking Quebec and Montreal, its largest city and last stronghold before surrender to the British.

The Great Lakes-Seaway Trail region was a vital transportation and communication link between France and her colonies in North America. Key battles were fought at Fort Niagara, Oswego and Lake George. Soldiers camped at Seaway Trail stopovers—Sodus, Irondequoit and Braddock bays, for example—on their way to Niagara.

Fort Niagara, the first fort built by the French, was later used during the Civil War. It is a historic site today. Its original 18th-century buildings remain, and interpreters in period costume bring the fort events to life, sometimes in re-enactments.

Oswego had three forts: Oswego, Ontario and George. Fort Ontario State Historic Site traces the fort's history from the French and Indian War to World War II.

Events to note the French and Indian War anniversary are under way along the Seaway Trail.

Islands in the sun

The Thousand Islands in the St. Lawrence River are a fascinating collection of 1,864 islands, to be exact. Wealthy industrialists began building summer homes here in the 1870s, and large hotels soon went up to accommodate less affluent tourists.

Vacationers still flock to the region. Boat tours are launched out of Alexandria Bay, a hot spot with families and anglers. (It's been called one of the top 10 places to fish in the country.) Among the homes of the wealthy are two castles open to visitors.

Singer Castle, on Dark Island in Chippewa Bay, was built in 1905. Frederick G. Bourne, president of Singer Sewing Machine Co., owned the five-story granite castle with Spanish red tile roofs. Guided tours are held all summer through October.

Perhaps most intriguing is that visitors

can actually stay overnight here. A luxury suite in the castle is available for rent. Accommodations include a candlelight dinner and a private tour of the castle.

Boldt Castle on Heart Island near Alexandria Bay is a favorite stop on the islands tour. It was owned by George Boldt, proprietor of the Waldorf Astoria Hotel in New York City. The 120-room Rhineland castle was four years into construction when Boldt's wife died. He halted construction, never to return to the island, and Boldt Castle was never completed.

The island is open for exploration from May to October.

The Seaway Trail's Discovery Center in the quaint village of Sackets Harbor, less than three hours from Rochester, is a central place to learn about sites to see along the route. Visitors also can take in exhibits on lighthouses and the War of 1812 or browse the gift shop. ***Seaway Trail Discovery Center, Ray and West Main streets, Sackets Harbor, (800) SEAWAY-T, www.seawaytrail.com***

Boldt Castle on Heart Island near Alexandria Bay is a favorite destination of visitors touring the Thousand Islands (right). Re-enactments are popular attractions at historic forts along the trail.

Letchworth State Park   *C19, C20*
http://nysparks.state.ny.us/parks
Entrances in Perry, Castile,
Portageville and Mount Morris
493-3600
Before the north-flowing Genesee River reaches Rochester, it cuts a 17-mile swath through Letchworth, nicknamed the Grand Canyon of the East. Sixty-six miles of trails, both paved and natural, wind along the scenic gorge and take hikers near three major waterfalls. Be sure to visit the overlook for the Mount Morris Dam; since 1952, this major structure has prevented flood disasters that once plagued the Rochester area. The park offers winter and summer recreation opportunities, such as ice skating, whitewater rafting, snowmobiling, cross-country skiing, biking, kayaking and hot-air ballooning. The 90-year-old museum displays Native American artifacts and tells the story of the park's creation. Glen Iris Inn offers dining and overnight accommodations. Cabins, camp sites and a lodge also are available.

Niagara Region   *A17, 18*
www.niagara-lewiston.org
There's more to Niagara Falls than millions of gallons of water (and the occasional daredevil) spilling over a precipice. While you're here, take a side trip to Old Fort Niagara. France and Britain controlled Niagara 300 years ago from this imposing structure on the shore of Lake Ontario. The site of historic battles and trade is open year-round. You'll see musket demonstrations and living-history programs during the summer. The Castellani Art Museum at Niagara University holds nearly 4,000 works of art. Some of the artists may surprise you: Picasso, Roualt, Modigliani, Motherwell and DeKooning are represented. Check out the 100 American Craftsmen Festival June 2-4 at the Kenan Center in Lockport. Artists from across North America display and sell their creations. ArtPark in Lewiston is an indoor/outdoor venue offering theater and musical performances, festivals, hiking trails, fishing docks and picnic areas. And don't miss the Niagara Power Project

By day or after dark, few sights are as dramatic as Niagara Falls. For a close-up view, take a boat ride to the base of the falls.

Visitors Center, known as Power Vista. It is 4 miles downstream from the falls in the Niagara River Gorge. State-of-the-art interactive exhibits teach about hydroelectricity and its role in the area's history.

**Niagara-on-the-Lake,
Ontario, Canada**   *A17*
www.niagaraonthelake.com
This picturesque Canadian town is best known as the site of the Shaw Festival, one of the largest repertory theaters in North America. The festival stages the plays of George Bernard Shaw and his contemporaries in three theaters from April to November. Proud old homes and tree-lined streets attest to the town's history as a prosperous shipbuilding center. Nineteenth-

Lake Ontario lighthouses

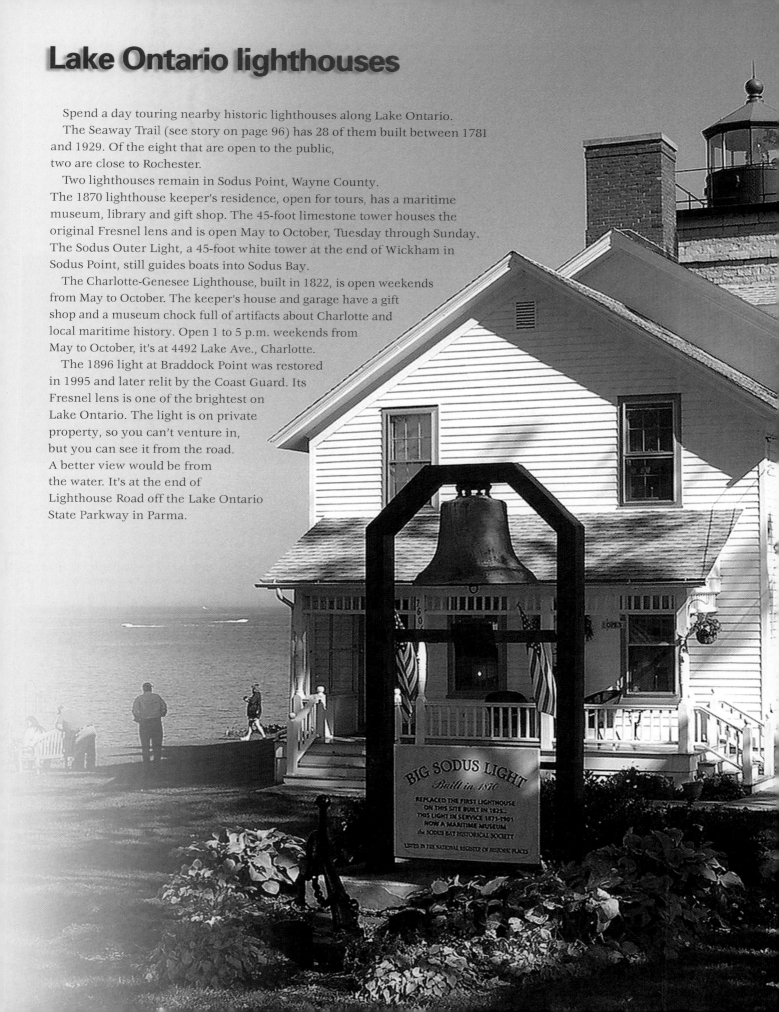

Spend a day touring nearby historic lighthouses along Lake Ontario.

The Seaway Trail (see story on page 96) has 28 of them built between 1781 and 1929. Of the eight that are open to the public, two are close to Rochester.

Two lighthouses remain in Sodus Point, Wayne County. The 1870 lighthouse keeper's residence, open for tours, has a maritime museum, library and gift shop. The 45-foot limestone tower houses the original Fresnel lens and is open May to October, Tuesday through Sunday. The Sodus Outer Light, a 45-foot white tower at the end of Wickham in Sodus Point, still guides boats into Sodus Bay.

The Charlotte-Genesee Lighthouse, built in 1822, is open weekends from May to October. The keeper's house and garage have a gift shop and a museum chock full of artifacts about Charlotte and local maritime history. Open 1 to 5 p.m. weekends from May to October, it's at 4492 Lake Ave., Charlotte.

The 1896 light at Braddock Point was restored in 1995 and later relit by the Coast Guard. Its Fresnel lens is one of the brightest on Lake Ontario. The light is on private property, so you can't venture in, but you can see it from the road. A better view would be from the water. It's at the end of Lighthouse Road off the Lake Ontario State Parkway in Parma.

century commercial buildings and converted residences house busy shops and restaurants. In addition to watching live theater, visitors can tour Niagara-region wineries and historic sites, such as Fort George. The area has plenty of shopping and golf courses, and Niagara Falls is 20 minutes away by car.

Seneca Falls   B22
www.nps.gov/wori
The women's rights movement began in 1848 in this central New York village. Today, the Women's Rights National Historical Park commemorates it. Four historical properties and a visitor center tell the story of how everyday people forged the battle for equal rights for women, including the right to vote. Though not involved at the outset, Rochester's Susan B. Anthony became the movement's leading voice for reform. The National Women's Hall of Fame honors outstanding leaders, including Madeleine Albright, Rosa Parks, Maya Angelou, Lucille Ball, Rosalynn Carter and many others.

Skaneateles   B23
www.skaneateles.com
This cozy village lies on the shores of a lake with the same Iroquois name (pronounced "skan-ee-ATlas"). Some 65 miles from Rochester, it's a charming place to visit any time of year. Enjoy the Skaneateles Antique and Classic Boat Show in late July. Dickens' Christmas, on four weekends after Thanksgiving, brings out carolers, sleigh rides and roasted chestnuts. Skaneateles also is the northeastern gateway to the Finger Lakes wine region, and it sits along Route 20, one of the best antiquing routes around. But if you find yourself rolling through in August, take advantage of the chamber music festival. Since 1980, world-renowned classical musicians have taken the

stage at this month-long event. Among the stars: violin prodigy and Grammy winner Hilary Hahn, Met soprano Korliss Uecker, pianist Diane Walsh and baritone Sanford Sylvan. Bring a picnic and a blanket for outdoor concerts at Brook Farm on Saturday nights. Enjoy weeknight shows at the First Presbyterian Church, tucked into the center of town across from the lake.

Sodus Point   A22
www.greatsodusbay.org
Catch a Great Lakes breeze in Sodus Point, Wayne County. Boaters love this hopping port on the southern shore of Lake Ontario. Settled in 1794, Sodus Bay was once a major Great Lakes shipping port. Today it's a popular gathering spot for boating enthusiasts. History buffs will find unique cobblestone homes, War of 1812 and Shaker community sites, and a lighthouse museum. (See the Seaway Trail feature on page 96.) Nearby Chimney Bluffs State Park draws visitors by foot and water. Besides boating, year-round outdoor sports include cross-country skiing, ice skating, freshwater fishing, biking, golfing and snowmobiling.

Syracuse   A24
www.syracuse.ny.us
If your passions run toward Division I basketball, Arts & Crafts design or the Erie Canal, spend the day in New York's central city. Syracuse played a leading role in the arts and crafts movement in the early 20th century; the Stickley brothers made their famous oak furniture here, and modern-day craftsmen carry on the spirit of the movement through a variety of media. (The company still operates a factory in Manlius.) With more than

30,000 screaming fans clad in orange, see the 2003 Division I national basketball champions, the Syracuse Orangemen, play in the Carrier Dome on campus. The Erie Canal Museum, housed in the canal's only remaining weighlock building, has hands-on exhibits and collections related to the famous waterway. The attached Syracuse Heritage Area Visitor Center provides lots of leads for further exploration. If you are in town Aug. 24 to Sept. 4, go to the 160th annual run of the New York State Fair. Last year, nearly 1 million people took in the show.

Toronto, Ontario, Canada
www.toronto.com
A trip to Toronto will take you longer than two hours—it's more like three—but it's worth every minute. Art, history and science museums, as well as major-league sports, abound in Canada's largest city. Its respected 710-acre zoo is home to more than 5,000 animals and is open all year. You'll find the Hockey Hall of Fame and the CN Tower, the world's tallest free-standing structure. Known for a diversity of ethnic restaurants, Toronto hosts the Gourmet Food and Wine Expo, Canada's biggest consumer food and wine show, in late November. Catch a Broadway show or a local play in the theater district; hotel/show packages are plentiful. Be sure to venture out into city neighborhoods, where cozy restaurants, bars and shops beckon. You might find a bed-and-breakfast on a brick-paved side street that's just right.

entertainment & *the arts*

Entertainment Districts

From East Avenue to the historic High Falls district, Rochester offers an almost dizzying array of nightlife options. Traditional bars and taverns, live music and theater, cafes and dance clubs—you'll find it all in the city after dark. Great food abounds, too.

For locations, match the map coordinates with the maps in front of the book. For addresses and phone numbers of restaurants, see the Dining Index on page 130. For additional live music venues, see "Places to Hear Live Music" on page 110.

Browns Race and High Falls BB2

Rochester once was known as the Flour City for all the wheat grinding it did in mills along the river. Today, Browns Race, a national register historic district, marks the spot. The area sits above the Genesee River gorge right next to the thundering High Falls. Visitors can view the falls day or night from the Pont de Rennes bridge, a pedestrian walkway named after Rochester's sister city in France. Other worthy stops: Center at High Falls Gallery and High Falls Museum, 60 Browns Race.

During the day, ad agencies, tech companies and engineering firms fill the former industrial buildings. At night, brick-paved streets make it a favorite location for outdoor concerts and festivals. Area bars and restaurants cater to soccer and baseball fans who come to High Falls before or after games at nearby Frontier Field. (The stadium sits in the shadow of Eastman Kodak Co.'s headquarters on State Street.) Later on, club hoppers come in search of the area's dance clubs.

RESTAURANTS
(For details, see the Dining Index on page 130.)

From an upscale dinner to a muffin and coffee, High Falls offers a variety of dining options. All are housed in repurposed factory buildings—with all the brick, wood and natural light you'd expect. **Jimmy Mac's Bar & Grill** is a neighborhood bar; you can dine on the patio overlooking the river gorge. **Triphammer Grill** serves eclectic cuisine in a cozy, upscale atmosphere—with seating indoors and outside overlooking the falls. **McFadden's Restaurant and Saloon** is an Irish pub serving soups, salads, sandwiches and wraps. Well-known dueling pianists perform at **Keys Martini & Piano Bar**, which serves everything from chicken wings to lobster tails. **Rubino's Italian Submarines** is open for lunch and early dinner. **Spin Caffe** serves coffee (roasted on-site) and light fare—with wireless Internet access. **High Falls Deli and Café** and **Hip Cup Coffee** are recent additions to the neighborhood.

Main thoroughfares: *State, Commercial and Platt streets*
Parking: *Meters on State Street (free after 5), High Falls Garage*

Among the nightlife options in Browns Race/High Falls is Keys Martini & Piano Bar on Mill Street.

BARS

Jimmy Mac's Bar & Grill: Casual bar. 104 Platt St.; 232-5230
Keys Martini & Piano Bar: Dueling pianos. 233 Mill St.; 232-KEYS
McFadden's Restaurant and Saloon: Irish pub. 60 Browns Race; 325-1250
Saddle Ridge Entertainment Resort: Country music, line dancing. 61 Commercial St.
Tiki Bob's Cantina: Nightclub, DJ music. 60 Browns Race; 325-2430
Triphammer Grill: Upscale eatery with bar area. 60 Brown's Race; 262-2700

Live music: Keys Martini & Piano Bar; McFadden's

Charlotte C12

Sandwiched between the suburbs of Greece and Irondequoit, Charlotte lies along Lake Ontario and the Genesee River. It is the northern tip of the city of Rochester. Being so far from the city proper, it feels more like a seaside village than a city neighborhood. This is truer now more than ever, with recent improvements in lighting, landscaping and walkways throughout the business district.

The focal point of Charlotte is Ontario Beach Park, which lies at the end of Lake Avenue. It has a sandy beach with lifeguards on duty, a boardwalk and a fishing pier. Children love the historic carousel. The park's shady lawn area is popular for grilling and picnicking; tables and shelters are available. Touring the Charlotte-Genesee Lighthouse and museum is a fun way to learn about Rochester's nautical past. Take a drive along Beach Avenue to see some of Rochester's

Charlotte (pronounced "shar-lot") is a city neighborhood on Lake Ontario. Its bars and restaurants bring people out long after the beach crowd has gone home.

nicest waterfront homes.

Nothing beats the beach on a warm summer night. Bring a blanket or lawn chair for free weekly concerts at the Performance Pavilion. Walk out on the fishing pier for an incredible sunset view, watch the boats return for the night—and top it all off with a custard treat.

RESTAURANTS
(For details, see the Dining Index on page 130.)

Bars and restaurants in Charlotte draw the boat crowd for lunch, dinner and lively happy hours on outdoor decks. For steaks and seafood, try **Gordon's Steak and Crab House** and **Schooner's Riverside Pub**. You can find lighter fare at **Leadbelly Landing**, **Scuttlebutt's**, **Windjammers** and **Bellanca's Portside Restaurant**. **Nola's Waterfront Barbeque** is a Cajun and barbecue establishment that brings in national musical acts. **Pelican's Nest Restaurant** serves a wide range of American cuisine. Some restaurants in Charlotte have been in business for decades: **Abbott's Frozen Custard** has scooped creamy cones in Charlotte since the 1920s. **LDR Char Pit** has served burgers and fries for nearly 60 years. And **Mr.**

Dominic's, an Italian restaurant, has earned destination status in its nearly 30-year run.

Main thoroughfare: Lake Avenue where it ends at the lake
Parking: Meters on Lake Avenue (free after 5) and free area lots

BARS

Leadbelly Landing: Decks, daily fish fry. 4776 Lake Ave.; 663-3210
Pelican's Nest Restaurant: Hopping night scene; seasonal. 566 River St.; 663-5910
Penny Arcade: Live rock. 4785 Lake Ave.; 621-7625
Schooner's Riverside Pub: Live music on the waterfront. 70 Pattonwood Drive; 342-8363
Windjammers: Beer and pub fare. 4695 Lake Ave.; 663-9691

Live music: Nola's Waterfront Barbeque; Penny Arcade; Schooner's Riverside Pub

East End CC6

The East End is driving a renaissance in 24/7 city living with its own stamp of jazzy/bluesy sophistication. The cultural heart of Rochester, it is centered on East Avenue and stretches through side streets north to Main Street. New condos, townhouses and restaurants, some carved out of car dealerships that once filled the area, have brought renewed energy to this downtown neighborhood. Anchoring the East End is the Eastman School of Music on Gibbs Street, whose students and faculty perform at Eastman Theatre, Kilbourn Hall and area cafes such as Java's and Spot Coffee. The Rochester Philharmonic Orchestra plays in Eastman Theatre, which has just completed a dramatic renovation. Blackfriars Theatre, the Little Theatre and Rochester Contemporary lend additional flavors of visual and theatrical art.

Standout local musicians and touring marquee acts headline local clubs, including Milestones Restaurant & Music Room. The bar scene ranges from the upscale lounge at Max of Eastman Place to casual watering holes such as Richmond's and Salinger's. The East End is just a short walk to East & Alexander, another hot night spot.

RESTAURANTS
(For details, see the Dining Index on page 130.)

Restaurants in the East End rank among favorites for cuisine that is out of the ordinary. **Max of Eastman Place** is known for seasonal dishes that spotlight locally produced foods. Cozy **Restaurant 2 Vine**, with its open kitchen and sprawling bar, draws big crowds every weekend. **Tournedo's Restaurant** is a steakhouse in the Inn on Broadway. **Alexandria**, serving Greek cuisine, is a favorite

stop for theater- and concert-goers. **Golden Port Dim Sum**, **House of Sushi** and **Lin's Garden Chinese Restaurant** offer affordable Asian cuisine. Office workers pile into **Rosey's Italian Café** for lunch during the week. For a diner-style breakfast or lunch, go to **Mitch's Restaurant**, **Flour City Diner** or **Center Stage Café**. You'll find pub food at **Richmond's** and **Matthew's East End Grill**. For lighter fare, try **Orange Glory Café**, **Little Theatre Cafe** (with live jazz on weekends), **Stromboli Express**, **Java's** and **Little Bakery**. **Java's**, **Spot Coffee** and **Backstage Coffee House** (located inside the Eastman School) are popular with students and professionals.

Main thoroughfares: East, Main, Gibbs and Chestnut streets
Parking: MetroCenter Garage (enter at Swan, Scio and Main), East (free after 5) and side streets

BARS

Alexandria: Full bar in a Greek restaurant. 120 East Ave.; 232-6180
Eastman Lounge: Casual bar, salsa lessons. 109 East Ave.; 232-6000
Havana Moe's Beer & Wine Lounge: Casual bar, cigar lounge. 125 East Ave.; 325-1030
Joey's: Neighborhood tavern. 561 E. Main St.; 325-9223
Little Theatre Café: Café serving wine and

More than 15 bars, including Soho East (left), are within easy walking distance of one another in the East & Alexander entertainment district.

beer. 240 East Ave.; 258-0413
Matthew's East End Grill: Casual, outdoor seating. 200 East Ave.; 454-4280
Max of Eastman Place: Upscale bar, live music. 387 E. Main St.; 697-0491
Milestones Restaurant and Music Room: Live entertainment, casual bar. 170 East Ave.; 325-6490
Restaurant 2 Vine: French bistro and bar; 24 Winthrop St.; 454-6020
Richmond's: Bar, live music, late-night menu. 21 Richmond St.; 454-4612
Salinger's Bar: Bar, pool table, darts. 107 East Ave.; 546-6880
Tara Lounge: Casual, piano and gay bar. 153 Liberty Pole Way; 232-4719

Live music: Java's; Little Theatre Café; Max of Eastman Place; Milestones; Montage Grille and Music; Richmond's; Spot Coffee

East & Alexander DD7

Alexander Street is one of the city's longest-running nightspots. In the past couple of years, its energy has spread around the corner to East Avenue, making East & Alexander a prime destination for partygoers. A relatively sedate business district by day, the area comes alive at night, drawing professionals from across the age spectrum. Slow-moving cars are as likely to be Volvo station wagons as chickmobiles. Live and DJ music resonates from practically every restaurant and watering hole, and all the clubs are within easy walking distance of one another.

RESTAURANTS
(For details, see the Dining Index on page 130.)

Some of the city's trendiest and most attractive restaurants are right here at East & Alexander. They serve Mexican, continental and fusion cuisine in beautifully restored and renovated spaces. **Mex** has converted a 19th century house into a colorful Latin American bistro. The **Bamba Bistro** is enjoying renewed vitality. With new owners, Rochester's grandame has a new name, a revitalized menu and an interior makeover. Situated in a factory loft, **Soho East** draws well-dressed crowds for drinks and late-night dancing. **Cosmo 344** is a new restaurant in the same building. Downstairs at **Daisy Duke**, country fans ride the mechanical bull. **Veneto Wood Fired Pizza and Pasta** is in demand for its homey Italian dishes. The wait staff at the **Old Toad** sport real British accents and the menu to match. **Rubino's**, a citywide favorite for imported Italian foods, prepares sandwiches and soups during the day. For late-night hots and hamburgers, there's **Roc City Hots**.

Main thoroughfares: East and Alexander streets
Parking: Free on Alexander, East (after 5) and side streets. Pay lot behind Old Toad on Alexander links to East and Union.

BARS

Alexander Street Pub: Bar, grill and dance club. 291 Alexander St.; 262-3820
The Bamba Bistro: Upscale lounge and patio. 282 Alexander St.; 244-8680
Bar Fly: Bar connected to Karma 355. 359 East Ave.; 232-5630
Blue Room: Martinis, casual, outdoor deck. 293 Alexander St.; 232-2230
Five 50 Pub & Grill at Strathallan Hotel: 550 East Ave.; 461-5010
Coyote Joe's: East Avenue and Alexander

Street; 232-7170
Daisy Dukes: Country music, mechanical bull. 336 East Ave.; 325-4441
Karma 355: Contemporary bar, DJ. 355 East Ave.; 454-7010
Mex Restaurant, Bar & Patio: Full bar and restaurant with Mexican flair. 295 Alexander St.; 262-3060
Monty's Korner: Imported drafts and soccer on the telly. 355 East Ave.; 263-7650
Muther's: DJ dancing, drag shows. 40 S. Union St.; 325-6216
The Old Toad: Authentic British pub. 277 Alexander St.; 232-2626
Pig-N-Whistle: 7 Lawrence St. 546-6150
Riffs: Wine and piano bar. 330 East Ave.; 325-2010
Soho East: Light and airy modern bar, DJ. 336 East Ave.; 325-7720
Whiskey Bar & Lounge: DJ dancing, pool table. 315 Alexander St.; 232-7550

Live music: The Old Toad; Monty's Korner; Whiskey Bar & Lounge

Monroe Avenue in the city C4, D4

Stretching from the Inner Loop to Culver Road, Monroe Avenue has a funky, eclectic style with deep roots in hippie culture. The avenue serves as "Main Street" for the neighborhood. Urban energy is evident around the clock. Shops are open late on weekends, offering unusual clothing, shoes, poster art, jewelry, antiques and used books. College students frequent the area's sports bars and dance clubs—and then stop at its late-night eateries to refuel. Night spots along Monroe Avenue include Bug Jar, Monty's Krown, J.D. Oxford's, Jeremiah's Tavern and Woody's.

RESTAURANTS
(For details, see the Dining Index on page 130.)

Monroe Avenue is one of the single best locations in Rochester for sheer diversity of menu choices at reasonable prices. Among the cuisines: Indian (**India Cafe, Raj Mahal**), Mediterranean (**Olive Tree, Aladdin's Natural Eatery** and **Oasis Mediterranean Bistro**), Vietnamese (**Dac Hoa, Le Lemon Grass**), fusion (**Lola Bistro**), Chinese and Japanese (**Ming's II, Plum House Japanese Restaurant, Hunan Wok**) and vegetarian (**New Health Cafe**).

A number of Rochester establishments serve excellent martinis, including Tapas 177 Lounge, Martini Grille and Blue Room.

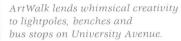

ArtWalk lends whimsical creativity to lightpoles, benches and bus stops on University Avenue.

Avenue mainstay **Jeremiah's Tavern**, which offers a full menu, is best known for its Buffalo wings and Friday-night fish fry. **Basta Pasta** serves up American Italian. **Mark's Hots** and **Gitsis Texas Hots** are great places for inexpensive diner food and fascinating people-watching, especially late at night. For pizza and subs, there's **Corky's Craving Parlor, Acme Bar & Pizza, Domino's, Gina's Sub Shop, Mark's Pizzeria, Pizza Hut** and **Sal's New York Pizzeria. Country Sweet** offers popular chicken and ribs. Bagels, doughnuts, sandwiches and soups are made fresh at **Bruegger's Bagel Bakery** and **Dunkin' Donuts**. For coffee and snacks, try **Starbucks**. If in the midst of all this home cooking you still want only fast food, Monroe Avenue has **Arby's** and **McDonald's**.

Main thoroughfare: Monroe Avenue
Parking: Free on Monroe and side streets. (Choose your spot carefully; tow trucks take their job seriously.)

BARS

Acme Bar & Pizza: Neighborhood bar serving pizza. 495 Monroe Ave.; 271-2263
The Avenue Pub: Gay bar. 522 Monroe Ave.; 244-4960
Bug Jar: Live alternative music and DJ. 219 Monroe Ave.; 454-2966
Damian's: Beer pong and drink specials. 81 Marshall St.; 232-1320
Enright's Thirst Parlor: Neighborhood tavern. 582 Monroe Ave.; 271-0170
J.J. Flynn's: Casual bar. 470 Monroe Ave.; 244-7077
J.D. Oxford's Pub: Darts, full bar. 636 Monroe Ave.; 256-0580
Jeremiah's Tavern: Casual dining, bar. 1104 Monroe Ave.; 461-1313
Monty's Krown: British pub, live music. 875 Monroe Ave.; 263-7650
O'Callaghan's: Contemporary Irish pub, deck. 470 Monroe Ave.; 271-7190
Spike's: Neighborhood bar. 655 Monroe Ave.; 242-4880
The Sports Page Restaurant and Bar: Sports bar and restaurant. 499 Monroe Ave.; 271-8460
Woody's: Sports bar. 236 Monroe Ave.; 546-6900

Live music: Bug Jar; Lola Bistro; Monty's Krown

Neighborhood of the Arts C5

In the Neighborhood of the Arts, converted factories house studios for dancers and visual artists. Post-war apartment buildings, multifamily Victorians and charming cottages line the area's many side streets. In the middle of it all is Memorial Art Gallery at 500 University Ave. Known for a comprehensive collection

spanning 50 centuries, the museum hosts traveling exhibitions and operates a popular gift shop and restaurant, plus the Clothesline Arts Festival in September. Next door, School of the Arts offers student and community performances in music and theater. (Actor Taye Diggs and musician Tweet are alumni.) Take a stroll down University and check out ArtWalk, Rochester's outdoor interactive art museum. The award-winning ArtWalk features sidewalk imprints, artistic benches, tiled light poles, sculptures and bus shelters from MAG to George Eastman House. Nearby are the Visual Studies Workshop, 31 Prince St., and Village Gate Square, 274 N. Goodman St., a converted factory housing public art along with shops and offices. Next door at Anderson Alley Artists, 250 N. Goodman St., some 40 artists share three floors in an old manufacturing building. Artists open their studios to the public from 1 to 4 p.m. the second Saturday of each month from October to June. They work on bookbinding, jewelry, mixed media, painting, ceramics and more. Writers & Books, the region's literary center at 740 University Ave., keeps a calendar jammed with readings and classes in—you guessed it—writing and literature.

RESTAURANTS
(For details, see the Dining Index on page 130.)

This neighborhood is known more for its artistic pursuits than dining choices. However, the few restaurants that call NOTA home are well-respected and popular. Options include **California Rollin'** (sushi), **Edibles Restaurant** (eclectic fine dining), **Feta Chinni** (Greek/Italian), **Cutler's Restaurant** (American), **Mamasan's** (Thai and Vietnamese), **Salena's** (Mexican) and **Starry Nites Café** (chef-prepared café fare).

Main thoroughfares: University Avenue and Goodman Street
Parking: In lots surrounding Village Gate Square, and on University, Goodman and side streets

BARS

Bachelor Forum: Motorcycle gay bar. 670 University Ave.; 271-6930
Edibles: Restaurant and small bar. 704 University Ave.; 271-4910
Feta chinni: Restaurant and bar. Village Gate Square, 274 N. Goodman St.; 254-3382
Salena's: Restaurant serves beer, tequila, margaritas, wine. Village Gate Square, 274 N. Goodman St.; 256-5980
California Rollin': Restaurant serving beer, wine and sake. Village Gate Square, 274 N. Goodman St.; 271-8990

Live music: Starry Nites Café

Park Avenue C4, 5

Between Culver Road and Alexander Street, Park Avenue is a tree-shaded, residential neighborhood. Restaurants, salons and shops are tucked among Victorian homes on the mile-long route.

Village Gate Square is a former factory converted to offices, restaurants and artists' studios in the Neighborhood of the Arts.

Bistros and cafes make up the majority of Park Avenue businesses; the biggest concentration is near Berkeley Street. Al fresco dining turns the sidewalks into patios during the summer. Besides restaurants, there are antique dealers and gift shops, plus convenience stores and a laundromat that serve the students and professionals who live in nearby apartments. A wine shop offers happy-hour tastings.

In this relaxed environment, you may forget you're inside city limits. Take a stroll down side streets and head north a block to see the mansions of East Avenue, one of the country's premier preservation districts. These were the grand homes of the leaders who shaped Rochester.

RESTAURANTS
(For details, see the Dining Index on page 130.)

Park Avenue is a wonderful place to work on your laptop in a cafe, or to meet a friend for coffee or dinner. The list of possibilities is long. For Italian, try **Bacco's Ristorante** for lunch or dinner; for pizza and takeout meals, try **Chester Cab Pizza**, **Cobbs Hill Pizza** and **Pontillo's Pizzeria**. **Café Cibon** and **Spin Caffe** serve light meals and desserts with coffee; **Cibon** has wine and beer too. **Montana Mills Bread Co./Java Joe's** and **Baker Street Bakery** are the street's bread purveyors. **Classy Cookie & Deli**, **Park and Oxford Cafe and Delicatessen**, and **Park Place Deli** prepare sandwiches and desserts. The American fare at **Jines** and

Charlie's Frog Pond is popular with the breakfast crowd. **Big Apple Café** and **First Taste Grill** offer fresh bistro fare. Find Asian cuisine at **Esan Thai Restaurant**, **K.C. Tea & Noodles**, **Kobay Japanese Restaurant**. **Hogan's Hideaway** is known for its soups, sandwiches, stir fry and beer. **La-Tea-Da** is a new lunch and tea room. If you crave a gyro, lentil soup or other Mediterranean dish, **Sinbad's** is the place. **Nathan's Old-Fashioned Soups** cooks up daily specials for takeout. And **Park Avenue Pub** has been a favorite destination for generations of Rochesterians in search of fine American food.

Main thoroughfare: Park Avenue
Parking: Free lot at Wilson Farms, free on-street on Park and alternating-sides parking on side streets

BARS

Café Cibon: Bistro fare, wine and martinis. 688 Park Ave.; 461-2960
Hogan's Hideaway: Casual dining, bar. 197 Park Ave.; 442-4293
Martini Grille: Dinner and martinis. 176 S. Goodman St.; 244-6526
Park Avenue Pub: Fine dining, full bar. 650 Park Ave.; 461-4140

*Tapas 177 Lounge in St. Paul Quarter
has Latin music, Salsa lessons and
a monthly wine tasting.*

Park Bench: Neighborhood bar and restaurant.
725 Park Ave.; 244-3267
Prepps: Casual bar. 729 Park Ave.; 271-7925

St. Paul Quarter *BB3*

On St. Paul and Water streets, between the
Inner Loop and Main, hulking brick factories once
housed Rochester's venerable clothing
companies and tool-and-die shops. This is where
the city became a manufacturing center of
national repute. A hundred years later, the St. Paul
Quarter was the first city neighborhood to convert
these factories into loft apartments, tech startups
and a growing number of bars and restaurants.

The early-evening crowd can find martinis
and dinner in the quarter's eclectic eateries. St.
Paul also is home to an impressive collection of
dance clubs like Liquid Nightclub, Club Klymax
and the Liquor Room, and Rochesterians come
here to let loose to salsa, techno or the live
offerings of touring bands. Tucked behind St.
Paul on a tiny side street not far from the river,
Water Street Music Hall brings rising stars and
established bands with a loyal following.

RESTAURANTS
(For details, see the Dining Index on page 130.)

Eateries in the St. Paul Quarter may not be
as plentiful as other neighborhoods, but what
they lack in numbers they make up for in
variety. **Sienna Contemporary Grill & Bar**

serves regional American cuisine in an upbeat,
contemporary setting. Eat at the bar or in the
downstairs dining room at **Tapas 177 Lounge**;
you'll find wild game and seafood on the menu.
Lively Caribbean flavors mark the lunches and
early dinners served at **L.J.'s II Jamaican
Cuisine**. **Pane Vino Ristorante** has moderately
priced Italian, an extensive wine list and a view
of the Genesee River. **Toasted Head Bar &
Grill** offers gourmet dinners and late-night
drinks. **Table Seven Bistro & Lounge** has
wood-fired pizza. Open for breakfast and lunch,
Lacagnina's Deli has hot and cold sandwiches
and a daily soup special.

*Main thoroughfares: St. Paul and Andrews
streets*
*Parking: Genesee Crossroads Garage (69
Andrews St.), meters on St. Paul and Andrews
(free after 5). Some surface lots, but check the
signs: Tow-away zones are strictly enforced.*

BARS

The Club at Water Street: Dancing, live
entertainment. 204 N. Water St.; 325-5600
Club Klymax: Live comedy, reggae, hip hop.
40 St. Paul St.; 232-8690
Liquid Nightclub: Dancing. 169 St. Paul St.;
325-5710
The Liquor Room: Late-night bar. 155 St. Paul
St.; 454-7750
Table Seven Bistro & Lounge: Bar and bistro.
187 St. Paul St.; 232-4305
Tapas 177 Lounge: Dancing and dining.
177 St. Paul St.; 262-2090
Toasted Head Bar & Grill: Casual bar.
187 St. Paul St.; 232-4305

Water Street Music Hall: National and regional
bands. 204 N. Water St.; 325-5600

Live music: The Club at Water Street; Club
Klymax; Tapas 177; Water Street Music Hall

South Wedge *D4*

The city's most ethnically diverse
neighborhood is home to some 60,000 people.
Just south of downtown on the east side of the
Genesee, the South Wedge is a great place to
see some of the oldest homes in the city, from
cottages to sprawling Victorians. Residents
range from old-timers who've lived here their
whole lives to college students and young
professionals who like the urban village
atmosphere. (Frederick Douglass owned two
homes in the area; 271 Hamilton St. still stands,
and a sign at Robinson Drive marks the general
locale of his South Avenue home.) South
Avenue runs through the heart of the Wedge.
The neighborhood is undergoing renewal, from
the tip of the Wedge at Mt. Hope and South all
the way down to the Ford Street Bridge. In the
middle of it all is House Parts, a museum of a
store packed with clawfoot tubs, solid-cherry
doors, leaded-glass windows and other relics of
Rochester's architectural past. Baobab Cultural
Center is an Africa-centered gathering place in
the Historic German House. And don't miss
Stars and Stripes Flag Store; proceeds benefit
war veterans in the Rochester area.

RESTAURANTS
(For details, see the Dining Index on page 130.)

The South Wedge has restaurants to satisfy a

variety of tastes, from meat lovers (Cajun barbecue at **Beale Street Café**) to vegetarian (**Skippy's Vegetarian Restaurant**). Newcomers **Dashen Ethiopian Restaurant and Bar** and **Ly Lou's Pearl of the Orient** bring a world-class flavor to the street. Grab a slice or a pasta dinner for takeout at **Little Venice Pizza** or a sandwich at **Julienne** or **Open Face Sandwich Eatery**. If you're in the mood for bread and pastries, try **Cheesy Eddie's**. **Daily Perks Coffeehouse** and **Women's Coffee Connection** serve the brew night and day, respectively.

Main thoroughfares: South Avenue and Gregory Street
Parking: Free on South (after 5) and side streets

BARS

Beale Street Café: Cajun and blues bar. 693 South Ave.; 271-4650
Caverly's: Authentic Irish pub. 741 South Ave.; 278-1289
The Keg: Lower level of the German House, 315 Gregory St.; 473-5070
Lux Lounge: Board games, pool table, funky art. 666 South Ave.; 232-9030
MacGregor's Grill & Tap Room: Bar and grill with wide beer selection. 381 Gregory St.; 271-3592

Live music: Beale Street; Daily Perks

More places to dance

The popular entertainment districts such as East & Alexander and St. Paul Street aren't the only places to go out dancing. Here are some other dance clubs in the city and the suburbs.

Steel Music Hall/Pulse Nightclub: 1509 Scottsville Road, Chili; 436-7573
Taylor's Nightclub of Pittsford: 3300 Monroe Ave., Pittsford; 381-3000

The Arts
Music

Nothing says Rochester like music. It's all around you here: in coffee shops and pubs, at the ballpark and church. While we may not all sing the same tune, most of us enjoy music of one kind or another. It's the common denominator that brings Rochesterians together. This was the vision of one man who brought music to the forefront of life in this city.

A legacy of music

As he built Eastman Kodak into an international company in the early 20th century, George Eastman amassed a fortune that he used to build the cultural treasures of Rochester. He gave generously to education and the arts, allowing the University of Rochester to establish a music school and a downtown performance hall. Eastman School of Music today enjoys an international reputation and a top rank among music schools

in the country. Its faculty are world-renowned musicians and composers, and students go on to stellar careers as performers and educators. Among its best-known graduates are baritone William Warfield, opera star Renee Fleming and big-band legend Mitch Miller. Fleming and Miller also grew up in Rochester.

In funding the construction of Eastman Theatre in 1922, Eastman gave the city one of its most beautiful buildings. Part of the Eastman School complex, the neo-Classical structure was designed by New York architects McKim, Mead and White. The rich interior includes murals by Ezra Winter and a replica of a commissioned Maxfield Parrish painting, "Interlude: The Lute Players." (The original is on permanent loan to the Memorial Art Gallery.)

The theater became the home of the Rochester Philharmonic Orchestra, which Eastman also founded in 1922. The RPO is known nationally for quality musicianship and a dedication to community education.

Something for everyone

Eastman believed strongly in the power of music to build community, and Rochester has

carried that forward. The Eastman School, along with Hochstein School of Music and Dance, anchors a huge network of community groups, from small, ethnic ensembles to classical orchestras. In many of these groups, local residents perform alongside music school faculty and students. There are town orchestras and choruses, lessons in instrument and voice and live shows that light up Rochester bars and concert halls every night of the week. With so many local kids growing up surrounded by music, it's no surprise we have

such an active music scene. Check out City newspaper for weekly show listings.

Homegrown talent

Rochester has brought the world its own legends of song. The 1950s and '60s were the heyday of Rochester jazz. Gap and Chuck Mangione, lifelong residents, collaborated with bassist (and high school classmate) Ron Carter, saxophonist Pee Wee Ellis, Chick Corea, Steve Gadd, Joe Romano and Frank Pullara. Cab ("Minnie the Moocher") Calloway was born here, as was Foreigner's Lou Gramm, who still lives in town. Other Rochester musicians whose talents were heard on the world stage are the Rascals' Gene Cornish; Joe English, drummer for Paul McCartney's Wings; R&B musician Tweet; and punk rocker Wendy O. Williams.

Live music, Rochester style

Rochester's musical roots might be more of the tuxedo-and-baton set, but we serve up heaping platefuls of blues, rock, jazz, Cajun and folk too. Dinosaur Bar-B-Que, in a converted downtown rail station; Beale Street Cafe, in the

The music of Rochester-based Atomic Swindlers has been featured on XM Satellite Radio and ManiaTV.

South Wedge; and Nola's Waterfront Barbeque, in Charlotte, offer Southern blues with the ribs and pork sandwiches to match. Milestones, with well-known acts that run the gamut from zydeco to reggae to roots rock, is a good bet any night of the week. If you're in the mood for jazz or folk, check out coffee joints Java's and

Spring in the air? It's time for jazz

The buzz of the East End hums louder in June.

Small musical ensembles peg out a tight beat for passersby. Drivers slow down to take a look. Music lovers stream from club to club.

Welcome to the **Rochester International Jazz Festival**—quickly becoming a signature event on the world jazz scene. More than 65,000 people attended the festival in 2005, making it one of the nation's largest and fastest-growing music festivals, and more are expected at this year's event June 9-17.

Woody Allen and his New Orleans Jazz Band will open the festival June 9 with a benefit concert for the New Orleans Musicians Hurricane Relief Fund.

"Rochester is one of the most gracious and knowledgeable music cities in the world," says festival producer (and tenor saxophonist) John Nugent, who also heads up the Stockholm Jazz Festival. "It didn't surprise me when Dave Brubeck said of his (first) concert here, 'In all my years of touring the world, this could be one of the best performances I've ever given.' The synergy between audiences and artists was magical."

Craig Roberts and Jumpin' Jive Band perform on the Jazz Street stage during the 2005 festival (top). Multiple-Grammy winner Chaka Khan was one of the headliners in Eastman Theatre (above).

RIJF attracts all styles of creative and improvised music from around the world—as well as America's own art form, jazz, of course. The 2006 lineup will bring 120 shows and more than 600 musicians, including a number from New Orleans as a tribute to the musicians of that city.

A list of some of RIJF's previous marquee shows in Eastman Theatre reads like a Who's Who in Jazz: Brubeck, Tony Bennett, Madeleine Peyroux, Sonny Rollins, George Benson, Chick Corea, Chris Botti and other multiple-Grammy winners. The more intimate shows, usually SRO, have featured rising stars like Norah Jones and Claudia Acuna.

And, as always, there will be scores of international bands that are wildly popular in their home countries but little-known here. Showgoers will hear unusual, eclectic stuff—some of it for the first time in this country.

"There are groups you won't get to hear in Miami, New York, Chicago or anywhere else," Nugent says. "Groups are coming from overseas—Japan, Sweden, Cuba, Korea, Brazil, Africa, all over the world—specifically to play at Rochester International Jazz Festival. People are starting to understand the diversity and magnitude of this event."

As in the Montreal Jazz Festival, RIJF shows happen in multiple venues around the city. Most are in Rochester's bustling East End: the festival's Big Tent, Milestones Music Room, Max of Eastman Place, Kilbourn Hall at the Eastman School of Music, Montage Grille, Milestones and the Little Theatre. The festival also offers free concerts on outdoor stages on Gibbs Street and East Avenue both weekends.

The jazz festival continues to expand around the city. A new venue this year is the *Mary Jemison*, a replica canal boat that tours the Genesee River and Erie Canal. Dixieland jazz cruises will be held June 15-17. Shows also have been added at the Dryden Theatre at George Eastman House, June 12-14, and the Memorial Art Gallery, June 9-11.

If you buy a Club Pass ($85), you can take your pick of three shows a day for nine days. It also buys you admission to the popular after-hours jam sessions at the State Street Bar and Grille in the Crowne Plaza Rochester. Talk about magic:

A quintet led by Wallace Roney (left), a protégé of Miles Davis, was one of the most highly anticipated shows at the 2005 festival.

artists of diverse musical styles jamming together, many for the first time, in the hotel bar until the wee hours.

In town for only a day or two? You can buy single-show tickets for $15 to $25.

Celebrating jazz in Rochester on a big scale makes so much sense, it's a wonder it hasn't been done before: Jazz legends have been calling Rochester home for years, among them Chuck (flugelhorn) and Gap (piano) Mangione, Jeff Tyzik (trumpet), Gerry Niewood (sax), Steve Gadd (drums), and Esther Satterfield and Cab Calloway (vocals). The Eastman School of Music has a reputable jazz program.

Given the size and knowledge of the crowds and the quality of the music, you won't believe the jazz festival is in only its fifth year.

Rochester International Jazz Festival, June 9-17, 2006, 234-2002, www.rochesterjazz.com

Of his nearly soldout show in Eastman Theatre, trumpeter Chris Botti's online "Road Report" said: "The crowd was fantastic, the sound was amazing—perhaps the best I have ever heard them sound."

The Rochester Philharmonic Orchestra, led by popular conductor Christopher Seaman, plays in the Estman Theatre and in special appearances around the world.

Daily Perks. Or listen in on a Golden Link Folk Singing Society weekly jam session. Take in an acoustic set at Little Theatre Cafe, where an Eastman student or faculty member is likely to be behind the mic.

MUSICAL GROUPS

The following are a sample of local performers in traditional and classical music. In addition, Rochester has dozens of working bands playing all genres: reggae, rock, blues, salsa, pop, metal, jazz, R&B, hip-hop, punk, roots rock and hybrids. Call or check local listings for show schedules.

Eastman School of Music: The Eastman School is one of the top music schools in the country. Student and faculty performances, many of them free, pack the calendar throughout the year. Eastman Theatre and Kilbourn Hall host recitals and performances by orchestra and wind ensembles, jazz and studio ensembles, vocal groups, and experimental and new music groups. 274-1000; www.rochester.edu/Eastman

Fiddlers of the Genesee: Dedicated to preserving the old-time fiddle music of the Genesee Valley, the group performs at festivals, concerts and other gatherings. Open jam sessions are held each week. 234-3582; www.fiddlersofthegenesee.org

Finger Lakes Choral Festival: A chorus of 200 performs the Mozart Grand Mass in C Minor in July at the Hochstein Performance Hall and at Chautauqua Institution. www.fingerlakeschoral.org

Golden Link Folk Singing Society: Folk musicians perform in concerts, workshops and free Tuesday-night "sing-arounds." 234-5044; www.goldenlink.org

Irish Musicians Association: Musicians celebrate Ireland with dances, workshops and concerts. Open jam sessions are held at area pubs twice a month. 234-ERIN

Gamelan Lila Muni: The percussion orchestra plays the bright sounds of Balinese music on gongs, metallophones, recorders and drums. Performances feature sacred and secular music, along with dances and instrument demonstrations. The group is part of Eastman's Community Education Division. Eastman School of Music, Rochester; 274-1100

Madrigalia: Madrigalia's 18 chamber singers perform 16th and 17th century madrigals and motets, plus secular and sacred choral music. 234-4283; www.madrigalia.org

Mercury Opera Rochester: Working in concert with Eastman School of Music, this group is a recent merging of Rochester Opera Factory, Opera Rochester and the Opera Theatre Guild; 473-6567

New Horizons Concert Band and Orchestra: Some of the seniors in these groups are playing for the first time; others are picking up an instrument they set aside years ago. The two groups play concerts around the community throughout the year. The brainchild of Eastman professor emeritus Roy Ernst, the program has expanded to more than 60 bands in the United States and Canada. Eastman School of Music; www.newhorizonsband.com

Rochester Chamber Orchestra: RCO plays chamber orchestra music from the 17th century to the present in Hochstein Performance Hall. Eastman faculty supported its creation 40 years ago and participate today. www.roch.com/rco

Rochester Gay Men's Chorus: The 20-year-old group performs popular and classic tunes throughout the year at area venues. 423-0650; www.thergmc.org

Rochester Oratorio Society: Singing in festivals around the world, this group of 200 links with the biggest names in classical music, including Leonard Bernstein and David Zinman. A Christmas performance of Handel's Messiah has been a tradition for 50 years. 473-2234; www.rossings.org

Rochester Philharmonic Orchestra: The RPO is considered one of the nation's premiere orchestras. It performs in Eastman Theatre, the Finger Lakes Performing Arts Center and other regional venues. The group tours and records extensively, and is heavily involved in community outreach and education. Guest musicians frequently perform with the RPO, including opera star Renee Fleming, a Rochester native, and cellist Yo-Yo Ma. 454-2100; www.rpo.org

Rhythmic Revolution: This youth percussion group works at community service, music and youth development. www.rhythmicrevolution.org

The Smugtown Stompers: Sporting an old-time Rochester nickname, this group celebrates America's musical heritage with performances around the country. Blues, ragtime, jazz and pop music from 1890 to 1930 have been staples since the band's start in 1958. www.dynrec.com/smugtown

PLACES TO HEAR LIVE MUSIC

You can find music happening every night of the week in bars, clubs, restaurants and coffee shops around town. Looking for some smooth jazz or blues to listen to over a latte? Or does loud and fast rock-n-roll sound more like it? We'll show you the places where you're most likely to catch a tune flying by.

For additional venues, see Entertainment Districts, pages 102 to 107. See the Entertainment Districts for DJ/dance clubs.

Clubs and Cafes

Barnstormer's Pub: 800 Jefferson Road, Henrietta *F12*; 272-1550

Barristers Pub & Meeting Place: 36 W. Main St., Rochester *CC3*; 232-2240

California Brew Haus: 402 W. Ridge Road, Greece *D12*; 621-1480

Chesapeake Coffee Co.: 98 W. Main St., Victor *B21*; 924-8410

Clark House: Shadow Pines Golf Club, 600 Whalen Road, Penfield *E14*; 385-3700

Dinosaur Bar-B-Que: 99 Court St., Rochester

Opera star Renee Fleming, a soprano, grew up in Rochester.

DD4; 325-7090

Dr.'s Inn: 1743 East Ave., Rochester *E13*; 271-0820

Earthtones Coffeehouse: 1217 Bay Road, Webster *D14*; 671-3060

Fat Moe's: 4419 Dewey Ave., Greece *C12*; 663-1860

Froggy's On the Bay: 1129 Empire Blvd., Penfield *D14*; 288-1080

Glengarry Grill: 4400 Nine Mile Point Road, Fairport *E15*; 377-7250

Barber Shop Singing: 58 E. Main St., Webster *D15*; 265-9540

Honeoye Pub: 4940 E. Lake Road, Honeoye *B21*; 229-4535

Lodge at Woodcliff: Route 96, Perinton *G14*; 381-4000

Java Junction Coffee Roasters & Bakery: 56 Main St., Brockport *D7*; 637-9330

Johnny's Irish Pub: 1382 Culver Road, Rochester *D13*; 224-0990

Josie's Country Jukebox: 5435 W. Ridge Road, Spencerport *C9;* 352-4505

Juniper Beans: 61 N. Main St., Honeoye Falls *B21*; 582-1830

Mcghan's Nearly Famous Pub: 11 W. Main St., Victor *B21*; 924-3660

Moonshine Barbeque: 125 White Spruce Blvd., Brighton *F12*; 272-1090

Norton's Pub: 1730 Goodman St., Rochester *D13*; 266-3570

Rab's Woodshed: 4440 Lake Ave., Rochester *C12*; 663-4610

The Roost: 4853 W. Henrietta Road, Henrietta *G12*; 321-1170

Six Pockets: 716 E. Ridge Road, Rochester *D12*; 266-1440

Slammer's Bar and Grill: 4650 Dewey Ave., Rochester *C12*; 663-4455

Smokin' Joe's Bar & Grill: 425 Lyell Ave., Rochester *B2*; 647-1540

Spender's: 1600 Lyell Ave., Rochester *D11*; 458-1040

Steel Music Hall/Pulse Nightclub: 1509 Scottsville Road *F11*; 436-7573

T.C. Hooligan's: 134 Greece Ridge Center Drive, Greece *D11*; 225-7180

Taylor's Nightclub of Pittsford: 3300 Monroe Ave., Pittsford *F13*; 381-3000

Thali of India: 3259 S. Winton Road, Henrietta *F13*; 427-8030

Zamar Café: 15 E. Main St., Webster *D15*; 265-1080

Performance Halls

Auditorium Center: 875 E. Main St., Rochester *B5*; 423-0295

Blue Cross Arena: 1 War Memorial Square, Rochester *DD3*; 758-5300

Brodie Fine Arts Building: SUNY College at Geneseo, School of Performing Arts, 1 College Circle, Geneseo *B20*; 245-5833

Six Flags Darien Lake Performing Arts Center: 9993 Allegheny Road, Darien Center *B19*; 599-4641

Eastman Theatre: 60 Gibbs St., Rochester *CC6*; 274-1100

Finger Lakes Performing Arts Center: Finger Lakes Community College, Canandaigua *B21*; 222-5000

Harro East Ballroom: 400 Andrews St., Rochester *BB5*; 454-0230

Hochstein School of Music and Dance: 50 N. Plymouth Ave., Rochester *CC2*; 454-4596

The world-famous Garth Fagan Dance troupe celebrates its 35th year in 2006.

Kilbourn Hall: Eastman Theatre, 26 Gibbs St., Rochester *CC6*; 274-1100

MCC Theatre: Monroe Community College, Building 4, 1000 E. Henrietta Road, Brighton *F12*; 292-2060

Roberts Cultural Life Center: Roberts Wesleyan College, 2301 Westside Drive, Chili *E9*; 594-6008

Strong Auditorium: University of Rochester River Campus, Wilson Boulevard, Rochester *E21*; 275-2121

Tower Fine Arts Center: SUNY College at Brockport, Holley Street, Brockport *D7*; 395-ARTS

Callahan Theatre: Nazareth College Arts Center, 4245 East Ave., Pittsford *F13*; 389-2170

Other places where music hangs out

These shops and museums frequently host live musical performances.

Abundance Cooperative Market: 62 Marshall St., Rochester *C4;* 454-COOP

Barnes & Noble Booksellers: 3349 Monroe Ave., Pittsford *F13*; 586-6020. 330 Greece Ridge Center Drive, Greece *D11*; 227-4020. 1070 Ridge Road, Webster *D14*; 872-9710

The Bop Shop: Village Gate Square, 274 N. Goodman St., Rochester *C5*; 271-3354

Borders Books Music & Café: 1000 Hylan Drive, Henrietta *F12;* 292-5900. 30 Square Drive, Victor *B21*; 421-9230

George Eastman House Dryden Theatre: 900 East Ave., Rochester *C5*; 271-4090

House of Guitars: 645 Titus Ave., Irondequoit *D5*; 544-9928

Lakeshore Record Exchange: 370 Park Ave., Rochester *C5*; 244-8476

Memorial Art Gallery: 500 University Ave., Rochester *C5*; 473-7720

Record Archive: 1880 East Ave., Rochester *E13*; 244-1210

Rochester Public Market: 280 N. Union St., Rochester *B4*; 428-6907

Visual Studies Workshop: 31 Prince St., Rochester *C5*; 442-8676

Dance

In a city full of music, can dancing be far behind? Rochester has long been a regional center for modern and classical dance performance and instruction. Many of our companies have been together for 25 years or more. Rochester dance ensembles emphasize education, participation and community involvement. Classes in dance and choreography, taught by patient pros, are available to children and adults. Tony Award-winner Garth Fagan bases his troupe in downtown Rochester.

DANCE TROUPES

Borinquen Dance Theatre: This regional ethnic dance company performs for a blend of African, Taino and Spanish influences with contemporary Latin movement. Borinquen, whose dancers are preteens and high schoolers, is the ensemble-in-residence at Hochstein. Hochstein School of Music, 50 N. Plymouth Ave., Rochester; 454-4596

Elizabeth Clark Dance Ensemble: The ensemble offers workshops and classes for the community, as well as professional performances of original choreographic works. Elaine P. Wilson Pavilion, 3646 East Ave., St. Thomas' Episcopal Church, 2000 Highland Ave., Brighton; 442-5988

Garth Fagan Dance: This award-winning modern dance troupe is led by Garth Fagan, whose choreography awards include a Tony for Broadway's "The Lion King." The company rehearses in an East End studio and performs all over the world. 50 Chestnut St., Rochester; 454-3260; www.garthfagandance.org

Hallmark Danceworks: Working with visual artists, filmmakers and composers, Hallmark develops original choreography and performs contemporary dance in regional venues. 358 Mulberry St., Rochester; www.hallmarkdanceworks.org

Hendrick Dance Project: Provides dance arts to city children and teens. 34 Elton St., Rochester; 235-3960

Park Avenue Dance Co.: Independent choreographers present their work through this 25-year-old modern-dance repertory. 15 Vick Park B, Rochester; 461-2766; www.parkavenuedancecompany.org

Rochester City Ballet: The ballet delights local schoolchildren and adults with its popular annual performance of "The Nutcracker." The company's repertoire includes traditional favorites as well as new works; it has premiered 20 ballets. Former members dance with the New York City Ballet, American Ballet Theatre and other distinguished companies. 1326 University Ave., Rochester; 461-5850; www.rochestercityballet.org

Belly Dance With Babanesh: The troupe performs contemporary belly dance and Middle East folk dances in venues throughout the area. 6482 County Line Road, Ontario; 265-2346; www.saharashimmer.com

SUNY College at Brockport Department of Dance: Brockport's dance program offers performances during the school year through a variety of ensembles. Students are preparing for professional careers in dance and choreography. 350 New Campus Drive, Brockport; 395-2153; www.brockport.edu/dance/index.html

SUNY College at Geneseo School of Performing Arts: Geneseo's student dance organization, Orchesis, offers several performances on campus during the academic year. Dancers also work with area dance students. Brodie Fine Arts Building, 1 College Circle, Geneseo; 245-5833

University of Rochester, The Program of Movement and Dance: The program's Performing Artist Series brings artists and educators to workshops, demonstrations and performances on campus. 121 Lattimore Hall, Rochester; 273-5150; www.rochester.edu/College/dance/index.html

PARTICIPATORY DANCE

Da Igramo Folk Ensemble: Rochester-area dancers perform folk music and dance from around the world. 442-6264

Country Dancers of Rochester: Dance to contra and English country dances in a smoke- and alcohol-free setting. (315) 587-2152; www.ggw.org/cdr

Rochester Swing Dance: Dedicated swing dance fans follow the music around town: zydeco, jazz, blues and other swinging music performed by regional bands. Newcomers are welcome; if you're getting your feet wet, get on the dance floor for the introductory swing lesson at the start of the show. Various area locations; 244-2815; www.rochesterswingdance.com

Theater

The hometown of Philip Seymour Hoffman, Robert Forster and Taye Diggs buzzes with spirited live theater every night of the week, all year long. First-rate professional theaters and smaller community groups offer dramas, musicals, comedies and cutting-edge new works. Geva Theatre Center, the most attended regional theater in New York State, and Downstairs Cabaret Theatre Center create productions that draw actors and directors from around the country. Blackfriars Theatre, located in the city's East End, has been staging productions for more than 50 years. The JCC Center for the Arts stages plays, an annual musical and solo performances in its 300-seat Hart Theatre.

Celebrating 35 years

Garth Fagan likes living in Rochester

With a list of awards as long as one of his dancer's lean limbs, choreographer Fagan could live and work anywhere in the world. Yet the founder of Garth Fagan Dance remains committed to keeping his company headquartered in Rochester.

"I love the sense of community; I love the sophistication," he says after wrapping up afternoon rehearsal at the troupe's Chestnut Street studio. "I like the (city's) size and the sense of calm I get when I come home."

Since choreographing Disney's "The Lion King" for the stage in 1997, Fagan has won every major award in his field, including the Tony, Outer Critics Circle, Drama Desk, Astaire and Olivier. These honors have intensified the spotlight on his groundbreaking style of movement, which intertwines elements of ballet, jazz and Afro-Caribbean dance with stork-like balances, fluid step sequences and gravity-defying jumps.

Dance Magazine senior editor Allan Ulrich calls Fagan a formidable innovator who began influencing choreographers long before the world tour of "The Lion King."

"In the last few years amongst choreographers of color, there's been extraordinary interest in going back to cultural roots," Ulrich says from his office in California. "In some ways, (Fagan) is a pathfinder, and he's a great original because he was doing this a decade ago."

Despite being away much of the year touring with the troupe or refining the choreography for new productions of "The Lion King," Fagan still looks to places near Rochester for creative inspiration.

"I like to be in a very quiet place, where I can really run a million ideas and images through my mind, juxtapose them and have them collide," he says. "I sometimes like driving in the hinterlands for that process—with just some good music and beautiful scenery—like down the Oatka Trail, which is one of the most beautiful places, or Letchworth Park.

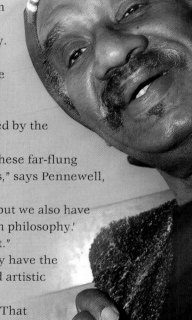

"When I was younger and not as wise, I was always looking for the great, grand inspiration," Fagan adds. "Now that I'm more mature and experienced, I realize that simple, subtle things can inspire me to do great work and to make poignant statements about life."

Nicolette Depass, a native of Jamaica who joined the troupe in 1994, says she shares Fagan's enthusiasm for this community.

"As dancers who travel around the world, we are ambassadors (of) Rochester," she says. "We carry that pride with us—that we're from Rochester—because it is a wonderful place to live."

Rehearsal director and dancer Norwood Pennewell says he is touched by the support local dance enthusiasts have shown the troupe over the years.

"There will be occasions where we will actually see people from Rochester in these far-flung places, and before we even talk to them, there's such a joy and pride in their eyes," says Pennewell, who joined the company in 1978.

"We have a major responsibility as ambassadors to Rochester," Pennewell adds, "but we also have a responsibility to adhere to the basic principle of what it is to be involved in 'Fagan philosophy.' And that really is just to learn and observe, and be open and vulnerable and honest."

Now in his late 40s and injury-free for more than 25 years, Pennewell will likely have the opportunity to dance for another decade, thanks to his boss' rigorous training and artistic point of view.

"My technique was designed to keep dancers dancing longer," Fagan explains. "That was a conscious effort on my part because I like plurality in life, and I love to look at a stage and see a community of people dancing."

Garth Fagan Dance, 50 Chestnut St., Rochester; 454-3260;
www.garthfagandance.org

LIVE THEATER

Blackfriars Theatre: 28 Lawn St., Rochester. 248 East Ave., Rochester (box office) *CC6*; 454-1260; www.blackfriars.org

Bristol Valley Theater: 151 S. Main St., Naples *C21*; 374-9032; www.bvtnaples.org

Downstairs Cabaret Theatre Center: 540 E. Main St., Rochester *BB6*; 20 Windsor St., Rochester *BB6*; 172 W. Main St., Rochester *DD2*; 325-4370; www.downstairscabaret.com

Geva Theatre Center: 75 Woodbury Blvd., Rochester *DD5;* 232-1366; 325-1411 TTY; www.gevatheatre.org

JCC Center for the Arts: 1200 Edgewood Ave., Brighton *F13*; 461-2000; www.inforochester.com/theater.htm

Monroe Community College Department of Visual and Performing Arts: 1000 E. Henrietta Road, Brighton *F12*; 292-2047

Its closing date twice extended, the production of "A Chorus Line" in 2005 became the highest-grossing show ever at the Geva Theatre Center, the most attended regional theatre in New York.

Nazareth College of Rochester Arts Center: 4245 East Ave., Pittsford *F14*; 389-2525; www.naz.edu/dept/artscenter

Nazareth College of Rochester Department of Theatre Arts: 4245 East Ave., Pittsford *F14*; 389-2170; www.naz.edu/dept/theater_arts/index.html

Off-Monroe Players: 60 Bittner St., Rochester *BB4*; 232-5570

RAPA Playhouse: 727 E. Main St., Rochester *BB7*; 325-3366

Rochester Broadway Theatre League: Traveling Broadway shows. Auditorium Theatre, 885 E. Main St., Rochester *B5*; www.rbtl.org (tickets: www.ticketmaster.com/artist/840467)

Rochester Children's Theatre Inc.: 525 University Ave., Rochester *C5*; 385-0510

Shakespeare Players: Performances in Highland Bowl. 1200 South Ave. at Robinson Drive, Rochester *E3*; 234-7840

School of the Arts: 45 Prince St., Rochester *C5*; 242-7682

Shipping Dock Theatre: 31 Prince St., Rochester *C5*; 232-2250; www.shippingdocktheatre.org

University of Rochester International Theatre Program: University of Rochester River Campus, Rochester *E2*; 275-4088; www.rochester.edu/college/eng/theatre

ART HOUSE/INDEPENDENT FILMS

Cinema Theatre: 957 S. Clinton Ave., Rochester *D4*; 271-1785

Dryden Theatre: 900 East Ave., Rochester *C5*; 271-3361; 271-3362 TTY line; 271-4090 film line; www.eastmanhouse.org

Little Theatre: 240 East Ave., Rochester *CC6*; 258-0400; www.little-theatre.com

Visual arts

Since its first exhibit in 1823 (a display of a single painting, "Christ Rejected" by William Dunlap), Rochester has flourished as an active arts town. Today, the pool of local talent is fed by Rochester Institute of Technology's School for American Crafts and a host of non-profit arts organizations. The nearby Finger Lakes and Lake Ontario are popular subjects for painters; modernist painter Arthur Dove, born in Canandaigua in 1880, is known internationally for his distinctive landscapes. Among our notable artists: furniture maker Wendell Castle, sculpture artists Nancy Jurs and Albert Paley, glass artist Nancy Gong and the late painter Ramon Santiago. Our summer festivals bring out established and emerging artists to display and sell their work. See Special Events.

ART GALLERIES

Rochester

1570 Art Gallery: Valley Manor, 1570 East Ave., Rochester *E13*; 442-8470

Furniture as art, art as furniture

Want to make a statement with your furniture? If you live in or visit Rochester, this might be easier than you think.

Since the 1950s, graduates and faculty of the School for American Crafts at Rochester Institute of Technology have been making unusual, high-end furniture. This means we're more likely than most communities to find handmade pieces of a masterful, artistic quality.

"Rochester has a real heritage of custom furniture making," furniture maker Jeff Koopus says. "There's been a class of clientele who can afford custom work and that continues to this day, even with cutbacks at Kodak and Xerox."

Furniture designer Wendell Castle is internationally renowned for his furniture art—pieces that look like sculpture and function as furniture.

Custom pieces made in his Scottsville studio range in price from $12,000 for a small end table to $40,000 for a dining table.

If the prices sound unappetizing, consider this: Castle's earlier works are selling for 10 to 20 times their original price at Christie's, Sotheby's and other auction houses.

The studio recently built a sculptural, one-legged dining room table with some 500 LED lights on the underside and a matching buffet that hangs off the wall. Some installations are so customized they are built right into the home, such as a recently completed piece that houses a television and fireplace.

Castle's team also makes non-custom furniture in a LeRoy plant; a

dining table could carry an $8,000 price tag—but for a couple thousand more could be made taller, wider or with different leg shapes, for instance. While not custom, it's still quality, and Castle's name alone carries weight in the market.

A life of art

Metal sculptor Albert Paley's studio has been infested by animals. No, not the nasty rodent or insect type. Rather, a good portion of his 20,000-square-foot workspace is teeming with model crocodiles, seals, tigers and more.

That's because Paley—a professor at Rochester Institute of Technology, who is considered one of the world's finest forged metal sculptors—is creating a huge gate that will soon greet visitors at the St. Louis Zoo.

Visitors will be welcomed by no fewer than 60 animals fabricated from Corten steel.

"I love the work," says Paley, 62, who oversees a team of 15 artisans and administrative staff. "Throughout my career, I've been fortunate not to have to compromise what I do, and I've been given a fair amount of latitude by clients."

Indeed, something must be working right. Paley's creations span the globe—throughout the U.S. as well as in Korea, Japan, Australia, Ireland, Germany, England and France. At any point in time, Paley and his staff are working on 70 to 80 projects.

"I relish the whole creative process," says Paley, who in 1995 received Institute Honors from the American Institute of Architects. "I'm on an airplane every 10 days, creating a dialogue with clients. It's a very enriching and exciting career."

Miraculously, Paley holds this conviction despite a near-fatal work injury three years ago.

While working on a project, he found himself immersed in a propane explosion. "For 40 seconds, my entire body was completely engulfed in flames," he says. "I was on total life support for two weeks. In the months that ensued, one-third of my body skin needed to be grafted. If not for the burn unit at Strong Memorial Hospital, I would have died."

Following such a trauma, others might have called it quits.

Not Paley.

"This is my life, 24/7. I can't retire because that would be like retiring from life."

Artisanworks: 565 Blossom Road, Rochester *E13*; 288-7170; www.artisanworks.net
A/V: 8 Public Market, Rochester *B5*; 423-0320; www.artsoundspace.org
The Baobab Cultural Center: 315 Gregory St., Rochester *D4*; 546-4790; www.thebaobab.org
Rochester Clayworks: 203 Milburn St., Rochester *E13*; 244-1098
Center at High Falls: 60 Browns Race, Rochester *BB2*; 325-2030
Department of Rare Books, Special Collections and Preservation: Rush Rhees Library, University of Rochester River Campus, Rochester *E2*; 275-4477
The College of Arts and Sciences, Art & Art History: University of Rochester River Campus, Rochester *E2*; 275-9249
door7: 750 South Ave., Rochester *D4*
Gallery Blue: Medical Arts Building, 277 Alexander St., Suite 204, Rochester *DD7*; 703-6087
Gallery r: Rochester Institute of Technology, 775 Park Ave., Rochester *C5*; 242-9470
Genesee Arts Building: Genesee Center for the Arts & Education, 713 Monroe Ave., Rochester *D5*; 244-1730
Genesee Pottery: Genesee Arts Building, 713 Monroe Ave., Rochester *D5*; 271-5183
George Eastman House International Museum of Photography and Film: 900 East Ave., Rochester *C5*; 271-3361
Hartnett Gallery: Wilson Commons, University of Rochester River Campus, Rochester *E2*; 275-4188
Hungerford Gallery: 1115 E. Main St.,

Rochester *B5*
Jembetat Gallery of African Art: 645 Park Ave., Rochester *C5*; 442-8960
Link Gallery: City Hall, 30 Church St., Rochester *CC2*; 389-2530
MK Colling Gallery: Village Gate Square, 274 N. Goodman St., Rochester *B5*; 442-8946
Memorial Art Gallery: 500 University Ave., Rochester *C5*; 473-7720
My Sister's Gallery: The Episcopal Church Home, 505 Mt. Hope Ave., Rochester *D3*; 546-8400
Oxford Gallery: 267 Oxford St., Rochester *C5*; 271-5885
Ramon Santiago Studio: 115 Berkeley St., Rochester *C5*; 288-9110

The Rochester Contemporary: 137 East Ave., Rochester *CC6*; 461-2222
Terry Art Gallery: St. John's Home, 150 Highland Ave., Rochester *E3*; 271-5413
Visual Studies Workshop: 31 Prince St., Rochester *C5*; 442-8676
William Marten Gallery: Daily Record Building, 11 Centre Park, Rochester *CC1*; 262-6460
Williams Gallery: First Unitarian Church, 220 S. Winton Road, Rochester *E13*; 271-9070

Brighton

Mercer Gallery: Monroe Community College, 1000 E. Henrietta Road, Brighton *F12*; 292-2021

Fine oil paintings, such as this one at Nan Miller Gallery, can be found at galleries throughout the region.

Friendly Home Memorial Gallery: 3156 East Ave., Brighton *E13*; 381-1600
Nan Miller Gallery: 3450 Winton Place, Brighton *F13*; 292-1430

Brockport

Art Student Association Rainbow Gallery: SUNY College at Brockport, Brockport *D7*
Tower Fine Arts Gallery: SUNY College at Brockport, Brockport *D7*; 395-ARTS

Canandaigua area

All Things Art: 65 S. Main St., Canandaigua *B21*; 396-0087
Gallery on Main Street: 131 S. Main St., Canandaigua *B21*; 394-2780
Rochester Folk Art Guild: 1445 Upper Hill Road, Middlesex *B21*; 554-5464

Henrietta

Rochester Institute of Technology: 1 Lomb Memorial Drive, Henrietta *F11*
Bevier Gallery: James E. Booth Building, 73 Lomb Memorial Drive, Henrietta *F11*; 475-7680
Switzer Gallery: National Technical Institute for the Deaf, Lyndon Baines Johnson Building, 52 Lomb Memorial Drive, 2nd Floor, Henrietta *F11*
SPAS Gallery: Rochester Institute of Technology, 103 Lomb Memorial Drive, Henrietta *F11*; 475-5919

Pittsford

Casa Italiana: Nazareth College of Rochester, 4245 East Ave., Pittsford *F14*; 389-2468
Gallery Imprevu: 1478 Marsh Road, Pittsford *F14*; 248-0033
Lavery Library: St. John Fisher College, 3690 East Ave., Pittsford *E14*; 385-8133
Roselawn Galleries: 7 Schoen Place, Pittsford *F14*; 586-5441

Elsewhere in the region

Lockhart Gallery: McLellan House, 23 Main St., Geneseo *B20*
Mill Art Center and Gallery: 61 N. Main St., Honeoye Falls *B21*; 624-7740

OTHER PLACES WHERE ART HANGS OUT

Anderson Alley Artists: Artists' studios.

Gallery r on Park Avenue presents works by faculty and staff of Rochester Institute of Technology.

250 N. Goodman St., Rochesters *D5*
Barnes & Noble: Community Room, 3349 Monroe Ave., Pittsford *F13*; 586-6020
Bug Jar: 219 Monroe Ave., Rochester *EE6*; 454-2966
Casava Jamaican Restaurant: 420 Central Ave., Rochester *AA4*; 546-1184
Fairport Village Coffee: 120 Fairport Village Landing, Fairport *F15*; 377-5880
Greater Rochester International Airport: 1200 Brooks Ave., Chili *E11*; 464-6000
Little Theatre: 240 East Ave., Rochester *CC6*; 232-3906
Mood Makers Books: Village Gate Square, 274 N. Goodman St., Rochester *B5*; 271-7010
Rochester Institute of Technology: Outdoor sculptures, Henrietta *F11*
Studio 34: 34 Elton St., Rochester *C5*; 271-8290

Literary arts

There must be something about Rochester that stirs the literary soul: Successful, creative writers live here or have roots in the area, including John Ashbery, Andrea Barrett, Nicholson Baker, Joanna Scott and Joyce Carol Oates. From writing studios and living room couches all over the city, Rochesterians have won Pulitzer Prizes, Macarthur Fellowships, PEN/Faulkner awards, the National Book Award and the National Book Critics Circle Award. Not surprisingly, literary readings and discussions are popular events.

The Writers Forum: Edward Albee, Lucille Clifton and Rochester native John Ashbery are among hundreds of well-known poets, writers and critics who have participated in this popular reading series, considered one of the finest in the country. Launched by Brockport's English department in 1967, the forum has videotaped more than 200 discussions of the writing craft by major contemporary writers. SUNY College at Brockport, Department of English, 350 New

Campus Drive, Brockport *D7*; 395-5713; www.acs.brockport.edu/~wforum/Main.html
The Plutzik Series: UR has honored poet and former faculty member Hyam Plutzik since 1962, the year he died, with a reading series that features writers of fiction and poetry. Participating literary luminaries have included Allen Ginsberg, Gwendolyn Brooks, John Updike and James Baldwin. University of Rochester, Department of English, 404 Morey Hall, River Campus, Rochester *E2*; 275-4092; www.rochester.edu/College/ENG/plutzik
Rochester Arts & Lectures: This popular series brings noted authors to Rochester to discuss their writing. Recent guests have included Susan Orlean, Tony Kushner, Barry Lopez and Ann Patchett. The series is subscription-based, so call for ticket availability. Downtown United Presbyterian Church, 121 N. Fitzhugh St., Rochester (lecture location) *CC2*; 546-8658; www.artsandlectures.org
Writers & Books: One of the leading literary centers in the country, Writers & Books hosts readings and classes devoted to the craft of writing in all genres. Its annual event, "If All of Rochester Read the Same Book," brings residents together for reading and discussions related to one book, leading to a three-day residency by the author. Past selections have included "The Sweet Hereafter" by Russell Banks and "Name All the Animals," Alison Smith's memoir. Writers & Books is located in a renovated firehouse in the Neighborhood of the Arts. 740 University Ave., Rochester *C4*; 473-2590; www.wab.org

The Little Theatre, a five-screen non-profit movie house, shows independent flicks and hosts film festivals.

dining

Dining

Visitors remark on the large number of independent restaurants in the Rochester area. From fusion to international to homestyle comfort food, chefs have developed niche dishes in a diverse range of menus. You'll find restaurants offer New York cuisine: menus that follow New York's four seasons and feature fresh produce, herbs and spices from the area.

Unlike chains, local eateries offer a culinary experience you won't have anywhere else. But there's no predicting what you'll find when you get there. Even if you are adventurous, sometimes it's nice to be pointed in the right direction. So we've compiled a list of both chain and local restaurants, grouped by cuisine, that are quality establishments serving delicious food with friendly service. Advertisers' listings include a brief description, but these are all great places to eat. Bon appetit!

$ . . . . $0 - $14.99	B . . . . . . Breakfast
$$ . . . . . $15 - $19.99	L . . . . Lunch
$$$ . . . . . $20 - $29.99	D . . . . Dinner
$$$$ . . . . $30+	S . . . . Snack

American

BARBECUE & CAJUN

Beale Street Café: 693 South Ave., Rochester *D3*; 271-4650. L D $
Dinosaur Bar-B-Que: 99 Court St., Rochester *DD4*; 325-7090. L D $
Nola's Waterfront Barbecue Co.: 4775 Lake Ave., Rochester *C12*; 663-3375. L D $
Sticky Lips Pit BBQ: 625 Culver Road, Rochester *C6*; 288-1910. L D $
Unkl Moe's Bar-B-Que & Catering: 493 West Ave., Rochester *C1*; 464-8240. L D $

BISTRO

Charlie's Frog Pond: 652 Park Ave., Rochester *C5*; 271-1970. B L D $
First Taste Grill: 653 Park Ave., Rochester *C5*; 271-6220. L D $
Lola Bistro: 630 Monroe Ave., Rochester *D5*; 271-0320. D $$
Martini Grille: 176 S. Goodman St., Rochester *D4*; 244-6526. L D $$
Northfield Food & Drink: 3100 Monroe Ave., Pittsford *F13*; 641-0468. L D $$$

CASUAL DINING

The Brighton: 1881 East Ave., Rochester *E13*; 271-6650. L D $$
Charley Brown's Restaurant: 1675 Penfield Road, Rochester *E14*; 385-9202. L D $$
Coal Tower Restaurant: 9 Schoen Place, Pittsford *F14*; 381-7866. B L D $
Courtyard Cafe: Courtyard by Marriott Brighton, 33 Corporate Woods, Brighton *F12*; 292-1000. Courtyard by Marriott East, 1000 Linden Park, Penfield *E14*; 385-1000. Courtyard by Marriott West, 400 Paddy Creek Circle, Greece *D11*; 621-6050. B $
Crescent Beach Hotel: 1372 Edgemere Drive,

Rochester *C11*; 227-3600. L D $$$
Elmwood Inn: 1256 Mt. Hope Ave., Rochester *E3*; 271-5195. L D $
Fairport Village Inn: 103 N. Main St., Fairport *F15*; 388-0112. L D $
Food at Fisher's Station: 7548 Main St., Fishers *B21*; 742-3280. B L $$
Flaherty's Three Flags Inn: 1200 Bay Road, Webster *D14*; 671-0816. 113 Pittsford-Palmyra Road, Macedon *B21*; 223-1221. L D $$
Flour City Diner: 50 Chestnut St., Rochester *DD5*; 546-6607. B L $
Gitsis Texas Hots: 600 Monroe Ave., Rochester *D5*; 271-8260. B L D $
Greenhouse Cafe at the Holiday Inn Rochester Airport: 911 Brooks Ave., Rochester *E11*; 328-6000. B L D $$
Hicks & McCarthy Restaurant: 23 S. Main St., Pittsford *F14*; 586-0938. B L D $$

Hogan's Hideaway: 197 Park Ave., Rochester *C4*; 442-4293. L D $$
Houlihan's Restaurant: 10 Square Drive, Victor *B21*; 223-4680. L D $$
Jines Restaurant: 658 Park Ave., Rochester *C5*; 461-1280. B L D $
Joe's Hide-Away: 4464 Lake Ave., Rochester *C12*; 581-0783. B L $
Keys Martini & Piano Bar: 233 Mill St., Rochester *BB2*; 232-5397. L D $$
Lamplighter Restaurant: 831 Fetzner Road, Greece *C11*; 225-2500. L D $$

The Rochester area has hundreds of restaurants serving everything from Italian to Ethiopian cuisine. Here, a chef gets busy at the Grill at Strathallan on East Avenue in the city.

On the waterfront

Looking for a place to enjoy a meal and a drink on the waterfront? Rochester is surrounded by water, from Lake Ontario to the Genesee River to the fabled Erie Canal. New restaurants are opening all the time.

Here's a partial list of waterfront eateries in or near the city:

Lake Ontario: A wall of windows is all that separates the **Crescent Beach Hotel** dining room from the lake. Whether it's stormy or sunny, the view is impressive.

Irondequoit Bay: Newport House Restaurant on the west side and **Bazil's** on the south end have expansive views of sparkling Irondequoit Bay, an inlet of Lake Ontario.

Genesee River: Pelican's Nest Waterfront Cafe is on the river near where it meets Lake Ontario. It has an expansive deck and a lively happy hour popular with boaters. The **Triphammer Grill** and **Jimmy**

Mac's Bar & Grill in the High Falls/ Browns Race Historic District overlook the 96-foot High Falls, where the Genesee River tumbles north on its way to Lake Ontario. **River Club Restaurant** in the Crowne Plaza Rochester has an east-facing view of the river and Genesee Crossroads Park. Across the river, **Pane Vino Ristorante**, an Italian restaurant tucked away on North Water Street in the St. Paul Quarter, has a commanding view. **Dinosaur Bar-B-Que** overlooks the Genesee River downtown. It's housed in the old Lehigh Valley Railroad train station.

Erie Canal: The historic

Richardson's Canal House in Bushnell's Basin was built in 1818. It once was a hotel for canal travelers. **Harbor House Cafe** in the village of Fairport was opened by the owners of the Colonial Belle, a canal tour boat. Born in the city, **Aladdin's Mediterranean** restaurant added a Pittsford location some years ago. It fronts the canal in Schoen Place, near the dock for the Sam Patch tour boat.

For information on waterfront dining in the Finger Lakes: www.fingerlakes.org

Lindburgers: 2157 Penfield Road, Penfield *E14*; 388-9420. L D $

Lorraine's Lunch Basket: 777 Culver Road, Rochester *C6*; 442-6574. B L D $

The Original Candy Kitchen: 4069 W. Main St., Williamson *A22*; (315) 589-9085. B L D $

The Original Char-Broil House: 1395 Island Cottage Road, Greece *C11*; 663-3860. B L D $

Pelican's Nest Restaurant: 566 River St., Rochester *C12*; 663-5910. L D $

Perkins Restaurant & Bakery: 1175 Jefferson Road, Henrietta *F12*; 475-1770. 2130 Fairport-Nine Mile Point Road, Fairport *F15*; 377-1690. 2047 Chili Avenue, Gates *E11*; 697-0725. 1500 W. Ridge Road, Greece *D11*; 581-8510. B L D $$

Pineapple Jack's: Colonial Plaza, 507 Spencerport Road, Spencerport *D10*; 247-5225. L D $

Remington's Restaurant: 425 Merchants Road, Rochester *D13*; 482-4434. L D $$$

River Club at Crowne Plaza Rochester: 70 State St., Rochester *CC3*; 546-3450. L D $

Scuttlebutt's: 431 River St., Rochester *C12*; 621-4650. D $

Simply Crepes Café: 7 Schoen Place, Pittsford *F14*; 383-8310. B L D $$

Steamboat Landing Restaurant & Banquet Facility: Home of the Canandaigua Lady: 205 Lakeshore Drive, Canandaigua *B21*; 396-7350. L D $$

Timothy Patrick's: 916 S. Panorama Trail, Penfield *E14*; 385-4160. L D $

Windjammers: 4695 Lake Ave., Rochester *C12*; 663-9691. L D $

The Crystal Barn in Pittsford, housed in an 1860s barn, serves continental cuisine with Victorian elegance.

GRILLS & PUBS

Bathtub Billy's Sports Bar & Restaurant: 630 W. Ridge Road, Rochester *D12*; 865-6510. L D $
Bennigan's Grill & Tavern: Clarion Riverside Hotel, 120 E. Main St., Rochester *CC4*; 232-3090. B L D $$
Bogey's Wood-Fired Grill: 2500 Ridgeway Avenue, Rochester *D11*; 720-0880. L D $

Buffalo Wild Wings: 382 Jefferson Road, Henrietta *F12*; 427-9464. L D $
The Distillery: 1142 Mt. Hope Ave., Rochester *E12*; 271-4105. L D $
J.G. Crummers: 1665 Penfield Road, Penfield *E14*; 264-0310. L D $
Jeremiah's Tavern: 1104 Monroe Ave., Rochester *E13*; 461-1313. L D $
Jimmy Mac's Bar & Grill: 104 Platt St., Rochester *BB2*; 232-5230. L D $

MacGregor's Grill and Taproom: 381 Gregory St., Rochester *D4*; 271-3592. 7408 Pittsford-Palmyra Road, Fairport *F15*; 425-7260. 300 Jefferson Road, Henrietta *F11*; 427-8410. 607 Coldwater Road, Gates *E10*; 247-7860. 759 S. Main Street, Canandaigua *B21*; 394-8080. L D $
Matthew's East End Grill: 200 East Ave., Rochester *CC6*; 454-4280. L D $
McFadden's Restaurant and Saloon: 60 Brown's Race, Rochester *BB2*; 325-1250. D $
Michael's Valley Grill: 1694 Penfield Road, Rochester *E14*; 383-8260. D $$
The Old Toad: 277 Alexander St., Rochester *DD7*; 232-2626. L D $
O'Mally's Irish Sports Pub Holiday Inn: 911 Brooks Ave., Gates *E11*; 328-6000. D $
Pittsford Pub: 60 N. Main St., Pittsford *F14*; 586-4650. L D $
Rohrbach Brewing Co. Inc.: 3859 Buffalo Road, Chili *D4*; 594-9800. L D $
State Street Bar and Grill at Crowne Plaza Rochester: 70 State St., Rochester *CC3*; 546-3450. D $$
Tully's Good Times: 1225 Jefferson Road, Henrietta *F12*; 272-8900. L D $
Woody's: 248 Monroe Ave., Rochester *EE6*; 546-6900. L D $

Pushcart dreams

Wegmans' drive began with an ambitious produce hawker

Wegmans Food Markets Inc. began in 1916, an outgrowth of a family grocery store on Fernwood Avenue. Son Walter worked in his parents' store, while his brother, John, peddled fresh produce in the streets from a pushcart.

Wegmans' signature innovation began early: John soon opened Rochester Fruit & Vegetable Co., and Walter joined him.

"I think it was a sign that they wanted to grow and expand, the very earliest signs of innovation from the Wegman family," says Jo Natale, the chain's director of media relations.

By 1921, the brothers had bought Seel Grocery Co. and Mahatchke Fruit Store, both on Main Street, and expanded into general groceries and bakery operations. In 1930, they opened their first "superstore," a 20,000-square-foot operation on Clinton Avenue that had cafeteria seating for 300.

The Wegmans continued to innovate. In the 1930s, the store brought refrigerated display windows and vaporized water sprays to keep produce fresh—two Rochester firsts. In 1974, Wegmans' East Rochester store became one of the first in the country to use laser scanning to read UPC codes.

Since then the chain has expanded to 70 stores in five states. It employs 35,000 people and has been named to *Forbes* magazine's list of the best companies to work for nine years in a row, reaching No. 1 in 2005. Wegmans' employee benefits, work-scholarship program and customer service are regularly applauded by industry experts.

Consumers can't seem to get enough of the chain's huge selection, sophisticated atmosphere and bend-over-backwards customer service. This focus on the customer, CEO Danny Wegman once told *Forbes* magazine, is "nearly telepathic."

Wegmans is so popular that the company in 2005 received 3,600 requests to open a new location and 3,500 shopper compliments.

These days, buses bring international tour groups to the 130,000-square-foot flagship store in Pittsford. The chain carries 70,000 items, including hundreds of cheeses from around the world, more than 700 varieties of produce, and gourmet meals hot and ready to pick up on the way home from work.

After nearly 90 years and numerous purchase offers, Wegmans remains family owned and operated. Walter's son, Robert Wegman, is chairman; his son Danny is CEO, and Danny's daughter Colleen is president.

www.wegmans.com

Woody's II: 2758 W. Henrietta Road, Henrietta *F12*; 424-6440. L D $

Zebb's Deluxe Grill and Bar: 1890 S. Clinton Ave., Brighton *E12*; 271-1440. L D $

FINE DINING

Avon Inn: 55 E. Main St., Avon *B20*; 226-8181. B (Sunday) D $$

Belhurst Castle – White Springs Manor: 4069 Route 14S, Geneva *B22*; (315) 781-0201. L D $$$

Bernard's Grove: 187 Long Pond Road, Greece *C11*; 227-6405. L D $$

The Big Tree Inn: 46 Main St., Geneseo *B20*; 243-5220. L D $$$

Bristol Harbour Resort: 5410 Seneca Point Road, Canandaigua *B21*; (800) 288-8248. B L D $$

The Clark House at Shadow Pines: 600 Whalen Road, Penfield *E14*; 385-3700. D $$$

Doubletree Hotel Rochester Bistro: 1111 Jefferson Road, Henrietta *F12*; 475-1510. B L D $$$

Edibles Restaurant: 704 University Ave., Rochester *C6*; 271-4910. L D $$

Erie Grill at the Del Monte Lodge: 41 N. Main St., Pittsford *F14*; 419-3032. B L D $$$

Gatherings at the Daisy Flour Mill: 1880 Blossom Road, Rochester *E13*; 293-2840. D $$$

The Grill at Strathallan: 550 East Ave., Rochester *C4*; 454-1880. B L D $$$

Grinnell's Restaurant: 1696 Monroe Ave., Brighton *E6*; 244-3710. D $$$

The Holloway House Restaurant: Routes 5 and 20, Bloomfield *B21*; 657-7120. Open April through early December. L D $$

Humphrey House Restaurant: 1783 Penfield Road, Penfield *E14*; 385-2685. L D $$$

Joey B's: 400 Packetts Landing, Fairport *F15*; 377-9030. D $$

Johnson House Restaurant: 19 S. Main St., Churchville *F8*; 293-1111. D $$

Lincoln Hill Inn: 3365 East Lake Road, Canandaigua *B21*; 394-8254. D $$$

Bushnell's Basin retains its 19th century charm in several buildings along the Erie Canal. This one houses Finger Lakes Coffee Roasters, a wholesale and retail operation that started in 1996.

Max Chophouse: 1456 Monroe Ave., Rochester *E12*; 271-3510. D $$$

Max of Eastman Place: 25 Gibbs St., Rochester *CC6*; 697-0491. L D $$$

Moscow's Eclectic Dining: 3208 Latta Road, Greece *C11*; 225-2880. D $$$

The Newport House: 500 Newport Road, Irondequoit *D13*; 467-8480. L D $$$

Nicole's at Canandaigua Inn on the Lake: 770 S. Main Street, Canandaigua *B21*; 394-7800. B L D $$

Park Avenue Pub: 650 Park Ave., Rochester *C5*; 461-4140. D $$$

Red Osier Landmark Restaurant: 6492 Main Road, Route 5, Stafford *B19*; 343-6972. D $$$

Relish!: 4135 Mill Street, Pultneyville *A22*; (315) 589-4512. D $$

Schooner's Riverside Pub: 70 Pattonwood Dr., Charlotte *C12*; 342-8363. L D $$

Sienna Contemporary Grill and Bar: 151 St. Paul St., Rochester *BB4*; 546-4070. D $$$

Tastings: 3195 Monroe Ave., Pittsford *F13*; 381-1881. L D $$$

Thendara Inn & Restaurant Boat House: 4356 E. Lake Road, Canandaigua *B21*; 394-4868. D $$$

Triphammer Grill: 60 Browns Race, Rochester *BB2*; 262-2700. L D $$

Asian

(also see Indian)

The Aja Noodle Co.: 2602 Elmwood Ave., Brighton *E6*; 244-1052. L D $

Bay Tree: 260 Park Ave., Rochester *E13*; 242-8540. L D $

California Rollin': Village Gate Square, 274 N. Goodman St., Rochester *C5*; 271-8990. 1000 North River St., Rochester. *C13*; 271-8920. L D $

Cantonese House: 3159 S. Winton Road, Henrietta *F13*; 272-9126. L D Dim sum on weekends $

Dac Hoa Restaurant: 230 Monroe Ave., Rochester *C4*; 232-6038. L D $

Esan Thai Restaurant: 696 Park Ave., Rochester *C5*; 271-2271. L D $

Flavors of Asia: 831 S. Clinton Ave., Rochester *D4*; 256-2310. L D $

Garden Restaurant: 1750 Monroe Avenue, Brighton *E13*; 241-3070. L D $$

Golden Dynasty Chinese Restaurant: Tops Plaza, 1900 S. Clinton Ave., Brighton *E4*; 442-6340. L D $

Golden Port Dim Sum: 105 East Ave., Rochester *CC6*; 256-1780. L D $

House of Poon: 2185 Monroe Ave., Brighton *E13*; 271-7371. L D $

House of Sushi: 101 East Ave., Rochester *CC6*; 546-2480. L D $

Jade Palace Chinese Restaurant: 602 Old Ridge Road, Webster *D14*; 671-5400. L D $

Joy Luck Garden Chinese Restaurant: Panorama Plaza, Penfield *E14*; 264-0990. L D $

K.C. Tea & Noodles: 360 Park Ave., Rochester *C5*; 271-1061. L D $

The King and I: 1455 E. Henrietta Road, Henrietta *F12*; 427-8090. L D $

Kobay Japanese Restaurant, Sushi on Park: 690 Park Ave., Rochester *C5*; 271-1060. L D $

Le Lemon Grass: 942 Monroe Ave., Rochester *D5*; 271-8360. L D $

Mamasan's: 309 University Ave., Rochester *BB7*; 262-4580. L $

Bruegger's Bagel Bakery has a location in the newly expanded Pittsford Community Library.

Martusciello Bakery & Deli: 2280 Lyell Ave., Rochester *E11*; 247-0510. S $
Montana Mills/Great Harvest Bread Co.: 210 Park Ave., Rochester *C5*; 697-0400. Twelve Corners Plaza, 1890 Monroe Ave., Brighton *E13*; 242-7544. S $
Patisserie Jean-Claude: Perinton Hills Mall, Fairport *F15*; 223-3150. B L S $
Rich Port International Baked Goods: 5 Public Market, Rochester *C3*; 232-6570. B S $
Savoia Pastry Shoppe: 2267 Clifford Ave., Rochester *D13*; 482-1130. S $

Coffee shops

Boulder Coffee Co.: 100 Alexander St., Rochester *DD7*; 454-7140. S $
Café Cibon: 688 Park Ave., Rochester *C5*; 461-2960. L D $
CanalTown Coffee Roasters: 1805 East Ave., Rochester *E13*; 271-6690. 6 S. Main St., Pittsford *F14*; 248-0390. S $
Cole & Parks Bakery, Café & Coffee Co.: 607 Rowley Road, Victor *B21*; 924-8710. B L S $
Daily Perks: 389 Gregory St., Rochester *D3*; 271-2340. S $
Earthtones Coffee House: 1217 Bay Road, Bay Centre, Webster *D14*; 671-3060. S $

2800 Monroe Ave., Pittsford *F14*; 461-3290. L D $
Pattaya Thai Restaurant: 1843 Penfield Road, Penfield *E14*; 383-6088. L D $
P. F. Chang's China Bistro: 820 EastView Mall, Victor *B21*; 223-2410. L D $$
Plum Garden: Pittsford Plaza, 3349 Monroe Ave., Pittsford *F13*; 381-8730. L D $
Plum House : 686 Monroe Ave., Rochester *D4*; 442-0778. L D $$
Seoul Garden Korean Restaurant: 2805 W. Henrietta Road, Henrietta *F12*; 424-2220. L D $
Shanghai Chinese Restaurant: 2920 W. Henrietta Road, Henrietta *F12*; 424-4000. L D Dim sum on Sunday $
Tokyo Japanese Restaurant: 2930 W. Henrietta Road, Henrietta *F12*; 424-4166. L D $$

Bagels & pastries

Bagel Bin: 2600 Elmwood Ave., Brighton *E13*; 461-4475. B L S $
Bagel Land: 1896 Monroe Ave., Brighton *E13*; 442-3080. B L S $
Baker Street Bakery: 745 Park Ave., Rochester *E13*; 241-3120. B L S $
Balsam Bagels: 288 N. Winton Road, Rochester *E13*; 482-5080. B L $
Bruegger's Bagel Bakery: (partial listing) 2496 W. Ridge Road, Greece *D11*; 723-9590. SouthTown Plaza, Henrietta *F12*; 424-6110. 133 Midtown Plaza, Rochester *CC5*; 232-8980. 548 Monroe Ave., Rochester *D4*; 256-3410. 585 Moseley Road, Fairport *F15*; 223-0450. 1950 Empire Blvd., Webster *D14*; 671-0720. B L D S $
Cheesy Eddie's: 602 South Ave., Rochester *D4*; 473-1300. S $
Gruttadauria Bakery: 1600 W. Ridge Road, Greece *C3*; 454-6979. S $
The Little Bakery: 89 Charlotte St., Rochester *CC7*; 232-4884. S $
Malek's Brighton Bakery: 1795 Monroe Ave., Brighton *E6*; 461-1720. S $

A burger and fries beckon at Black & Blue, a popular steak and seafood restaurant in Pittsford Plaza.

Fairport Village Coffee: 6 N. Main St., Fairport *F15*; 377-5880. S $
Finger Lakes Coffee Roasters: 616A Pittsford-Victor Road, Bushnell's Basin *F14*; 249-9310. Pittsford Plaza, 3349 Monroe Ave., Pittsford *F13*; 385-0750. S $
Java's: 16 Gibbs St., Rochester *CC6*; 232-4820. L S $
Montana Mills/Great Harvest Bread Co.: 210 Park Ave., Rochester *C5*; 697-0400. L S $
Spin Caffe: 2 State St., Rochester *CC3*; 454-6340. 739 Park Ave., Rochester *C3*; 506-9550. 229 Mill Street, Rochester *BB2*; 232-1070. L S $
Spot Coffee: 200 East Ave., Rochester *CC6*; 613-4600. B L S $
Starbucks: 1380 Mt. Hope Ave., Rochester *E3*; 271-7330. 680 Monroe Ave., Rochester *D5*; 244-4545. 1930 Monroe Ave., Brighton *E6*; 442-6410. 2900 Monroe Ave., Pittsford *F13*; 381-2140. 5 State St., Pittsford *F14*: 586-8290.

1100 Jefferson Road, Henrietta *F12*; 424-2190. 2150 W. Ridge Road, Greece *D11*; 723-3220. 2255 E. Ridge Road, Irondequoit *D13*; 342-1460. 1806 Penfield Road, Penfield *E14*; 383-0250. 6720 Pittsford-Palmyra Road, Fairport *F15*; 223-4240. S $
Starry Nites Café: 696 University Ave., Rochester *C5*; 271-2630. L D S $
Women's Coffee Connection: 642 South Ave., Rochester *D4*; 442-2180. B L S $

Caribbean

Chimo's Sandwich Shop: 1038 N. Clinton Ave., Rochester *D12*; 266-1405. L D $
El Conquistador: 1939 Clifford Ave., Rochester *D13*; 288-4160. L D $
L J's II Jamaican Cuisine: 38 St. Paul St., Rochester *CC4*; 232-5420. L D $

Continental

Bamba Bistro: 282 Alexander St., Rochester *DD7*; 244-8680. L D $$$
Crystal Barn: A "hidden treasure" in fine dining! A pleasant blend of crystal chandeliers and Victorian motifs set in an authentic 1860 country barn—an unusually comfortable and elegant atmosphere for a unique dining experience. Savor an original contemporary culinary creation or enjoy exquisite traditional cuisine at its best. 2851 Clover St., Pittsford *F13*; 381-4844. L D $$$
Cutler's Restaurant: Memorial Art Gallery, 500 University Ave., Rochester *C5*; 473-6380. L D $$$
E.J.'s at the Rochester Marriott Airport Hotel: 1890 W. Ridge Road, Greece *D11*; 225-6880. B L D $$$
Hedges 9 Mile Point Restaurant: 1290 Lake Road, Webster *C15*; 265-3850. L D $$$
Horizons Restaurant at the Lodge at Woodcliff: 199 Woodcliff Drive, Fairport *G14*; 248-4825. B L D $$$
The Mundo Grill: 2833 Monroe Ave., Brighton *E13*; 442-2840. L D $$$
Phillips European Restaurant: 26 Corporate Woods, Brighton *F12*; 272-9910. L D $$$
Restaurant 2 Vine: 24 Winthrop St., Rochester *CC6*; 454-6020. L D $$
Richardson's Canal House: 1474 Marsh Road, Pittsford *F14*; 248-5000. L D $$$
The RIT Inn & Conference Center: 5257 W. Henrietta Road, Henrietta *F11*; 359-1800. B L D $$

Dining Spotlight

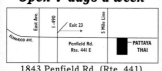

A world of cuisines

Rochester's dining scene has big-city variety

If you're hungry for something different but can't decide what mood your taste buds are in, welcome to Rochester, where dining out is a favorite pastime for many.

"Rochester has an incredible diversity of ethnic restaurants," says Michael Warren Thomas, a local food critic. "That's what I hear from people who come to our area. They're surprised at how many different ones we have."

The quality of the cuisine also is impressive, he adds. "People who travel to New York City have told me our ethnic restaurants are better than the very good ones in New York that they search out."

Rochester has quite a few **Indian** restaurants that are "all very good," Thomas says. One of the newest is Tandoor in Henrietta. Its sister restaurant, Thali of India, serves food from many different regions of India. Other favorites are India House and India House Café, Raj Mahal, India Palace and India Café.

A new **Thai** restaurant opens seemingly every year, much to the delight of Rochesterians, who can't seem to get enough ginger and coconut curry. "You could have a full week of different Thai restaurants," Thomas says. "There are excellent ones across the board."

The King and I in Henrietta is often the first on people's lips, but other favorites are Esan on Park Avenue, Puket Thai on Empire Boulevard, Pattaya Thai on Penfield Road and Thai Taste on Mt. Hope Avenue.

A growing number of restaurants are offering multi-ethnic **Asian** menus including Thai, Chinese and dim sum. Flavors of Asia and Golden Port Dim Sum have loyal followings.

For **Japanese** and **sushi** cravings, try California Rollin', a hopping joint in Village Gate Square; House of Sushi near Eastman School of Music in the city; Shiki on South Clinton Avenue; Tokyo in Henrietta; and sister restaurants Plum House on Monroe Avenue in the city and Plum Garden in Pittsford.

The flavorful, sometimes spicy dishes of **Ethiopia** can be found at Dashen and Abyssinia. "Ethiopian food is something everyone should try," Thomas says. "It's served on a single platter—no plates, no silverware."

Oddly, for a city where a quarter of the population has **German** roots, there are no strictly German restaurants. Swan's Market, a German sausage shop and meat market on Parsells Avenue, serves German lunches Wednesday through Friday. Ralf's European Meats & Delicatessen on Dewey Avenue does the same. The owner of Flour City Diner in the East End makes his own sausage based on the former owner's recipe.

The best place for **Greek** food in Rochester, Thomas says, is the nearly 30-year-old Olive Tree on Monroe Avenue in the city. "I try to go in every month or so." Olive's Greek Taverna in Pittsford is another intimate option.

For authentic **Mexican** cuisine in the Rochester area, foodies agree El Rincon, in Sodus and Canandaigua, is the best. Chilango's in Spencerport also is a critics' favorite. Everything is homemade from scratch.

Like many cities in the Northeast, Rochester has an abundance of **Italian** restaurants. Thomas likes Ristorante Lucano on East Avenue for its homemade, authentic Italian food. Rocky's on Jay Street and Mr. Dominic's in Charlotte have been serving up cozy Italian American food to generations of Rochesterians.

Olga's, on East Ridge Road in Irondequoit, serves **Polish** and **Eastern European** food like pierogies and cabbage rolls. **Jamaican** restaurant LJ's Jamaican Cuisine on St. Paul Street has a loyal following. Critics like **Pakistan** House in Henrietta. The Old Toad on Alexander Street serves authentic **British** pub fare. Popular **Mediterranean** cuisine is served at Aladdin's, Sinbad's and, with a Turkish influence, Mediterranean Cuisine next door to Olga's in Irondequoit.

Thomas has assembled a searchable database of more than 800 restaurants in Greater Rochester. He updates it every month or two (except for hours, so call ahead). It's available to download at his web site, www.savorlife.com.

Biaggi's Ristorante Italiano has a location at EastView Mall in Victor.

Rooney's Restaurant: 90 Henrietta St., Rochester *D4*; 442-0444. D $$$
Tapas 177 Lounge: 177 St. Paul St., Rochester *BB4*; 262-2090. D $$
Warfield's Restaurant & Bakery: 7 W. Main St., Clifton Springs *B21*; (315) 462-7184. L D $$
Winfield Grill: 647 N. Winton Road, Rochester *E13*; 654-8990. L D $$

Ethiopian

Abyssinia: 80 University Ave., Rochester *BB6*; 262-3910. L D $
Dashen: 503 South Ave., Rochester *D4*; 232-2690. D $

Greek

Mykonos Cafe: 3423 Winton Place, Rochester *E13*; 475-0040. B L D $
Mykonos Express Greek Cuisine: 1330 Mt. Hope Avenue, Rochester, *F13*; 271-5220. L D $
Olive's Greek Taverna: Northfield Commons, 50 State St., Pittsford *C14*; 381-3990. L D $
The Olive Tree: 165 Monroe Ave., Rochester *EE6*; 454-3510. L D $$

Hots & hamburgers

Bill Gray's Restaurant: (partial listing) 941 Hard Road, Webster *D14*; 671-0584. Perinton Square Mall, Fairport *F15*; 223-1820. 2987 Buffalo Road, Gates *E11*; 247-3940. 1650 Penfield Road, Penfield *E14*; 385-3450. 3240 Chili Ave., Rochester *C4*; 889-8260. 4870 Culver Road, Seabreeze *C13*; 266-7820. 1225 Jefferson Road, Henrietta *F12*; 424-2350. L D $
Don's Original: 4900 Culver Road, Seabreeze *C13*; 323-1177. 2545 Monroe Ave., Brighton *E13*; 244-2080. 2055 Fairport-Nine Mile Point Road, Penfield *E15*; 377-1040. L D $
LDR Char Pit: 4753 Lake Ave., Rochester *C12*; 865-0112. B L D $
Nick Tahou Hots: 320 Main St. W., Rochester *DD1*; 436-0184. 2260 Lyell Ave., Gates *E11*; 429-6388. B L D $
Roc City Hots: 336 East Ave., Rochester *DD7*; 232-4687. L D $
Schaller's Brighton: 2747 W. Henrietta Road, Brighton *F12*; 427-7810. L D $
Schaller's Drive-In: 965 Edgemere Drive, Greece *B11*; 865-3319. L D $
Schaller's Ridge Road: 559 E. Ridge Road, Irondequoit *D12*; 544-2097. L D $
Tom Wahl's Restaurant: (partial listing) 283 E. Main St., Avon *B20*; 226-2420. 643 Pittsford-Victor Road, Pittsford *G14*; 586-4920. Marketplace Mall, Henrietta *F12*; 427-0460. EastView Mall *B21*; 425-4860. 40 Greece Ridge Center, Greece *D11*; 227-2950. L D $
Vic & Irv's Hots and Burgers: 4880 Culver Road, Seabreeze *C13*; 544-7680. L D $

Indian

India Café: 651 Monroe Ave., Rochester *D4*; 256-1210. L D $

Save room for the funnel cake a la mode at Bazil Restaurant.

India House Restaurant: 998 S. Clinton Ave., Rochester *D4*; 461-0880. 7343 Pittsford-Victor Road, Victor *B21*; 742-2030. L D $

India Palace: Tops Brighton Plaza, 1900 S. Clinton Ave., Brighton *E4*; 271-2100. L D $

Raj Mahal: 324 Monroe Ave., Rochester *C4*; 546-2315. L D $

Tandoor of India: Jefferson Plaza, 376 Jefferson Road, Henrietta *F12*; 427-7080. L D $

Thali of India : 3259 S. Winton Road, Henrietta *F13*; 427-8030. L D $

Italian

Agatina's Restaurant & Party House: 2967 Buffalo Road, Gates *E10*; 426-0510. L D $$

Bacco's Ristorante: 263 Park Ave., Rochester *C5*; 442-5090. D $$

Bazil Restaurant: A casual Italian kitchen is the newest Italian restaurant addition to Rochester. We have traditional Italian items, such as veal saltimbocca, chicken marsala, fish fry, Italian stone oven pizzas, homemade lasagna and more. You can also create your own pasta dish—choose your pasta, sauce and toppings. All dinner entrees include all-you-can-eat salad and breadsticks. For dessert, try our famous carnival-style funnel cake! Full bar and wine list. Outdoor seating available in season. 749 E. Henrietta Road, Henrietta *F12*; 427-7420. 1384 Empire Blvd., Webster *D13*; 697-2006. L weekend D $$

Bellanca's Portside Restaurant: 4768 Lake Ave., Rochester *C12*; 663-8488. L D $$

Benucci's Contemporary Italian Cuisine: 3349 Monroe Ave., Pittsford *F13*; 264-1300. L D $$

Biaggi's Ristorante Italiano: Serving fresh, affordable Italian cuisine, including award-winning pastas, salads, steaks, chicken, veal, fresh fish and seafood. Extensive wine list. Comfortable atmosphere. Casual dress. Children always welcome. Open 11 a.m. daily. Credit cards and reservations are accepted. Call for private events. 818 EastView Mall, Victor *B21*; 223-2290. L D $$

Bocaccinis Bistro & Bar: Perinton Square Mall, 6720 Pittsford-Palmyra Road, Fairport *F15*; 421-8200. L D $$

DaVinci Restaurant: 1500 W. Ridge Road, Greece *D11*; 663-3360. L D $$

Mario's Via Abruzzi: Rochester's most authentic Italian dining experience. The atmosphere captures the sights and sounds of Italy, with strolling accordion players every Saturday evening and satellite-fed Italian festive music every night. Family operated for over 23 years. Serving dinners seven days a week and our famous Sunday brunch from 10 a.m. until 3 p.m. Full bar, 2000 to 2002 Wine Spectator Award of Excellence wine list and after-dinner cordials. Fresh seafood specials daily, veal, chicken, steaks, filets, calamari, homemade pasta and much more. Reservations recommended. 2740 Monroe Ave., Brighton *E13*; 271-1111. D $$

Mr. Dominic's on the Lake: 4699 Lake Ave., Charlotte *C12*; 865-4630. L D $$

NapaGino's Restaurant: 2200 Penfield Road, Penfield *E14*; 377-2570. L D $

Northside Inn: 311 N. Washington St., East Rochester *E14*; 248-3470. L D $

Palladio at the Hyatt Regency Rochester: 125 E. Main St., Rochester *CC4*; 423-6767. B L D $$

Pane Vino Ristorante: 175 N. Water Street, Rochester *BB3*; 232-6090. L D $$

Pasghetti's Casual Italian Cuisine: 211 N. Main St., East Rochester *E14*; 586-2340. B L D $$

Perlo's: 202 N. Washington St., East Rochester *E14*; 248-5060. D $$

Pomodoro Grill & Wine Bar: 1290 University Ave., Rochester *C6*; 271-5000. L D $$

The most-requested pies at Veneto Wood Fired Pizza & Pasta are the Greek, the pollo and the basic margherita.

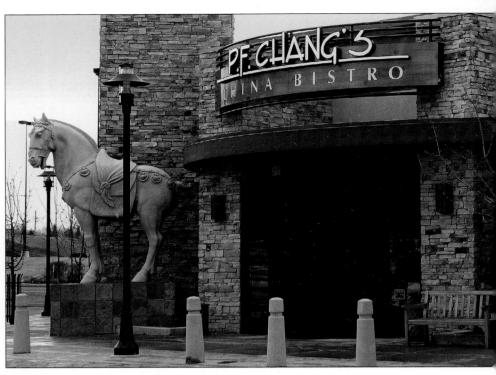

P.F. Chang's China Bistro, part of a chain out of Arizona, does a bustling business in EastView Mall.

Portobello Ristorante: 2171 W. Henrietta Road, Henrietta *F12*; 427-0110. L D $$
Proietti's Italian Restaurant: Webster Plaza, 980 E. Ridge Road, Webster *D14*; 872-2330. D $$$
Red Fedele's Brook House: 920 Elmridge Center Drive, Greece *D11*; 723-9988. L D $
Ricci's Family Restaurant: 3166 Latta Road, Greece *C11*; 227-6750. L D $
Ristorante Lucano: 1815 East Ave., Rochester *C4*; 244-3460. L D $$
Rocky's: 190 Jay St., Rochester *AA1*; 232-9717. L D $
Romano's Macaroni Grill: 760 Jefferson Road, Henrietta *F12*; 427-8230. L D $
Roncone's Restaurant: 1749 East Ave., Rochester *E13*; 244-1160. L D $
Tuscany's Italian Trattoria: Culver Ridge Plaza, 2255 E. Ridge Road, Irondequoit *D13*; 266-5510. L D $$

Kosher

Brownstein's: 1862 Monroe Ave., Brighton *E13*; 442-2770. *Rabbi Henry Hyman, Cong. Ahavas Achim. Baked goods only.*
Chabad Café: 1037 S. Winton Road, Rochester *F13* ; 271-0330. *Rabbi Dovid Mochkin.*
Dunkin' Donuts: 1760 Monroe Ave., Brighton *E13*; 271-6940. *Rabbi Shaya Kilimnick, Cong. Beth Sholom.*
Freshens Yogurt: EastView Mall, Victor *B21*; 425-8930. *Chicago Rabbinical Council.*
Friendly's: 2717 Monroe Ave., Pittsford *F13*; 442-6400. *KVH — Vaad HaRabonim of New England. Ice cream only.*
Geulah's Kosher Cafe and Deli: Jewish Community Center, 1200 Edgewood Ave., Rochester *F13*; 461-2000. *Rabbi Henry Hyman, Cong. Ahavas Achim.*
Jewish Home of Rochester Cafeteria: 2001 S. Winton Road, Rochester *F13*; 427-7760. *Rabbi Shaya Kilimnick, Cong. Beth Sholom.*
Krispy Kreme Doughnuts: 1150 Jefferson Road, Henrietta *F12*; 424-7370. *Rabbis Shaya Kilimnick and Chaim Hisiger.*
Lipman's Kosher Market: 1482 Monroe Ave., Brighton *E13*; 271-7886. *Rabbi Chaim Hisiger, Rochester Kosher Service.*
Malek's Brighton Bakery: 1795 Monroe Ave., Brighton *E13*; 461-1720. *Rabbi Shaya Kilimnick, Cong. Beth Sholom.*
Nosh Kosher Deli: Douglass Hall, University of Rochester *E12*; 275-3978. *Rabbi Eric Grosser.*

Mediterranean

Aladdin's Natural Eatery: 646 Monroe Ave., Rochester *D4*; 442-5000. 8 Schoen Place, Pittsford *F14*; 264-9000. L D $
Alexandria Mediterranean Cuisine: 120 East Ave., Rochester *CC6*; 232-6180. L D $
Basha Mediterranean Eatery: 798 S. Clinton Ave., Rochester *D4*; 256-1370. L D $
Brio Mediterranean Bistro: 3400 Monroe Ave., Pittsford *F13*; 586-7000. L D $$

Oasis Mediterranean Bistro: 687 Monroe Ave., Rochester *D4*; 473-0050. D $
Sinbad's Mediterranean Cuisine: 719 Park Ave., Rochester *C5*; 473-5655. L D $

Mexican/South American

Chilango's Mexican Restaurant: 42 Nichols St., Spencerport *D9*; 349-3030. L D $
Desert Moon: 1475 E. Henrietta Road, Henrietta *F12*; 424-2990. L D $
Don Pablo's Mexican Kitchen: 780 Jefferson Road, Henrietta *F12*; 424-6860. L D $
El Rincon Mexicano: 6974 Old Ridge Road, Sodus *A22*; (315) 483-4199. 5 Beeman St., Canandaigua *B21*; 394-3580. L D $
Juan & Maria's Empanada Stop: Rochester Public Market, 280 N. Union St., Rochester *B5*; 325-6650. B L $
Los Amigos Mexican Restaurant: 1859 Penfield Road, Penfield *E14*; 385-1410. L D $
Mex Restaurant : 295 Alexander St., Rochester *DD7*; 262-3060. D $
Paola's Burrito Place and Mexican Grill: 1921 South Ave., Rochester *F3*; 271-3655. L D $
Salena's Mexican Restaurant: Village Gate Square, 274 N. Goodman St., Rochester *C5*; 256-5980. L D $

Pizza

Rochester has way too many pizza places to list here. Your best bet is to check the yellow pages for detailed listings and coupons. When you call to order, don't be shy: Ask if they make New York style (thin and crispy) or a lighter, breadier crust. We have plenty of both here. Single local shops make some of the best pizza around, but local chains have established a neighborhood presence: Pontillo's Pizzeria, Mark's Pizzeria and Salvatore's Pizza, to name a few. If you would rather go with a tried-and-true chain, you'll find Pizza Hut, Domino's Pizza, Papa John's Pizza and Pizzeria Uno. The

following are local dine-in restaurants that specialize in wood-fired, gourmet pizzas.

Great Northern Pizza Kitchens: 1918 Monroe Ave., Brighton *E6*; 244-7437. 2750 Ridge Road W., Greece *D11*; 458-7437. 14 S. Main St., Pittsford *F14*; 586-7437. L D $
Panzari's Italian Bistro: 321 Exchange Blvd., Rochester *EE3*; 546-7990. L D $
Pizza Café: Suburban Plaza, 2199 E. Henrietta Road, Henrietta *F12*; 334-2321. D $
Veneto Woodfired Pizza & Pasta: 318 East Ave., Rochester *CC7*; 454-5444. L D $

Steak & seafood

Black & Blue Steak & Crab: Pittsford Plaza, 3349 Monroe Avenue, Rochester *F13*; 421-8111. L D $$$
The Cartwright Inn Restaurant: 5691 W. Henrietta Road, West Henrietta *G11*; 334-4444. L D $$
Castaways: 244 Lake Road, Webster *C13*; 323-2943. L D $$
Conesus Inn: 5654 E. Lake Road, Conesus *B20*; 346-6100. D $$$
Joe's Mendon House: 1369 Pittsford-Mendon Road, Mendon *B21*; 624-7370. D $$
Gordon's Steak & Crab House: 155 Pattonwood Drive, Irondequoit *C12*; 323-2722. D $$
Hawthorne's Restaurant: 3500 East Ave., Rochester *E13*; 385-4959. L D $$
Max Chophouse: 1456 Monroe Ave., Rochester *E12*; 271-3510. D $$$
Oatka Steak and Seafood Restaurant: 17 Main St., Scottsville *G10*; 889-7350. D $$$
Outback Steakhouse: 1180 Jefferson Road, Henrietta *F12*; 424-6880. 1954 Ridge Road W., Greece *D11*; 453-0640. D $$
Peter Geyer's Steak House at the Brookwood Inn: 800 Pittsford-Victor Road, Bushnell's Basin *G14*; 248-9300 or 248-9000. B L D $$$
Pittsford Seafood Restaurant and Raw Bar: 510 Monroe Ave., Rochester *C4*; 271-1780. L D $$

Red Lobster: 655 Jefferson Road, Henrietta *F12*; 424-2060. 1515 W. Ridge Road, Greece *D11*; 663-8360. L D $$

Rick's Prime Rib House: 898 Buffalo Road, Chili *E11*; 235-2900. L D $$$

Schoen Place Prime Rib & Grill: Northfield Commons, 50 State St., Pittsford *F14*; 586-5286. D $$$

Scotch 'n' Sirloin: Rochester's steakhouse since 1972. Serving millions of satisfied customers the finest steaks, fresh seafood and specialty dishes in our rustic, Vermont-style setting. Our Midwestern corn-fed USDA Choice beef is aged and hand-cut on our premises. Our seafood is brought in daily from the Boston seaport. Extensive wine list. 3450 Winton Place, Brighton *F13*; 427-0808. D $$$

Shamrock Jack's Steak & Seafood: 4554 Culver Road, Irondequoit *C13*; 323-9310. L D $$

Streb's Steak & Seafood House: 4464 W. Ridge Road, Greece *D10*; 352-1400. D $$$

Tournedos: 26 Broadway, Rochester *CC6*; 269-3888 L D $$$$

Subs, soups & sandwiches

Bagel Bin: *See Bagels & Pastries*
Balsam Bagels: *See Bagels & Pastries*
Bee-Licious Foods: Powers Building, 16 W. Main St., Rochester *CC3*; 454-5920. B L $
Brownstein's Deli & Bakery: 1862 Monroe Ave., Brighton *E6*; 442-2770. B L $
Bruegger's Bagel Bakery: *See Bagels & Pastries*
Camille's Sidewalk Cafe: 657 Park Ave., Rochester *C5*; 442-4986. Pittsford Plaza, 3349 Monroe Ave., Pittsford *E13*; 383-5660. B L D $
Classy Cookie & Deli: 111 Park Ave., Rochester *C4*; 271-5309. L S $
Corky's Craving Parlor: 1136 Monroe Ave., Brighton *D5*; 461-0090. L D $
DiBella's Old-Fashioned Submarines: (partial listing): 1900 S. Clinton Ave., Brighton *E4*; 256-2060. 420 Jefferson Road, Henrietta *F12*; 475-1831. 1900 Empire Blvd., Webster *D14*; 787-1320. L D $
Fox's Gourmet Delicatessen Restaurant: 3450 Winton Place, Suite 15, Henrietta *F13*; 427-8200. L $
The Full Belly Deli: 1225 Jefferson Road, Henrietta *F12*; 292-0210. B L $
Julienne's Catering: 429 South Ave., Rochester *D4*; 232-3290. L $
Little Theatre Café: 240 East Ave., Rochester *CC6*; 258-0400. D $
Magnolia's Market & Deli: 366 Park Ave., Rochester *E13*; 271-7380. L D S $
Nathan's Old-Fashioned Soups: 691 Park Ave., Rochester *C5*; 461-3005. L S $
Open Face Sandwich Eatery: 651 South Ave., Rochester *C3*; 232-3050. L D $
Orange Glory Cafe: 240 East Ave., Rochester *CC6*; 232-7340. L $
Palermo's Sub Station: Brighton-Pittsford Plaza, 3349 Monroe Ave., Pittsford *E13*; 218-9500. 3545 Buffalo Road, *E11*; 594-8400. L D $
Pickle Nicks Submarines: 1601 Howard Road, Gates *E11*; 426-7827. 339 Jefferson Road, Henrietta *F12*; 697-1802. L D $
Rubino's Italian Submarines: (partial listing) 349 W. Commercial St., East Rochester *B3*; 387-0760. 362 State St., Rochester *BB1*; 454-

3850. 1304 E. Ridge Road, Irondequoit *D13*; 544-5680. L D $
Starry Nites Café: 696 University Ave., Rochester *C5*; 271-2630. S L D $

Vegetarian/veggie options

The Aja Noodle Co.: 2602 Elmwood Ave., Brighton *E6*; 244-1052. L D $
Aladdin's Natural Eatery: 646 Monroe Ave., Rochester *D4*; 442-5000. 8 Schoen Place, Pittsford *F14*; 264-9000. L D $
Basha Mediterranean Eatery: 798 S. Clinton Ave. Rochester *D4*; 256-1370. L D $
Basta Pasta: Bring your own wine. 741 Monroe Ave., Rochester *D5*; 442-4599. L D $
Breathe Yoga & Juice Bar: 19 S. Main St., Pittsford *F15*; 248-9070. S L $

Brio Mediterranean Bistro: 3400 Monroe Ave., Pittsford *F13*; 586-7000. L D $$
India House Vegetarian Cafe: 1009 S. Clinton Ave., Rochester *C4*; 271-0242. L D $
The King and I: 1455 E. Henrietta Road, Henrietta *F12*; 427-8090. L D $
Mamasan's: 309 University Ave., Rochester *BB7*; 262-4580 L $. 2800 Monroe Ave., Pittsford *F14*; 461-3290. L D $
New Health Cafe: 288 Monroe Ave., Rochester *D4*; 325-1831. B L $
Oasis Mediterranean Bistro: 687 Monroe Ave., Rochester *D4*; 473-0050. L D $
Sinbad's Mediterranean Cuisine: 719 Park Ave., Rochester *C5*; 473-5655. L D $
Skippy's Vegetarian Restaurant: 742 South Ave., Rochester *C3*; 271-7590. L D $

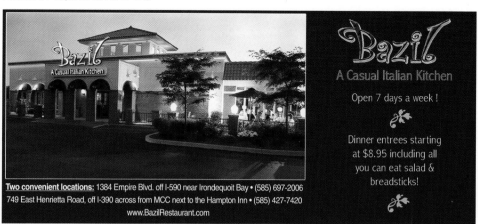

Dining Index

shopping

Shopping

In the 19th century, the phrase "Rochester made" was synonymous with quality craftsmanship, particularly in clothing and shoes. This emphasis on quality remains in the homegrown stores that have bloomed here in the years since. Local retailers have built international reputations for well-made merchandise and an abiding concern for the customer.

Shop owners keep tabs on customer tastes and industry trends. The result is merchandise with a unique Rochester flair. We're known particularly for handmade artwork, crafts, jewelry and clothing. Some stores feature one-of-a-kind items made by artists who live in the area, as well as the nearby Finger Lakes, Adirondack Mountains and New England. Others import crafts directly from artists overseas.

With its healthy per-capita income and employment levels, Rochester has become known as a market receptive to leading chain retailers, especially in recent years. Like the smaller, independent shops, area malls and plazas constantly expand and refresh their offerings in tune with trends and consumer demand. So no matter what you are looking for, you are bound to find it here.

Popular shopping destinations

MONROE AVENUE

Beginning at the Inner Loop near Strong Museum and ending six miles away in the suburb of Pittsford, Monroe Avenue is one long shopping district. We've divided it into three sections:

Oxford Square

This strip of Monroe in the city bills itself as a shopper's "mallternative." The street offers a variety of unusual clothing, gifts, shoes, poster art, books and antiques. Archimage is a street institution. The store is crammed with bongos and other musical instruments, Japanese dishes, gag gifts, toys, journals, jewelry, clothing and lots more from around the world. At Aaron's Alley, you'll find vintage and funky clothing. If you are a fan of used books, Brownbag Bookshop and Rick's Recycled Books have plenty to offer. Poster Art and Mercury Poster carry thousands of posters, prints and cards.

Brighton

On the stretch through Brighton, Monroe Avenue is lined with locally owned shops that have been serving the neighborhood for half a century or more. Along with kosher delis, bagel shops, tailors and salons, you'll find home furnishings, clothiers, shoe stores and gift shops. Among the highlights: Tuthill Lighting is a third-generation family business. Working with the Smithsonian, Tuthill restored the lighting in the George Eastman House. Cooks' World is a favorite stop for amateur chefs. The gourmet kitchen store, which has a popular online retailing component, carries cookware, cutlery, appliances and gifts.

Pittsford

As you cross the town line into Pittsford, you'll find local shops dotted among popular big-box retailers and plazas. The Bird House offers garden and bird-sanctuary gifts and accessories. Cornell Jewelers and Mann's Jewelers are family businesses with national reputations and roots in the city. Inspiration Designs sells designer women's apparel from New York. And this is where you'll find the largest local Wegmans. The Rochester-based grocery chain, praised for customer service and gourmet-food selection, is a popular stop for visitors. One World Goods, in Pittsford Plaza, sells fair-trade crafts, home accessories and toys made around the world.

PARK AVENUE

Not far from Monroe Avenue lies this winding, tree-shaded street. Surrounded by neighborhoods full of rambling Victorians, Park Avenue has a relaxed ambience that belies its city location. Pockets of shopping can be found between Alexander Street and Culver Road. Parkleigh anchors the corner at Park and Goodman. This Rochester landmark began life as a pharmacy; these days it sells an eclectic mix of goods, from Joseph Schmidt chocolates to the MacKenzie-Childs collection. Across the street, A Step Apart carries men's and women's shoes (and apparel) by Kenneth Cole, Diesel, Think! and more. Talulah Petunia sells antiques and gifts. East of Goodman Street on Park, the Dutch Market sells Dutch and Indonesian gifts and food. Eleventh Hour Gift Shop features jewelry, journals, gifts for kids and lots of cookbooks. Jembetat African Art Gallery has tribal art and jewelry. Stocked with wines from around the world, Wine Sense

Cornell's Jewelers, founded in 1923, is one of only 125 couture stores in the country.

offers free tastings twice a week.

CANAL TOWNS

Pittsford

When Monroe Avenue reaches the village of Pittsford, it becomes State Street. The village has retained much of its 19th and early 20th century charm. Small shops line both sides of Main and State, and the north side of the Erie Canal. Each of these areas is fine for browsing and strolling.

Take State Street over the canal and turn left. This is Northfield Commons, where you'll find Harmony in Wood, which has sold handmade wooden toys, clocks, boxes and other gifts for more than 30 years. Pottery and handcrafts can be found at the Pedestal. The Map Shop carries globes, flags and—you guessed it—maps of all kinds. Just west on the canal is Schoen Place, where tour boats dock and people feed the ducks. Among the shops here is Towpath Bike Stop, which not only sells bikes and apparel but rents out bikes for long rides on the canal. Naples Creek Leather sells Birkenstock and other shoe lines. Mostly Clay is full of gift possibilities in pottery, jewelry and leather.

Fairport

In this Erie Canal town, you'll find interesting shops and the relaxed pace to enjoy them.

Visitors combine a lunch in the park with a stroll along the water, and then head down Main Street for some shopping. It's a great place to find unusual gifts and antiques.

Lombardi's Gourmet Imports and Specialties carries a complete line of Portmeirion products and Paul Cardew teapots. Cooking gear and foods are in abundance. Located in a Victorian house, the Toy Soldier is full of fun stuff for kids. Besides home furnishings, Diane Prince Furniture carries gifts and collectibles, including Dedham Pottery and Byer's Choice Ltd. Anything Goes and One Enchanted Evening have racks of quality clothing at consignment prices. Gift shops include Fairport Antiques.

Spencerport

West of the bustle of Greece's commercial strip, West Ridge Road takes a step back in time and rolls through farmland. Along this road, you'll find Ridge Antiques and Willowcreek Antiques. While you're out, stop at Towpath Park in Spencerport, which has a picnic shelter and benches. Pleasure boats often dock or stay overnight here along the canal.

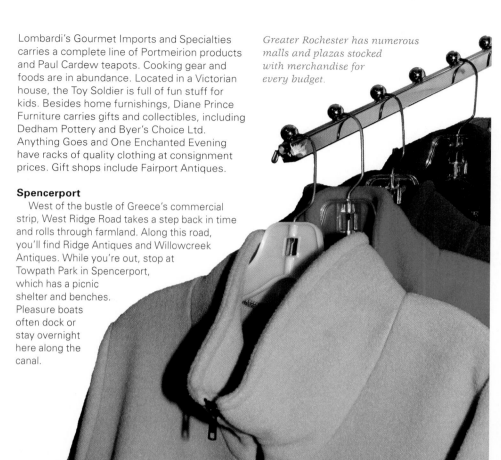

Greater Rochester has numerous malls and plazas stocked with merchandise for every budget.

A visit to Craft Company No. 6, located in a former city firehouse, is a feast in color and design.

Brockport

This canal village is home to a State University of New York campus. Its well-kept Victorian mansions and cottages line streets that lead the way to Brockport's business district. Lift Bridge Books is a favorite for book lovers, and Tea for Two has tea, jams, jellies and soaps. In town and the surrounding area, antique collectors seek out Lone Pine Collective. Hurd Orchards in nearby Holley has been featured in *Martha Stewart Living*

magazine. Have a picnic in Harvester Park and check out the Park Avenue lift bridge over the canal.

MALLS AND PLAZAS

Feel like malling? Rochester has several major shopping centers to choose from. **EastView Mall** and the surrounding area in Victor, off I-490 near I-90, is busy with expansion, offering many of the most popular retailers. **Pittsford Plaza** on Monroe Avenue and smaller nearby plazas house independent and chain retailers. Henrietta has major chains on Jefferson Road, Hylan Drive, and East and West Henrietta roads; the **Marketplace**, right in the center of all the action, was the area's

first regional mall when it was built in the early 1980s. Nearby **SouthTown Plaza** remains a strong visitor attraction and recently received a facelift. Along Chili Avenue in Gates you'll find a revived and expanded **Westgate Plaza**. It's a short drive down Brooks Avenue to the Greater Rochester International Airport. The **Mall at Greece Ridge Center**, on Ridge Road in Greece, was created with the blending of the former Long Ridge and Greece Towne malls during the 1990s. It anchors a busy retail corridor along West Ridge Road in Greece. On East Ridge Road in Irondequoit, **Culver-Ridge** and **Ridgeview Plazas** are busy. Target and other national retailers can be found at the newly revitalized **Medley Centre**. In Webster, Barnes & Noble, Dick's Sporting Goods, Target and Kohl's can be found in the **Towne Center at Webster** on Holt Road. In downtown Rochester, **Midtown Plaza** was the nation's first enclosed downtown mall when it was built in the 1950s. **Waterloo Premium Outlets**, off I-90 near Waterloo, is a popular shopping spot for tour groups and locals.

Antiques & collectibles

All That Jazz Antique & Collectible Co-op: 1221 Empire Blvd., Webster *D14*; 224-0340
Antiek Journeys: 340 Culver Road, Rochester *C6*; 271-8890
The Antique Barn: 499 E. Ridge Road, Irondequoit *D13*; 266-5520
Antiques & Old Lace: 1290 University Ave., Rochester *C6*; 461-1884
Craft Antique Co-op: 3200 W. Ridge Road, Greece *D11*; 368-0670
Echoes of Time: 17 S. Main St., Pittsford *F14*; 586-5310
Fairport Antiques & Rainy Day Mercantile: 62 N. Main St., Fairport *F15*; 377-4140
Green Door Antiques: 1534 Monroe Ave., Rochester *E13*; 271-2460
House Parts: 540 South Ave., Rochester *D4*; 325-2329
International Art Acquisitions Inc.: 3300 Monroe Ave., Pittsford *F13*; 264-1440
ReHouse Inc.: 1473 E. Main St., Rochester *B5*; 288-3080
Ridge Antiques: 5236 W. Ridge Road, Spencerport *C9*; 352-4721
Rochester Antique Market and Galleries: 155 Monroe Ave., Rochester *C4*; 262-4643
Talulah Petunia's: 39 S. Goodman St., Rochester *C4*; 244-7720
Willowcreek Auction Service & Antiques: 5377 W. Ridge Road, Spencerport *C9*; 352-1760

Apparel—children's

Babies R Us: 2335 Marketplace Drive, Henrietta *F12*; 424-7170
Black Sheep: 34 S. Main St., Pittsford *F14*; 248-3960
Forever Kids: 2695 W. Ridge Road, Greece *D11*; 227-8530
The Rugged Bear: Pittsford Plaza, 3349 Monroe Ave., Pittsford *F13*; 586-2440
Simon's Baby Furniture Co.: 461 W. Ridge Road, Greece *D12*; 865-9615. 3400 Monroe

Ave., Pittsford *F13*; 264-9250
Small Wonders: Frontier Commons, 1225 Jefferson Road, Henrietta *F12*; 272-0670

Apparel—general

Aaron's Alley: 662 Monroe Ave., Rochester *D4*; 244-5044
Abercrombie & Fitch: EastView Mall, Victor *B21*; 223-4520. The Marketplace, Hylan Drive, Henrietta *F12*; 272-1670
Banana Republic: EastView Mall, Victor *B21*; 223-9250. The Marketplace, Hylan Drive, Henrietta *F12*; 272-8450
Cohoe's: Pittsford Plaza, Pittsford *F13*; 218-0230
Dave Brown the Hatter: 3054 W. Henrietta Road, Henrietta *F12*; 475-1613
Eddie Bauer: EastView Mall, Victor *B21*; 425-9860
Lands' End Inlet: 2000 Miracle Mile Drive, Henrietta *F12*; 424-3500
Naples Creek Shoes and Leather: 10 Schoen Place, Pittsford *F14*; 586-9070
Pittsford Pendleton Shop: 1 S. Main St., Pittsford *F14*; 264-0010

Apparel—men's

Adrian Jules Ltd. Custom Clothier: 1392 E. Ridge Road, Irondequoit *D13*; 342-7160
Hickey-Freeman Co. Inc.: 1155 N. Clinton Ave., Rochester *A3*; 467-7021
Jos. A. Bank Clothiers: 1900 S. Clinton Ave., Rochester *E4*; 244-6920. 3240 Monroe Ave., Rochester *F13*; 381-6070
Mentality: 21 State St., Pittsford *B14*;

248-3870
Nahum Fine Clothing: 1498 Monroe Ave., Brighton *E6*; 442-9553
The Red Barn Gentlemen's Apparel: Pittsford Plaza, Monroe Avenue, Pittsford *F1*; 586-9409
RT Gentry: 1694 Penfield Road, Penfield *E14*; 248-0620
S&K Menswear: 319 EastView Mall, Victor *B21*; 223-2060. Greece Ridge Center, Greece *D11*; 225-6290. 540 Miracle Mile Drive, Henrietta *F12*; 272-1280
Up The Creek: 28 S. Main St., Pittsford *F14*; 381-3550

Naples Creek Shoes and Leather in Pittsford carries jackets, wallets, purses and footwear.

Apparel—shoes

A Step Apart: 235 Park Ave., Rochester *C5*; 241-3110
Annabelle's Closet: 808 S. Clinton Ave., Rochester D4; 271-7370
Bostonian Shoe Store: EastView Mall, Victor *B21*; 425-9980
DSW (Designer Shoe Warehouse): 1200

Miracle Mile Drive, Henrietta *F12*; 424-2260
Karizma Boutique: 676 Monroe Ave., Rochester *D5*; 271-0600
Shoe Concepts: 2947 Monroe Ave., Pittsford *F13*; 442-5020
Sullivan's Shoe Co.: 14 Edmonds St., Rochester *D4*; 442-8730
Uneeda Birkenstock: Cobblestone Court Drive, Victor *B21*; 475-1322

Apparel—women's

A Different Point of View: 2930 Monroe Ave., Pittsford *F13*; 264-1770
Ann Taylor: EastView Mall, Victor *B21*; 425-9650
Ann Taylor Loft: The Marketplace, Henrietta *F12*; 292-5640
Anything Goes: 136 Fairport Village Landing, Fairport *F15*; 223-3737
B'Younique: 1892 Monroe Ave., Brighton *E6*; 271-4060
CJ Banks: Greece Ridge Center, Greece *D11*; 225-1060. The Marketplace, Henrietta *F12*; 427-8380. EastView Mall, Victor *B21*; 223-0140
Cache: 741 EastView Mall, Victor *B21*; 425-3930
Chico's: 3240 Monroe Ave., Pittsford *F13*; 586-6860
Christopher & Banks Division of Brauns: Greece Ridge Center, Greece *D11*; 227-0490.

The Marketplace, Henrietta *F12*; 424-2560. EastView Mall, Victor *B21*; 421-3800
Elaine's of Pittsford: 32 S. Main St., Pittsford *F14*; 383-8140
Ewe Too: 15 S. Main St., Pittsford *F14*; 264-9670
Inspiration Designs: 3122 Monroe Ave., Pittsford *F13*; 383-8790
Juliana's: 2209 Monroe Ave., Brighton *E13*; 271-1830
L'Avant Garbe: 19 State St., Pittsford *F14*; 248-0440
One Enchanted Evening: 280 Packett's Landing, Fairport *F15*; 425-1166
Sissy's: 7 S. Main St., Pittsford *F14*; 383-8512
SJ's: Nestled amid vintage antiques in a historic 19th century home in the heart of the village of Pittsford, SJ's offers a unique collection of clothing, sterling silver jewelry, leather goods, shoes and accessories for women, men and your home. 25 S. Main St., Pittsford *F14*; 248-0640
Suzanne's Distinctive Fashions: 40 State St., Pittsford *F14*; 383-1810
Talbots: 66 Monroe Ave., Pittsford *F13*; 586-5642. 1110 Long Pond Road, Greece *C11*; 453-0750

Art galleries

For more listings, see the Entertainment & the Arts section.

Nan Miller Gallery: Nan Miller, owner and international art publisher, has resources to provide clients with the finest selection of art available. The gallery carries styles from abstract to impressionism as well as pop to realism. For 35 years, Miller and her staff have been committed to helping clients enhance their homes and offices. 3450 Winton Place, Brighton *F13*; 292-1430

Books

Barnes & Noble Booksellers: Pittsford Plaza, 3349 Monroe Ave., Pittsford *F13*; 586-6020. 330 Greece Ridge Center, W. Ridge Road, Greece *D11*; 227-4020. Towne Center at Webster, 1070 Ridge Road, Webster, *D14*; 872-9710
Borders Books Music & Café: 1000 Hylan Drive, Henrietta *F12*; 292-5900. 30 Square Drive, Victor *B21*; 421-9230
Brownbag Bookshop: 678 Monroe Ave., Rochester *D5*; 271-3494

Works of art from around the world can be found at Nan Miller Gallery in Brighton.

Fagan Books: 6883 Routes 5 & 20, East Bloomfield *B21*; 657-7096
Houghton Book Shop: Village Gate Square, 274 N. Goodman St., Rochester *C5*; 454-2910
Lift Bridge Book Shop: 45 Main St., Brockport *D7*; 637-2260
Mood Makers Books: Village Gate Square, 274 N. Goodman St., Rochester *C5*; 271-7010
Rick's Recycled Books: 739 Monroe Ave., Rochester *D5*; 442-4920
Yankee Peddler Book Shop: Village Gate Square, 274 N. Goodman St., Rochester *C5*; 271-5080

Candy & confections

Andy's Candies: 1100 Hudson Ave., Rochester *D12*; 266-5180. 1536 W. Ridge Road, Greece *D11*; 663-9190
Candy Caboose Fudge Factory: 52 Railroad St., Fairport *F15*; 377-3275
Candy Nation Plus Inc.: 20 Fairport Village Landing, Fairport *F15*; 377-0030
Encore Chocolates Inc.: 147 Pattonwood Drive, Rochester *C12*; 266-2970
Godiva Chocolatier: EastView Mall, Victor *B21*; 223-9290
Goodie Shoppe: 83 North Ave., Webster *D15*; 872-6460
The Nut House: 1520 Monroe Ave., Brighton *E6*; 244-9510
Peter's Sweet Shop: 880 S. Clinton Ave., Rochester *D4*; 442-6770
Stever's Candy Shop: 623 Park Ave., Rochester *C5*; 473-2098
Watson's Candies: 725 Pittsford-Victor Road, Pittsford *F14*; 218-0520

Florists

Arena's Florist Inc.: 260 East Ave., Rochester *CC6*; 454-3720
Blanchard Florist: 3208 Latta Road, Rochester *C11*; 254-1200
Canalside Florists: 616 B Pittsford-Victor Road, Pittsford *F14*; 248-5115
Edgerton Floral Co.: 151 Park Ave., Rochester *C4*; 244-2222
Enright Florist: 1585 Dewey Ave., Rochester *D12*; 254-9330
Fioravanti Florist: 2279 Clifford Ave., Rochester *D13*; 482-1001
Kittelberger Florist & Gifts: 263 North Ave., Webster *C15*; 872-1823
Pittsford Florist: 41 S. Main St., Pittsford *F14*; 248-5860
Westfall Florists Inc.: 1092 Mt. Hope Ave., Rochester *E3*; 271-1100
Wisteria Flowers & Gifts: 360 Culver Road, Rochester *C6*; 271-0610

Rochester has dozens of wine shops, including Pittsford Wine & Spirits (above).

Gift & specialty shops

Animas Alta: 2930 Monroe Ave., Pittsford *E13*; 586-4730

Animas Traders: 975 S. Clinton Ave., Rochester *D4*; 271-4210

Archimage: 668 Monroe Ave., Rochester *D5*; 271-2789

Barnswallow: 2900 Monroe Ave., Pittsford *F13*; 586-6490

Bearly Country: 45 Schoen Place, Pittsford *F14*; 381-5540

Beers Of The World: 3450 Winton Place, Brighton *F13*; 427-2852

Bird House: 3016 Monroe Ave., Pittsford *F13*; 264-1550

Cooks' World: 2179 Monroe Ave., Brighton *E13*; 271-1789

Crabtree & Evelyn: EastView Mall, Victor *B21*; 425-3450. 215 Park Ave., Rochester *C5*; 244-4842

Craft Company No. 6: Don't miss award-winning Craft Company No. 6. Eight rooms and outdoor courtyard are filled with American and Canadian handcrafted jewelry, gifts and home/garden accessories. 785 University Ave., Rochester *C5*; 473-3413

Create A Gift: 3180 Latta Road, Greece *C11*; 225-3182

The Creator's Hands: 81 Brown's Race, Rochester *BB2*; 235-8550

A Different Point of View: An unrivaled collection of clothing, personal accessories and giftware. Choose from our wide assortment of clothing from Eileen Fisher, ISDA and Sarah Pacini; accessories from Kate Spade, Vera Bradley and Brighton; jewelry from Ed Levin, Wasabi and Saundra Messenger; and giftware from Orrefors, Kosta Boda and Casa Fina. Shop in a relaxed, warm atmosphere—and, of course, gift wrap is always free! 2920 Monroe

CRAFT COMPANY No.6

Sticks.object art and furniture sold exclusively at Craft Comany No.6 in upstate NY.

handmade in the USA and Canada

Located in a Victorian firehouse on ArtWalk ~ one block from the George Eastman House ~ in the **Neighborhood of the Arts**

785 University Avenue
473-3413

www.craftcompany.com

Eight reasons to buy local

Every city has its claims to fame—here are a few of Rochester's:

Adrian Jules suits

Adrian Jules Ltd. Custom Clothier's hand-sewn, custom-tailored suits are worn by people in the public eye—top actors, politicians and professional athletes. Staff are regularly on the road to work one-on-one with clients—drafting a personal pattern, taking measurements and using a CAD system to create the perfect fit. *Town and Country* magazine calls Adrian Jules one of the top tailors in the United States. The shop is a multiple blue-ribbon winner from the Custom Tailors and Designers Association. *1392 E. Ridge Road, Irondequoit* **D12**; *(800) 295-SUIT; www.adrianjules.com*

◀ Cool Whip

When it was introduced by General Foods in 1966, Cool Whip was meant to be a timesaver in the kitchen. Millions of tubs of the creamy whipped topping (a delicious blend of tropical oils, sugar and suspicious stabilizers) have been sold since. The taste debate continues: Cool Whip, or real whipped cream? Today Kraft Foods owns the brand and produces all of it at a plant in nearby Avon. Coincidentally, Jell-O gelatin was invented in LeRoy, just down the road. *140 Spring St., Avon* **B20**; *226-4400*

▼ Dave Brown hats

Master hatter Dave Brown is one of fewer than 50 custom hat makers working in the United States. His creations appear regularly on the heads of music, movie and sports celebrities, from George Clooney to Sting. Oscar-winning Hollywood costume designers hire him repeatedly; recent projects include "Memoirs of a Geisha," "Road to Perdition" and "Goodnight and Good Luck." *3054 W. Henrietta Road, Henrietta* **F12**; *475-1791; www.davebrownhats.com*

Genny Cream Ale ▶

Plenty of upstaters have memories of fathers and uncles holding sweating cans of Genny Cream Ale at family picnics on hot July afternoons. A product of High Falls Brewing Co. LLC (formerly Genesee Brewing Co.), Genny Cream came on the scene in 1960. Rochesterians (one-quarter of whom are German) love beer. At the turn of the 20th century, 50 breweries operated here. High Falls bills Genny Cream as having "the flavor of a fine ale and the smoothness of a premium lager." We just know it was "Dad's beer" back in the day. Today it is enjoying renewed popularity: It's carried in 32 states and Canada. *445 St. Paul St., Rochester* **AA3**; *263-9446; www.highfalls.com*

Hickey Freeman suits ▶

Known around the world for its quality menswear, Hickey Freeman Co. Inc. got its start here in 1899. Jacob Freeman and Jeremiah Hickey built a state-of-the-art factory in northeast Rochester, recruiting skilled tailors from large U.S. cities and abroad. The factory is still humming, its craftspeople turning out garments made of the finest Italian and British textiles. The suits they make have a reputation for excellent fit and drape. You could buy a Hickey Freeman suit at Saks, but why? Check out the factory store while you're here. *1155 N. Clinton Ave., Rochester A3; 467-7021; www.hickeyfreeman.com*

▼ Kodak cameras

Kodak's popular digital cameras aren't made in Rochester, but the photo giant is based here, in a headquarters building that towers over State Street. The company's EasyShare digital cameras rank high in customer satisfaction for connectivity, performance, cost and appearance. Kodak started in the back room of a bank building downtown. In the 130 years since, it has become one of the most recognizable brands in the world for photography, medical imaging and graphic communications. *343 State St., Rochester BB1; (800) 242-2424; www.kodak.com*

Terry bicycles ▶

Georgena Terry soldered a love for biking with her skills as a mechanical engineer to build Terry Precision Bicycles. The Macedon company makes bikes that fit women. Most bicycles are made to fit men's torsos, shoulders and legs—producing aches and pains in the women who ride them. Terry sold 20 bikes for women in 1985; today the company is a multimillion-dollar firm with an international reputation. *1657 East Park Drive, Macedon B21; (800) 289-8379; www.terrybicycles.com*

▼ Zweigle's White Hots

Forbes calls them "a kind of American *boudin blanc*." Made of beef, pork and veal, these dogs are white. You can find them elsewhere, mostly in Western New York, but Zweigle's was the first to put them in a stadium: They're the official hot dog of the Buffalo Bills. Served the Rochester way, a white hot is topped with chopped raw onions and meat sauce; sometimes cheddar cheese and mustard are involved. They taste great with beans too. *651 N. Plymouth Ave., Rochester E12; 546-1740; www.zweigles.com*

Mann's Jewelers is a 75-year-old family operation. The store is known around the state for unusual designer jewelry.

Ave., Pittsford *E13*; 264-1770
Eleventh Hour Gift Shop: 622 Park Ave., Rochester *C5*; 256-1450
The Glue Factory: 3252 Union St., North Chili *E9*; 594-0857
Harmony In Wood: 50 State St., Pittsford *F14*; 381-1992
Hurd Orchards: 17260 Ridge Road, Holley *A19*; 638-8838

Irish & Celtic Imports: Pittsford Plaza, 3349 Monroe Ave., Pittsford *F13*; 389-1790. Mall at Greece Ridge Center, Greece *D11*; 225-1050
Jembetat African Art Gallery: 645 Park Ave., Rochester *C5*; 442-8960
Lindsey's: 631 Pittsford-Victor Road, Bushnell's Basin *G14*; 248-8952
The Map Shop: Northfield Commons, 50 State St., Pittsford *F14*; 385-5850

Mostly Clay Inc.: 7 Schoen Place, Pittsford *F14*; 381-9990
Naples Creek Shoes and Leather: 10 Schoen Place, Pittsford *F14*; 586-9070
One World Goods: Pittsford Plaza, 3349 Monroe Ave., Pittsford *F13*; 387-0070
Onnie's Closet: 1336 Pittsford-Mendon Road, Mendon *B21*; 582-1072
Parkleigh: 215 Park Ave., Rochester *C5*; 244-4842
The Pedestal: 50 State St., Pittsford *F14*; 381-7640
People's Pottery: EastView Mall, Victor *B21*; 425-1140. Spring House Commons, Suite 1, 3025 Monroe Ave., Pittsford *F13*; 271-2740
Port of Pittsford Gifts: 10 Schoen Place, Pittsford *F14*; 383-9250
Possibilities: 585 Moseley Road, Fairport *F15*; 223-9690
RSVP Papers & Gifts: 1664 Monroe Ave., Brighton *E6*; 271-6070
Seasons of Fairport: 20A Fairport Village Landing, Fairport *F15*; 388-6756
Simply D'Vine: 672 Pittsford-Victor Road, Bushnell's Basin *G14*; 381-0360
Tessellations: 34 1/2 State St., Pittsford *F14*; 271-7920
Tradition Fine Judaic & Israeli Gifts: 932 S. Winton Road, Brighton *E6*; 244-3540

Gourmet food

The Dutch Market: 257 Park Ave., Rochester *C5*; 271-6110
Lombardi's Gourmet Imports and Specialties: 124 N. Main St., Fairport *F15*; (800) 784-6875
V.M. Giordano Imports European Cheese Shop: Rochester Public Market, 280 N. Union St., Rochester *B5*
Wegmans Food and Pharmacy: 3195 Monroe Ave., Pittsford *F13*; 586-6680
Williams-Sonoma: EastView Mall, Victor *B21*; 425-9810

Home furnishings & accessories

Amish Outlet & Gift Shop: 3530 Union St., North Chili *E9*; 889-8520
Country Curtains: 900 S. Panorama Trail, Penfield *E14*; 383-1010
Diane Prince Country Furniture & Gifts: 23 Liftbridge Lane East, Fairport *F15*; 388-0060
Houseworks: 3450 Winton Place, Henrietta *F13*; 427-7620
Maitlins: 3246 Monroe Ave., Pittsford *F13*; 586-4660
Stickley Audi & Co.: EastView Mall, Victor *B21*; 425-2302
Tuthill Lighting: 1689 Monroe Ave., Brighton

E6; 271-5877

Jewelry

45 East Fine Jewelers: 45 East Ave., Rochester *C4*; 454-0060

Blueground Jewelry: Pittsford Plaza, Pittsford *F13*; 249-9040

Burke & Bannayan Jewelers: 1100 Long Pond Road, Greece *C11*; 723-1010

Cornell's Jewelers: Cornell's Jewelers, established in 1923, offers a lasting experience while providing a lifetime of memories. Our passion is diamonds, although we understand that is not everyone's need. That is why we offer a wide selection of quality gold, silver and colored stones. 3100 Monroe Ave., Pittsford *F13*; 264-0100

Forsythe Jewelers Inc.: 66 Monroe Ave., Pittsford *F13*; 586-5954

The Gem Lab: 4098 W. Henrietta Road, Henrietta *F12*; 359-3900

James Salerno Jewelry Designers: 1 N. Main St., Pittsford *F14*; 385-4444

Jared's Galleria of Jewelry: 300 Hylan Drive, Henrietta *F12*; 424-3950

Karen Brown Custom Goldsmiths: 2171 Monroe Ave., Rochester *F13*; 473-6171

Mann's Jewelers Inc.: Family-owned jewelers since 1836, Mann's Jewelers has been serving the Rochester community since 1922. Providing competitive prices and more selection than 10 average stores combined, Mann's Jewelers has become the premier destination for the finest diamonds, Swiss watches, designer jewelry and distinctive giftware in Upstate New York. 2945 Monroe Ave., Pittsford *F13*; 271-4000

Northfield Designer Goldsmiths: 700 Park Ave., Rochester *C5*; 442-2260

Richard's Fine Jewelers: 1855 Monroe Ave., Brighton *E6*; 242-8777

Richard's & West Inc.: 1255 University Ave., Rochester *C6*; 461-3022

The Source: 3300 Monroe Ave., Pittsford *F13*; 586-9145. 2147 W. Ridge Road, Greece *D11*; 225-5445. 535 W. Ridge Road, Greece *D12*; 621-6280

West & Co. Jewelers Ltd.: 1229 Bay Road, Webster *D14*; 671-2410

Malls

EastView Mall: EastView has five major department stores and more than 170 specialty shops and restaurants, including the largest selection of upscale stores and restaurants, such as Williams-Sonoma Grand Cuisine, Pottery Barn Kids, J. Jill, Banana Republic, Coldwater Creek, P.F. Changs, Champs Americana, Ann Taylor, J. Crew, Build-A-Bear Workshop, Biaggi's Ristorante Italiano and Lord & Taylor. 7979 Pittsford-Victor Road, Victor *B21*; 223-4420

The Mall at Greece Ridge Center: This 1.6 million-square-foot shopping center is the

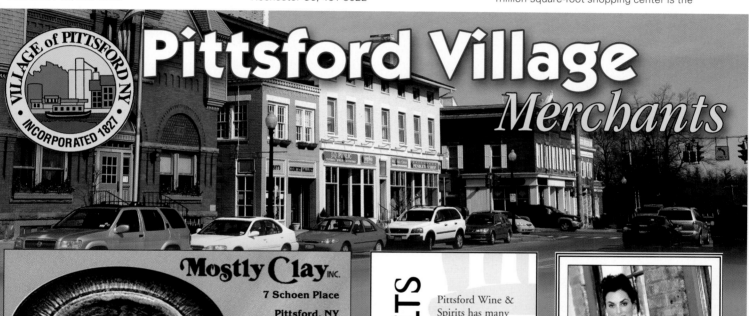

Purls of knitting

Devoted knitters don't let a little time on the road stop them. In fact, what better way to while away the hours waiting for a flight? Needle wielders in Rochester have yarn shops aplenty to keep their fingers flying. If you're searching for a truly different color or you left your knitting needles at home, check out these area suppliers.

Cloverleaf Farms: Hand-dyed yarns and fiber. 2559 S. Union St., Spencerport *A20*; 352-0852; www.cloverleaffarms.com

Expressions in Needleart: 110 S. Main St., Canandaigua *B21*; (888) 528-7666; www.expressionsinneedleart.com

Fine Fibers: Mohair "from hoof to finished goods." 665 Colby St., Spencerport *A20*; 352-5538; www.finefibers.com

Knit 'n' Purl: 1855 Monroe Ave., Brighton *E13*; 248-8339; www.knitnpurl.com

New York Knits: 1286 Blossom Drive, Farmington *B21*; 924-1950; www.newyorkknits.com

Sheep and Wool Shop: No longer any sheep, but lots of wool at a beautiful location. 4849 Cory Corners Road, Marion *A22*; (315) 926-5765

Spirit Work Knitting & Design: Large but welcoming,

big selection, online sales. 563 Titus Ave., Irondequoit *D12*; 544-9107; www.spiritworkknit.com

Village Yarn Shop: Tucked in the back of a bookstore at Midtown Plaza, the shop is bursting with yarn, supplies, books—the grandmother of area yarn stores. 200 Midtown Plaza, Rochester *CC5*; 454-6064

Wild Wools: Exclusive and luxury hand knitting yarns. 732 South Ave., Rochester *D4*; 271-0960; www.wildwools.com

Yarn Source: 2080 E. Henrietta Road, Henrietta *F12*; 334-5350

---

largest in Upstate New York with more than 140 specialty stores, four anchor stores and six big-box retailers, including Barnes & Noble, Dick's Sporting Goods, Marshalls, Bed Bath & Beyond, Burlington Coat Factory and Kaufmann's Home Store, and Rochester Athletic Club. 271 Greece Ridge Center Drive, Greece *D11*; 225-0430

The Marketplace: More than 140 stores and restaurants including Abercrombie & Fitch, Ann Taylor Loft, Banana Republic, Hollister, Tony Roma's and Yankee Candle. The Marketplace offers an array of merchandise and services for all family members. 1 Miracle Mile Drive, Henrietta *F12*; 475-0757

Medley Centre: 81 Irondequoit Mall Drive, Irondequoit *D13*; 266-4000

Midtown Plaza: 211 Midtown Plaza, Downtown Rochester *C4*; 454-2070

Pittsford Plaza: 3349 Monroe Ave., Pittsford *F13*; 424-6220

SouthTown Plaza: 3333 W. Henrietta Road, Henrietta *F12*

The Prime Outlets at Niagara Falls USA: 1900 Military Road, Niagara Falls *A17*; (800) 414-0475

Towne Center at Webster: Ridge Road and Holt Road, Webster *D14*

Waterloo Premium Outlets: 655 Route 318, Waterloo *B22*; (315) 539-1100

Westgate Plaza: Chili Avenue, Gates *E11*

Music

Analog Shop: 57 E. Main St., Victor *B21*; 742-2860

The Bop Shop: Village Gate Square, 274 N. Goodman St., Rochester *C5*; 271-3354

The Guitar Center: 1100 Jefferson Road, Henrietta *F12*; 424-2188

House of Guitars: 645 Titus Ave., Irondequoit *D12*; 544-9928

Lakeshore Record Exchange: 370 Park Ave., Rochester *C5*; 244-8476

Music Lovers Shoppe: 2229 Monroe Ave., Brighton *E13*; 242-0980

Record Archive: 1880 East Ave., Rochester *E13*; 244-1210

"Bloomfield Antique Country Mile," on Routes 5 and 20, is lined with shops such as this one.

Salons & spas

AE Spa – Andrea Esthetics Ltd.: 1855 Monroe Ave., Rochester *E13*; 461-4310

Brow Diva: 3025 Monroe Ave., Suite 103, Pittsford *F13*; 271-2950

The Clinic'ue: 2410 W. Ridge Road, Greece *D11*; 227-0612

Del Monte Lodge, a Renaissance Hotel & Spa: 41 N. Main St., Pittsford *F14*; 381-9900.

DermaSpa: 120 White Spruce Blvd., Rochester *F12*; 272-9346

Hollywood Hair and Spa: 8355 Lake Ave., Rochester *C12*; 615-8218

Luxe Spa: 2541 Monroe Ave., Brighton *E13*; 256-1050

Maxim Spa and Salon: 633 Park Ave., Rochester *C5*; 256-0838.

The Men's Room: 2320 Monroe Ave., Brighton *E13*; 461-5740

Oggi Domani Salon: 3400 Monroe Ave., Pittsford *F13*; 383-1340

Park Avenue Salon & Day Spa: 735 Park Ave., Rochester *D6*; 473-5040

Pharaoh's Hairum Inc.: 4112 W. Henrietta Road, Henrietta *F12*; 359-2249

Salon Brio: 665 Pittsford-Victor Road, Bushnell's Basin *F14*; 264-0250

Salon Enza: 1784 Penfield Road, Penfield *E14*; 218-0660

Salon Hermitage: 3122 Monroe Ave., Pittsford *F13*; 586-6880

RSVP Papers & Gifts carries traditional and trendy items (below). The weavers' names are stitched into the border of a rug at Thos. R. Paddock Oriental Rug Exchange (right).

Salon Lidori: 1343 Long Pond Road, Greece *D11*; 225-3420
Scott Miller: 3340 Monroe Ave., Pittsford *F13*; 264-9940
Scruples Lifestyle Center: 2175 Empire Blvd., Webster *D14*; 671-6000
Shear Ego Salon and Spa: Pittsford Plaza, 3349 Monroe Ave., Pittsford *F13*; 586-1781. 2833 W. Ridge Road, Greece *D11*; 225-4860
Spa Elan: The Lodge at Woodcliff, 199 Woodcliff Drive, Fairport *B21*; (800) 365-3065
Thrillz Spa and Salon: 3254 Monroe Ave., Pittsford *F13*; 586-9710
Water Lily: 2383 Monroe Ave., Brighton *E13*; 442-5140
World Hair: 121 Park Ave., Rochester *C4*; 473-5452

Smoke shops

Dewey Ave. Smoke Shop: 1405 Dewey Ave., Rochester *D12*; 458-8824
Havana House: 365 N. Washington St., Pittsford *F14*; 586-0620

Sporting/athletic shops

Bell Racquet Sports: 349 W. Commercial St., East Rochester *E14*; 385-9940
Big Oak Driving Range & Golf Shop: 441 N. Washington St., East Rochester *E14*; 586-0614
Dick's Sporting Goods: The Marketplace, Henrietta *F12*; 697-7400. Greece Ridge Center, Greece *D11*; 227-3730. Cobblestone Court, Victor *B21*; 223-1530. Towne Center at Webster, Webster *D14*; 872-1080
The Golf Tee: 1039 Ridge Road, Webster *D14*; 872-1390
Medved Running & Walking Outfitters: Pittsford Colony Plaza, 3400 Monroe Ave., Pittsford *F13*; 248-3420
Panorama Outfitters: 900 Panorama Trail, Penfield *E14*; 248-8390
The Park Ave. Bike Shop: 2900 Monroe Ave.,

Pittsford *E13* ; 381-3080. 600 Jay Scutti Blvd., Henrietta *F12*; 427-2110
The Ski Company Mountain Sports: 1225 Jefferson Road, Henrietta *F12*; 292-0580
Snow Country: Pittsford Plaza, Pittsford *F13*; 586-6460
The Soccer Shack: 2298 Monroe Ave., Brighton *E13*; 244-1460
Towpath Bike Stop: 3 Schoen Place, Pittsford *F14*; 381-2808

Toys

Build-A-Bear Workshop: EastView Mall, Victor *B21*; 425-2050
Ridge Road Station: 16131 W. Ridge Road, Holley *A20*; 638-6000

The Toy Soldier: 16 W. Church St., Fairport *F15*; 223-6170
Toys-R-Us: 1530-1550 W. Ridge Road, Greece *D11*; 621-7510. 654 Hylan Drive, Henrietta *F12*; 272-8697
Unique Toy Shop: 120 S. Main St., Canandaigua *B21*; 394-2319

Miscellaneous

Mercury Posters: 1 Sumner Park, Rochester *D4*; 271-3110
Pittsford Wine & Spirits: 3 Schoen Place, Pittsford *F14*; 218-0200
Wine Sense: 749 Park Ave., Rochester *D6*; 271-0590

Shopping Index

for more *information*

Emergency

Police, Fire, Ambulance **911**

Airlines

**Greater Rochester
International Airport**
1200 Brooks Ave., Chili
464-6000
www.rocairport.com

Air Canada
(888) 247-2262
(800) 361-8071 TTY
www.aircanada.com

AirTran Airways
(800) 247-8726
www.airtran.com

American Airlines/American Eagle
(800) 433-7300
(800) 582-1573 TTY
www.aa.com

**Continental Airlines/
Continental Express**
(800) 523-3273 domestic
(800) 231-0856 international
(800) 343-9195 TTY
www.continental.com

Delta Airlines
(800) 221-1212 domestic
(800) 241-4141 international
(800) 831-4488 TTY
www.delta.com

JetBlue Airways
(800) 538-2583
(800) 336-5530 TTY
www.jetblue.com

Northwest Airlines/KLM
(800) 225-2525 domestic
(800) 447-4747 international
(800) 328-2298
www.nwa.com

United Airlines
(800) 864-8331 domestic
(800) 538-2929 international
(800) 323-0170 TTY
www.united.com

US Airways
(800) 428-4322
(800) 622-1015 international
www.usairways.com

Automobile rentals

Alamo Rent A Car
(800) 327-9633
www.alamo.com

Avis Rent A Car
(800) 831-2847
www.avis.com

Budget Car Rental
(800) 527-0700
www.budget.com

Dollar Rent a Car
235-0772 Rochester rentals
(800) 800-4000 worldwide
www.dollar.com

Enterprise Rent A Car
(800) 736-8222
www.enterprise.com

Hertz Rent A Car
328-3700
(800) 654-3131 worldwide
www.hertz.com

National Car Rental
(800) 227-7368
www.nationalcar.com

Rent-A-Wreck
328-8332 Rochester
(800) 535-1391 worldwide
www.rent-a-wreck.com

Bus lines

Regional Transit Service
288-1700
(888) 288-3777
654-0210 TDD
Local bus service throughout Greater Rochester. Pick up schedules at: bus headquarters, 1372 E. Main St., Rochester; RTS information booth in Midtown Plaza, downtown Rochester; Rochester Public Library, 115 South Ave., Rochester; and banks, libraries and shopping facilities.
www.rgrta.org (printable format)

Greyhound Bus Lines
187 Midtown Plaza, Rochester
232-5121 station information
(800) 231-2222 fares/schedules
325-2974 package express

New York Trailways
187 Midtown Plaza, Rochester
232-5121 station information
(800) 295-5555 fares/schedules/package express
www.trailwaysny.com

Rail service

Amtrak
320 Central Ave., Rochester
454-2894 station information
(800) 872-7245 reservations/schedules
www.amtrak.com

Taxicab services

Airport Taxi
235-0508

Associate Taxi
232-3232

Century Cab Co.
235-7777

Corporate Airport Taxi
703-4222

Entertainment tickets

TicketExpress, local only
222-5000

TicketMaster, national
232-1900
www.ticketmaster.com

Government and organizations

City of Rochester
City Hall
30 Church St., Rochester
428-5990
428-7600 TTY
www.ci.rochester.ny.us

County of Monroe
County Office Building
39 W. Main St., Rochester
www.monroecounty.gov

Greater Rochester Enterprise Inc.
100 Chestnut Plaza, Suite 1910, Rochester
530-6200
www.visitrochester.com

Rochester Business Alliance Inc.
150 State St., Rochester
244-1800
www.rnychamber.com

Rochester Public Library
Central Library of Rochester
and Monroe County
115 South Ave., Rochester
428-7300
www.libraryweb.org

Rochester Riverside Convention Center
123 E. Main St., Rochester
232-7200
232-3362 event information
www.rrcc.com

Media

News radio
WHAM-AM 1180
WXXI-AM 1370—NPR

Print
City Newspaper
Free alternative newsweekly
www.rochester-citynews.com

Rochester Business Journal
Weekly business newspaper
www.rbjdaily.com

Rochester Democrat and Chronicle
Daily newspaper
www.democratandchronicle.com

Television
WROC-TV 8—CBS
R News—24-hour news, cable 9
WHEC-TV 10—NBC
WHAM-TV 13—ABC
WXXI-TV 21—PBS
WUHF-TV 31—Fox

Visitor information

Rochester Downtown Guides
Downtown Information Center
Corner East Main and St. Paul streets, Rochester
232-3420
www.rochesterdowntown.com
Monday - Friday, 8:30 a.m. - 5:30 p.m.
Saturday, 10 a.m. - 4 p.m. (May - October)
Maps and information about downtown restaurants, activities and entertainment

Greater Rochester Visitors Association
546-6810 (24-hour event line)
546-8484 (TTY)
(800) 677-7282
www.visitrochester.com
GRVA provides brochures, maps, calendars and schedules for area attractions at these locations:

Visitor Information Booth
Greater Rochester International Airport, Chili
First Floor
Brochures available 24 hours
Monday - Friday, 8 a.m. - 8 p.m.
Saturday, 10 a.m. - 6 p.m.,
Sunday, 10 a.m. - 5 p.m.

Downtown Visitor Information Center
45 East Ave., Suite 100, Rochester
546-3070
(800) 677-7282
Monday - Friday, 8:30 a.m. - 5 p.m.
Saturday, 10 a.m. - 4 p.m.
Sunday, 10 a.m. - 3 p.m.

Seneca Thruway Visitor Information Center
Seneca Rest Area, New York State Thruway westbound,
east of exit 45
Monday - Friday, 8 a.m. - 6 p.m.
Saturday and Sunday,
8 a.m. - 4 p.m.

Web sites

http://mcls.rochester.lib.ny.us/~rochhist
A rich resource of articles on the history of Rochester and Western New York

www.movingtorochester.org
For visitors considering a move to Rochester

www.real-rochester.com
A twentysomething guide to life in Rochester

www.roccity.org
Supporting the young adults of Rochester's business community

www.rochesterdowntown.com
Downtown neighborhoods, nightlife, restaurants and cultural attractions

www.rochestermadeforliving.com
All the reasons Rochester's climate is perfect— in more ways than one

www.visitrochester.com
Everything you need to plan your visit

index to *advertisers*

photo *credits*